PEOPLE POWER AND DEMOCRACY

PEOPLE POWER AND DEMOCRACY:

THE POPULAR MOVEMENT AGAINST MILITARY DESPOTISM IN NIGERIA, 1989-1999

by

Rita Kiki Edozie

Africa World Press, Inc.

Africa World Press, Inc.

First Printing 2002

Book Design: Jonathan Gullery
Cover Design: Ashraful Haque

Library of Congress Cataloging-in-Publication Data

Edozie, Rita Kiki.
People power and democracy : the popular movement against military despotism in Nigeria, 1989-1999 / by Rita Kiki Edozie.
p.cm.
Includes bibliographical references and index.
ISBN: 0-86543-916-8 (hard cover) -- ISBN 0-86543-917-6 (pbk.)
1. Nigeria--Politics and government--1984-1993. 2. Nigeria--Politics and government--1993- 3. Democracy--Nigeria--History--20th century. 4. Military government--Nigeria--History--20th century. I. Title.
DT515.842 .E36 2002
966.905'3--dc21

2002001081

Table of Contents

List of Diagrams

Dedication

Between June and September 1998, more than half of Nigeria's political prisoners were released from jail, where they had been persecuted for advocating democracy. Some were not so lucky; the five-year tyrannical regime silenced those who came up against it head to head.

People Power and Democracy is dedicated to the millions of Nigerians who chose not to condone tyranny during the country's unprecedented five-year (1993-1998) tyrannical regime that sought to promote authoritarianism and suppress the country's rich and longstanding tradition of pluralism and democratic space. These millions of Nigerians came together in the Nigerian pro-democracy movement.

May their commitment to the freedom of Nigeria live on!

Acknowledgments

People Power and Democracy could not have been written without the guidance and wisdom of the eclectic advisory committee that facilitated the book's scholastic development. It was especially a privilege and honor to have a pace-setting guru of African Politics and Global Studies chair this committee. Professor Zolberg's insights and comments brought to the present document a disciplinary expertise that was characteristic of the exciting founding years of African Politics.

A contemporary document, this book also remains equally indebted to the document's advisors, who specialize in democratic transitions, Nigerian politics and history, and social movement theory and civil society. For their guidance and input in these areas, I'd especially like to acknowledge professors Ehiedu Iweriebor, Chuck Tilly, David Plotke, Tony Pereira, Julius Ihonvbere, Stephen Ndegwa, and Mahmood Mamdani.

A final special thanks goes out to my family, friends, and the staff of Africa World Press, for their participation and support of this important case-record depicting African socio-political development.

Preface

In the 1990s, Africa's one time giant, Nigeria, had declined to the point of becoming just another African crisis-spot, a human rights abuser and a pariah nation. Political instability brought about the resurgence of an activist civil society involved in an intense struggle for democracy.

After the 1993 military annulment of the presidential election, which elected Chief Moshood Abiola as Nigeria's third democratically-elected leader, the Nigerian political landscape was pervaded by an expansive opposition to that decision. A movement that had been spearheaded in 1989 grew larger and more formidable against continued military rule. Deteriorating relations between civil society and the Nigerian military resulted in chronic political crises and instability.

Between 1989-1999 the Nigerian political landscape underwent an intense period of democratic struggles. Although this struggle has been a feature of Nigerian political history since the country's independence from Britain in 1960, the expression of the struggle in the 1990s was particularly intensified, more expansive, and took on a much more serious character than during previous phases of the country's history. The persistent defiance by the Nigerian military to pressures to return to democratic rule; the rampant abuse of human rights against pro-democracy activists; the increase of incidences of guerilla activity and of state terrorism; and the military's sustained attempt to co-opt civil societal segments into "buying-in" to its own transition-to-democracy program, are all reasons why between 1989-1999 Nigerian politics was accurately depicted as "The Dawn of a New Dark Age."[1] *People Power and Democracy*, looks at this 'dark ages' from the point-of-view of the Nigerian pro-democracy movement.

Foreword

Nearly two decades ago, Richard Sklar described Africa as "a veritable workshop of democracy" (1982; 1991, p. 250). Perhaps in this laboratory with its smokescreens, tortuous pain, and few successes, Nigeria is the foremost experiment. Often flawed in design, more often derailed by a shabby commitment by the civilian and military elite and by the well-known travails of the post-colonial state (e.g. malformed political cultures and dependent economies), democratic experiments in Africa have stalled repeatedly. In this book, Edozie deals with the question that has preoccupied students of Nigerian democracy: what is the trouble with Nigeria? (Achebe 1984; Osaghae 1998). Among the many books and articles that examine Nigeria's quest for democracy, Edozie's is a creative addition to the literature in its examination of the role of civic associations in the democracy experiment in Nigeria.

Edozie's major contribution is to highlight the underlying dynamics of the serial unraveling of the democratic experiment in Nigeria and the role of the civic associations in trying to reclaim more civil space for the practice of democracy and to resist persistent decline into dictatorship. Edozie's focus is on the civil arena and the role of popular movements, what she calls "people power." (Indeed, the reminiscence to the people's revolution against Ferdinand Marcos in the Philippines is not trite.) This book's best contribution is that it refocuses our attention onto the elemental level at which democracy must begin to be cultivated. The seemingly insurmountable monoliths of despotism such as the military, corruption, and maladjusted political cultures are best understood at the level they are most often experienced — the local level. Such local manifestations of the despotic state — in institutions, cultures, and structures — are also most effectively challenged, reformed, and reformulated through local organizations to *accommodate* democracy. (Which is probably all that can be expected of nascent democracies emerging from military despotism.)

Edozie's comparative case studies show the immensity of the task of challenging despotism in Nigeria — an already well-known fact; but the focus on the local level provides an even deeper, uncommon appreciation. Instructively, Nigeria's latest experiment with democracy under President Olusegun Obasanjo has faced more problems emanating from the nature of the Nigerian state as manifested at the local levels (e.g. religious and ethnic tensions) rather than the favorite boogey of democracy — the military.

No text is capable of examining fully the 'trouble with Nigeria' and this present text does not claim to do so. But it does offer a clearer understanding of (and cause for guarded optimism for) the potential in local civic associations as defenders and promoters of democracy in Nigeria. At the very least, this book is valuable in its counter to the endemic pessimism regarding Nigeria's democratic chances, and especially the genius of Nigerians to chart a path — probably muddled rather than modeled, tentative rather than definite — toward democracy. The comparative study of civil society organizations presented here contributes another useful and sturdy plank toward our understanding of democracy and democratization in Nigeria and, importantly, in the rest of Africa.

Stephen Ndegwa, Associate Professor -
Department of Government, College of William and Mary

CHAPTER 1

THE DEMOCRATIC MOVEMENT AGAINST MILITARY DESPOTISM

I. People Power

On July 1, 1993, a series of violent, nationwide strikes and demonstrations organized by Nigerian pro-democracy, human rights, labor, and professional organizations, to reinstate Nigeria's military-annulled presidential elections compelled the once popular military leader, General Ibrahim Babangida to unceremoniously step down after eight years in office. This historic act of defiance by civil society in post-independence Nigeria paradoxically marked the end of the "military democracy" of the Babangida regime. However, this event also aborted what had promised to be the Nigerian military's most successful transition-to- democracy program.

Before leaving office, though refusing to reinstate the "annulled" presidential election results in what has popularly become known as the "June 12" mandate, President Babangida instead installed an interim national government (ING), to guide a new transition-to- democracy program through new elections. However, continued strikes and demonstrations against the legitimacy of the military-installed interim government- as well as prolonged reaction against a continuing debilitating economy-ultimately crippled the arrangement, causing a state of socio-political disorder that led to the re-intervention of the military under General Babangida's successor, General Sani Abacha. This represented the official abrogation of Nigeria's third attempt at attaining democratic rule.

Nonetheless, unlike previous regime changes, this "palace

coup" was not welcomed by the Nigerian people. Ironically, despite the new regime's attempt to fully reestablish military rule and consolidate its regime among Nigerian civil society, the establishment of the Abacha military regime resulted in the intensification of demands, calling for a definitive end to military rule. The proliferation of these demands among civil society and their subsequent translation into an anti- military, opposition movement marked the beginning of a crusade to mobilize for the reinstallation of democratic governance in the country.

Marking the formal establishment of the "June 12" movement,[2] the period between 1993-1999 was characterized by the insurgency of pro-democracy organizations in Nigeria as well as by an international human rights campaign against the Nigerian military government sustained by NGOs abroad. These factors all contributed to the launching of the Nigerian pro-democracy movement, whose founding organizations included: the Campaign for Democracy (CD), the Committee for Defense of Human Rights (CDHR), the Civil Liberties Organization (CLO), the Movement for National Reformation (MNR), the Association for Democracy and Good Governance (ADGGN), the National Democratic Coalition (NADECO), the National Liberation Council (NALICON), the United Democratic Front of Nigeria (UDFN).

These organizations forged pro-democratic coalitions with already existing political and professional associations and sectors among civil society, such as the Nigerian Labor Congress (NLC), the Petroleum and Gas Senior Staff Association (PENGASSAN), the National Union of Petroleum and Natural Gas Workers (NUPENG),[3] the National Association of Nigerian Students (NANS), the Academic Staff Union for Universities (ASUU), the media and the clergy.

This network of pro-democratic alliances - through strikes, demonstrations, and the ideological critique of the regime by the media- sought to put pressure on the military regime to reinstate the election results that had declared Chief Abiola the winner. However, rather than to reinstate the democratically-elected government of Chief Abiola, in its traditional fashion, the Nigerian military pursued an agenda of intimidation, subversion, repression, and manipulation of the pro-democracy movement, as well as pursuing yet another state-led, constitutionally engineered, elaborate "transition-to-democracy" program. Civil disobedience among significant sectors of civil society in the form of pro-democracy opposition was suppressed and subverted by the Nigerian military through a series of arrests, detentions, incarcerations, and, in some cases, assassinations of key pro-democracy actors.

The state of politics in Nigeria between 1993-1999 lent credence to earlier predictions about the consequences of pro-longed military rule in Nigeria. For example, *The Review of African Political Economy*, a leading African journal, as early as 1986 predicted that, "In the final analysis, the struggle between authoritarianism and democracy is firmly on the agenda in Nigeria."[4]

II. The Nigerian Democracy Paradox

Studies on democratization and transition may assist in examining the nature of this struggle. Scholarship of the period on the subject[5] suggests that democracy needs to be supported by a wide range of associations and other organized collectivities capable of articulating the interests of their members as well as being able to mould and constrain the power of the state. A country well endowed with a vigorous civil society or associational life is expected to be favorably positioned for democratization. Conversely, a "weak" civil society explains the failure of democracy. Tocquevillean and later Gramscian conceptions of pluralist analyses of democracy argue that the density of autonomous organizations, a dense civil society, leads to democracy.

This book presents a case study for testing the emerging theories of democracy and civil society. It assesses the extent to which Nigerian democratic struggles are expressive of the social movement or consciousness for establishing, practicing and preserving democratic values and institutions in Nigeria. By so doing, I seek to address the prevalent notion among studies on civil society that the actions of popular movement organizations that emerged internationally from democratic struggles in the 1990s formed important components of the pressure for democratization during that decade.

The study spans thirteen years, 1986-1999, an era in which a new brand of civil society organization and activism was manifested in the growth and proliferation of scores of pro-democracy groups. Spearheading the pro-democracy movement by way of these organizations'[6] alliance with professional groups and other civil society sectors, the Nigerian pro-democracy movement vigorously and consistently over the entire period challenged the Nigerian military state for the desired objective of a re-democratized state.[7]

Nigeria is a significant case study of a single country undergoing democratic struggles, observed in the context of African comparative politics and international democratization studies for two reasons.[8] First, between 1993-1999, Nigeria became a prominent international case of political instability. By 1994, the international community- represented most forcefully by the actions and pronouncements of the Commonwealth Heads of Government Meeting (CHOGM), the United Nations, South Africa, Great Britain, Canada, and the United States- had repeatedly called on the government of Nigeria to "respect the rights of the Nigerian people to freely elect their government and to return to civilian government." What's more, during that period, Nigeria was categorized, alongside China, as a "major" international human rights abuser.[9]

Second, is Nigeria's uniqueness as a study for research within comparative African politics. Nigeria used to be considered the "Giant of Africa" in the 70s and 80s. In the 1960s, after successfully establishing democratic government during that period, Nigeria was predicted to become the world's largest "Black" democracy. In 1999, however, Nigeria still represented a case of late democratization in Africa- especially compared to African states with smaller economies and lower-levels of development.[10] Having once been in the forefront of economic development[11] and foreign policy,[12] as well as a country that has formulated elaborate transition-to-democracy models for the rest of Africa, it was disappointing to the international arena that Nigeria still remained under military dictatorship.[13]

Adding to the mystery of Nigeria's late democratization was the fact that the country also represented a unique contradictory case of state/civil society relations- one of the few nations in Africa demonstrating a long-standing and rich civil associational life, a history of deep democratic space, and, in fact, a highly developed practice with democratic regimes[14]. There had always been a rich but contradictory democratic tradition embedded in Nigerian civil society, organized around a relatively free press, a fairly developed judicial system, a strong culture of trade union struggle, and a "federalist" political system based on disparate centers of power and governed by "checks and balances."

Thus, ".... if Nigeria is so well endowed with associations, why does there exist so little democracy at the level of the state?", quizzed Bjorn Beckman who describes Nigerian politics as, "so much civil society; so little democracy" (Beckett and Young, 1997). A wide body of literature has emerged that seeks to understand the paradox of late democratization in the country. Richard Joseph asks, "Why did Nigeria, which has conducted perhaps the most extensive attempts of any developing nation to construct a constitutional democracy, fail so abysmally? If the Nigerian military governed the country during much of the post-civil war decade in a manner that allowed for a high level of openness and autonomy in civil society, how did this country end up being one of the few today still ruled by a military dictatorship?" (Beckett and Young,1997).

One group of scholars has sought to explain Nigeria's late democratization paradox. In their seminal study of the 1985-1993 transition-to-democracy program organized by the Babangida regime, Olagunju, Jinadu, and Oyovbaire[15] present the theory of "military rule as anti-politics." Referring to this notion as a culturally-imposed paradox, the authors explain that anti-politics has arisen as a result of the interlocking, cultural, economic, political, social and clientele networks which organizations in civil society have created.

Even within the twenty-three year tenure of military government, the Nigerian military sought to legitimize itself by drawing from this network of civilians and former politicians for a pool of experienced public servants. In turn, networks among civil society served as lobby groups and bases for recruitment into the military administrations in the country. According to the authors, the practice of anti-politics has kept tyrannical authoritarian rule at bay in Nigeria. In addition to providing the function of a "check" on the excesses of authoritarian military regimes, the very close and sometimes indistinguishable alliances and coalitions forged between civil society and the military state fostered the politicization of the Nigerian military, thereby undercutting the development of a sustainable and consolidated democratic government.[16]

The present study draws upon previous attempts to understand late democratization in Nigeria, especially drawing upon Olagunju's theory of the military as anti-politics. Re-conceptualizing this problem as the Nigerian democracy-paradox, the current study seeks to draw correlations among the mutually interpenetrative relationship between the Nigerian military and civil society; Nigeria's late democratization; and the efforts made by the Nigerian pro-democracy movement of the 1990's to generate a popular-based democratic transition.

The current study is written to respond to three related questions referred to above. The first two questions address the normative study of outcomes with regard to 'democratic struggles and civil society' derived from the Nigerian case. Here, the book assesses the extent to which Nigerian civil society has been expressive of the social movement or consciousness for establishing democratic institutions and advancing democratic values during the country's third phase of democratization. By attempting to determine democratic outcomes, the first question looks for tangible evidence demonstrating that democracy in Nigeria was advanced as a result of democratic struggles, organized by the popular groups selected for study.

This objective further assesses the organizational impact that the groups researched had on advancing democratization during the period studied. I determine democratic advancement by identifying how the organizations limited military-state power in Nigeria, particularly in the realization of a democratic transition. Moreover, I seek to determine democratic advancement by demonstrating concrete incidents in which the Nigerian democracy movement mobilized broader civil societal communities to advocate for democracy.

Following this theme, in this study, I also demonstrate the extent to which these organizations were able to advertise the vulnerability of the military regime, eroding the regime's legitimacy and ultimately inducing a positive response by the military regarding policy on democracy. The study demonstrates how the pro-democracy movement gradually undermined military credibility in the country's politics.

Determining democratic advancement also relates to my second question- also a normative concern- with regard to the organizational attributes, which link civil society struggles to democratic advancement. By applying a revised civil society-political liberalization thesis to the normative study of democratic struggles in Nigeria, the current study seeks to spell out the organizational conditions, which facilitate civil society's capacity to realize democratic outcomes. This second question seeks to determine the extent to which the pro-democracy organizations researched have been able to facilitate and expand the mobilization of social resistance among a broad spectrum of civil societal communities in Nigeria, thereby influencing democratic awareness and empowerment among such communities. Indicators demonstrating effective social mobilization of democratic awareness include incidents of the movement's agitation of civil society sectors to embark upon pro-democracy events and join the pro-democracy struggle.[17]

Finally, hinging upon the normative case and examining the contingent historical element of the Nigerian case study, the last question- an empirical concern- more narrowly focuses upon the thesis of democratic outcomes by seeking to determine whether long-standing, mutually interlocking civil-military relations in Nigeria- defined as the Nigerian democracy-paradox[18]- continued to undercut democratic sustainability and consolidation in the country's political landscape.

In determining the organizations' impact on the struggle for Nigerian democratization, I examine the movement's performance outcomes in relation to the Nigerian democracy paradox by looking at the extent to which democratic consciousness is embodied within the organizational structure of the movement. I critically compare and assess each organization's embodiment of elite and personal politics, both factors that affected the movement's ability to provide effective leadership and therefore successful democratic outcomes.

In sum, in this book, an examination of the resistance to democracy posed by Nigeria's military state has enabled me to formulate the problems that faced the 1990s "campaign for democracy" as well as to identify its central issues and principles.

Democratic Struggles in Civil Society

With democratization rapidly occurring in Latin America in the 1980s and in Africa and the Eastern European/Soviet bloc in the 90s, Samuel Huntington asserted that democratization was the most significant global development, especially in the Post-Cold War environment.[19] It is no wonder, therefore, that accompanying these global occurrences in the 1990's was a proliferation of studies examining this new wave of democratic transitions. However, differently from earlier studies on democratic transitions,[20] democratic transitions in Eastern Europe, the Former Soviet Union, Asia, and Africa, began to increasingly be analyzed through the paradigm of democratic struggles and the participation of civil society.[21]

As an example, in his study of global democratization, Larry Diamond points out that the "democratic revolution" is the cumulative achievement of tens and hundreds of thousands, sometimes millions of citizens who become actively involved in civic movements and independent media. In South Korea, Taiwan, Chile, Poland, China, Czechoslovakia, South Africa, *Nigeria* and Benin, extensive mobilization of civil society was a crucial source of pressure for democratic change. For this author, and many others, it was now clear that to understand democratic change around the world, one must study civil society.[22]

Diamond's representation of the contemporary 'democratic transition' approach to democratization draws from Barrington Moore's classical study on democracy *the Social Origins of Dictatorship and Democracy.* Moore observed that democracy is advanced through historical social struggle, pushed forward by the divergent interests of socio-economic groups. Democracy developed as a long and incomplete struggle to check the power of arbitrary rulers, to replace arbitrary rules with just and rational ones, and finally to obtain a share for the underlying population in the making of rules. Capitalizing on this approach to democratization, my own work is informed by a more recent study by Dietrich Rueschmeyer, John Stephen and Evelyn Stephens. This model examines popular struggle in democratic advancement, where advancement signified the capacity for civil-societal mobilization and organization against authoritarian rule.

Like these studies, I view democracy as a product of power. For this approach, democracy is significantly extended from the narrow scope of the political to the wider scope of the economic and social. Using this theoretical underpinning, my own study focuses on the interplay of shifting social sector constellations, showing how various social groups compete and struggle for democratic inclusion.

For Africa, the occurrence and study of democratic transitions and civil societal struggles has been particularly prominent since the late 80s, with the 90s being described as Africa's "second wave of liberalization." It became fashionable for academics to explain political instability and democratic breakdown in Africa through the nexus of state-society relations. This approach argued that the crisis of the African state fostered the emergence of social actors who devised various strategies to survive the nested crises of state action.[23] Democratic struggles, according to this perspective, were to be analyzed as part of the process of a state-society struggle, where civil society represents a counter-hegemonic reaction against an all pervasive, predatory—albeit 'soft' or 'weak'—state hegemony. [24]

With many African nations[25] having already heeded the "winds of change" by the mid-90s, many scholars predicted for Africa the transformation of the entire political, social and economic reality of the continent as a potential result of democratic struggles by African civil society.[26] To the extent that the Nigerian democratic struggle occurred in coincidence with the broader wave of popular sentiment for political change that swept Africa and other regions in the developing world, the literature on civil society- leveraging with it theories on social movements and democratic transitions- helps in understanding the features of the mass social mobilization advocating democratization in Nigeria. These studies have been especially helpful in determining the influence these democratic struggles can have on democratic transitions at the level of the authoritarian regime.

As a leading African nation, where democratic government continued to be elusive for three decades but where democratic struggles among civil society tended to be especially forceful and prominent, Nigeria represents an important case study for unraveling and testing theories of civil society. The Nigerian case demonstrates the increasing power of democratic ideology over authoritarian ideologies in Africa during the decade of the 90s.

III. Civil Society-Democratization

In the 1990's, the resuscitated 16th century Western European-originated concept of civil society [27] became an extremely popular concept for both the analysis of the social bases of political change in Africa, and for external policy support for processes of liberal democratic political reform. Naomi Chazan, the leading theorist of civil society and democracy in Africa asserted that,

"Civil society is the first and necessary step toward democracy in Africa."[28] Chazan's pace-setting studies on civil society in Ghana in which she famously referred to state-society relations in Africa as a "precarious balancing act," set the tone for research on civil society in Africa. This theme is best portrayed as the survival and consolidation of new democracies as predicated on a civil society that is active in delimiting state dominance (Chazan, 1992; Haberson 1994; Bratton 1994; Callaghy 1994). Chazan broadly defines civil society as, "The dynamic processes of interaction between the state and society, a straddling of constant movement between the official and unofficial, the private and the public, the rural and the urban, a precarious balance between state and society." [29]

However, the wide empirical and theoretical currency of civil society in the manner used by Chazan and others demonstrates that there still exists a large measure of ambiguity as to the concept's precise applicability to democratic struggles in Africa, especially the all-encompassing notion of civil society as one thing or the other. The concept's most formidable detractors find "civil society" as a conceptual variable to be diffuse, hard to define, empirically imprecise, and ideologically laden. [30] A significant point of the nature of this criticism concerns the "all-encompassing" notion of civil society as "society against the state" evidenced by Chazan's definition of civil society as, ".....autonomous societal groups that interact with the state but delimit and constrain its action"(Chazan, 1994). Whereas Chazan's definition rightly recognizes that civil society implies diverse, narrow interests sharing the space outside of the state; however, the definition requires more theoretical precision regarding the differentiation of civil society's diverse sectors and interests,[31] thereby necessitating the delineation of boundaries within civil society. Critics of Chazan's "civil society-applied-to-Africa paradigm" ask, "To what extent can we speak of the existence of civil society in Africa?" And more importantly, "What is the significance of this process, particularly in light of democratic struggles?" (Mamdani, 1995).

Also requiring more precise analysis is the civil-society-political liberalization thesis, a paradigm that links the growth of associational life and the growth of pressures for political reform. The bulk of more recent contemporary literature on civil society in Africa uses the civil society-political liberalization thesis to argue that civil society is at the heart of the democratization struggles in Africa. For Chazan and her followers, the relationship between civil society and democratization is assumed. Civil society is the prime engine of democratization, and the mere existence of civil society necessarily results in democratization.

Critics refute that there exists any empirical evidence demonstrating the automatic civil society - political liberation linkage. On theoretical grounds, leading such criticism is Mahmood Mamdani, who has labeled such assumptions as the programmatic agenda of international neo-liberal institutions.[32] After all, Mamdani argues, it is one thing to argue that civil society expands dramatically from the mid-1980's in Africa, but quite another to assert that the same "civil society" lies un-differentiatedly behind democratization. More broadly, one should ask: What are the boundaries of civil society? Which associations are eligible or involved in political transformation? Acknowledging that civil society may not behave as a change agent in all circumstances, by what means do we identify such agents.

A thesis study on social movement organizations[33] and civil society in Kenya by Stephen Ndegwa[34] provides a concrete case study, which more definitively refutes the automatic relation between civil society and democratization. Ndegwa's thesis further asserts that the automatic linkage is supported only in a vague sense and that the resurgence of civil society and its political activity in Africa does not automatically cause political liberalization.[35] Ndegwa challenges the supporters of the civil society-political liberalization thesis to more substantially support with empirical and theoretical evidence that organizations in civil society necessarily are central to opposing democratic governments (Ndegwa, 1996). In so doing, Ndegwa questions whether civil society necessarily behaves as a change agent in all circumstances.[36]

Ndegwa supports his criticism in his own study of civil society in Kenya (Ndegwa, 1996), in which he determined that organizations within civil society were not necessarily able or willing to advance democratization. Though acknowledging the impressive grassroots organizing of both NGOs researched in his study, Ndegwa warns that this merely signifies certain implications for democratization, and therefore the "promise of democracy" (Ndegwa, 1996), but is not evidence that democratization has been advanced. Presenting the organizational attributes of civil society as the most important features of organizations that make them crucial contributors to democratization, Ndegwa identifies four conditions that must obtain: organization, resources, alliances, and political opportunity. By stressing the aforementioned organizational features, Ndegwa successfully distinguishes among the configuration of power within civil society by linking the internal characteristics[37] of organizations in civil society to the broader collective claims by civil society- a necessary element in explaining democratic struggles.

By normatively delineating organizational attributes for research on "civil society," Ndegwa's study also draws upon the revelation of political opportunity structures[38] in the broader relations embedded in the tensions and contradictions of social change as well as in the encroaching state structures. By emphasizing the interplay between organizations among civil society and a state undergoing structural change, this model is able to identify the historical-institutional structure of the state and strategies it uses to deal with its challengers among civil society.

Underlining these structural determinants of state-society relations, Ndegwa differentiates civil society further by arguing that organizational power alone was not a sufficient condition for having impact upon democratization. It was necessary to examine each organization in historical perspective, examining the organizations' leadership to determine the extent to which organizations within civil society had embedded social cleavages, such as personal rule, within their own structures.

Ndegwa's conclusion was that of the two NGOs he studied, the more institutionalized one remained aloof when faced with clear opportunities to engage the state in ways that would advance the democratic ferment in Kenya. Persuasively, Ndegwa concludes that the progressive tendencies of some civil society organizations should therefore not mislead analysts into thinking that such organizations are naturally predisposed to democratic government or that all of civil society is progressive. Instead, it is the leadership that directs the political actions of civil society organizations, especially when decision-making has yet to be institutionalized.

The theoretical and empirical critique of civil society outlined above suggest the need to reexamine assumptions about the real and potential contributions of organizations in civil society to democratization in Africa. For example, Ndegwa's thesis implies that whereas definitions of civil society observe actors sharing the space outside of the state, these actors' interests may not necessarily be shared. The study shows that even though organizations may be expressed in or by some parts of civil society, they are not synonymous with the generic civil society.

Mamdani further suggests the more effective usage of the notion of social movements to analyze democratic struggles in contemporary Africa. Arguing that the social movement category is "the starting point around which universal studies anchor themselves" (Mamdani, 1995), the scholar's leading 1997 African Studies volume criticizes the work by researchers on civil society and democratization in Africa as surprisingly uninformed by the theoretical findings which have accumulated from international and cross-national analysis of social movements.[39] Drawing from the broader study of contentious politics (Tilly, 1981, 1978),[40] social movements are defined as "networks of informal interactions between a plurality of individuals, groups and/or organizations, engaged in political or cultural conflicts, on the basis of shared collective identities/interests." [41]

Acknowledging the significantly distinguishing features of the social movement category, Michael Bratton proposes a revised definition of civil society, which attempts to compensate for the lack of precision embodied in the concept by including social movements within his definition of civil society. Bratton states that, "*Civil society* is an *arena* where manifold *social movement organizations* from all classes attempt to constitute themselves in an ensemble of arrangements, so that they can express themselves and advance their interests."[42] In Bratton's revised definition, social movements serve as an effective theoretical framework for determining the linkages between civil society and democratic transitions due to the literature's ability to recognize the "emancipatory" character of civil society—defined as the concept's "agency" as an institutional basis for political action and struggle.[43] The social movement literature identifies agency among civil society, by selecting for analysis, only civil society organizations involved in political contention against the state and examining only civil society actors who are agents of political contention.

Social movements are instances of collective action, which vary in scale of mobilization. In turn, social movement organizations sometimes exist as part of loose, "structure-less" movements within civil society, where there exists shared support, among vast sectors of a society, for a desirable and possible claim.[44] Using the social movement method in an analysis of African democratic movements, one can distinguish between the broader democracy movement, which may include civil societal elements such as the media, the clergy, and professional organizations; and the social movement organizations—pro-democracy and human rights organizations—driving that movement. Thus, the organizational attributes reflected in a social movement imply a shared dynamic in a given direction and a core set of overriding values that bind different actors to the same broader goal. Whereas the only common thread uniting actors in civil society is the state of their "autonomy" from the state, a common thread uniting social movement organizations with broader elements among civil society is indeed the self-consciousness of their opposition or claim.

In this context, my own study will demonstrate that for civil society to effect transitions from authoritarian regimes, civil society must be expressive of the social movement or consciousness for establishing, practicing, and preserving democratic values and institutions. In their comparative study of democracy in advanced capitalist nations, central America and the Caribbean, Rueschmeyer, Stephens and Stephens (Capitalist Development & Democracy, 1992) argue that the development of democratic institutions and the effective role of the many in collective decision-making depend on these socio-economic power constellations, including the balance of class power, the power and autonomy of the state apparatus and its articulation with civil society, and the transnational structures of power.

My own book demonstrates how all three clusters interact with each other in complex ways in the Nigerian case; however, my thesis of democracy more narrowly focuses on the aspect of Rueschemeyer-Stephens model that emphasizes, "the power and autonomy of the state apparatus and its articulation with civil society." The Rueschmeyer study, while acknowledging the importance of a dense civil society as an establishment of a counterweight to state power, opts for a strategy of focusing on sectors of civil society that are organizationally and institutionally grounded- ergo social movements. As in my study, the Rueschmeyer study conceives of democracy as matter of power, adopted by some groups in civil society who operate in the context of a struggle for control over state power.

By seriously subjecting studies on civil society and democratic struggles to the disciplining of the concept, and by embracing the application and methods of the social movement literature,[45] the present study on democratic struggles in civil society in Nigeria is able to identify agents among associational life, select boundaries within civic associational life, and define conditions under which democratic struggles in Nigeria occur. Enhancing the theory of civil society by synthesizing it with the literature on social movements and democratic transitions, this study presents a theory for linking civil society to structural and organizational realities.

For the African studies school, the current study presents a more concrete relationship between civil societal resurgence in Africa and the continent's democratic transitions by showing the extent to which "agency" and the "emancipatory" efforts emerging among civil society sectors might affect Africa's remaining authoritarian states' inclination to democratize. In sum, *People Power and Democracy* provides evidence of a case study demonstrating that civil society is vibrant and active in Africa. Moreover, popular social movements are a proliferating and prominent feature of African democratic struggles, and are central to opposing undemocratic governments and to furthering and consolidating democracy in Africa.

IV. The Popular Movement Against Nigerian Military Despotism: the CD, NADECO, and the UDFN, 1986-1999

People Power and Democracy is based on research derived from a number of Nigerian academic and governmental research institutions, and from the offices of the pro-democracy organizations under consideration. The three organizations selected for research have all played dominant and pioneering roles in the Nigerian pro-democracy struggles. The book compares these three organizations in an effort to explore their social construction within the process of collective action as well as the dynamics of these groups' alliances and ideological orientations in relation to other civil society sectors.

First among these organizations, sometimes referred to as the instigator of the Nigerian democracy struggle, is the human rights-oriented Campaign for Democracy (CD). It is an umbrella group whose key affiliated groups- sometimes referred to as the CD Collective include: the Committee for Human Rights and Democracy (CDHR), the Civil Liberties Organization (CLO), the Constitutional Rights Project (CRP), and the Movement of the Survival of Ogoni People (MOSOP). These groups—through the leadership of the Campaign for Democracy—organized the popular resistance protests and demonstrations between July 5-7, 1993 and the stay-at-home protest on August 12-14, 1993, that resulted in the stepping down of General Ibrahim Babangida. This group initiated the pro-democracy movement in Nigeria, and its leader is the prominent social activist, Dr. Beko Ransome-Kuti.

The elite-oriented National Democratic Coalition (NADECO) became the dominant pro-democracy organization after the annulment of the Third Republic by the Abacha military regime. This organization is especially significant for its role in organizing rallies and lobby efforts in support of the reinstatement of Chief Abiola as the rightful winner of the June 12 elections, thereby becoming the most prominent force in the "June 12" movement. Representative of the elite, Nigerian political class opposing the Nigerian military, some of its leaders include former military personnel—Chief Alani Akinriade, and former Nigerian nationalist, Anthony Enahoro.

The United Democratic Front of Nigeria, UDFN, has been selected for the purpose of examining the Nigerian pro-democracy movement abroad. The UDFN brings together more than 100 Nigerian pro-democracy organizations located in the United States, Canada, the United Kingdom and other parts of Western Europe. The UDFN led the campaign for democracy abroad, articulating the goals of immediate democracy to the offices and institutions of western governments and international institutions. A prominent representative of this organization is UDFN chair, Nobel Prize-winner Wole Soyinka.

Other important sectors within civil society, whose coalition and alliance actions strengthened the democracy movement, include trade union and professional organizations—PENGASSAN, NUPENG, NLC, ASUU; as well as the media and the clergy.

Each organization is comparatively examined with regard to its organization, alliances, political opportunity, and resources.

Moreover, three components of social movement organizations are analyzed: actors (leaders) involved; values, beliefs, and claims articulated; and the actions (events) carried out(Tilly, 1978). This study concludes by demonstrating the direct impact of these organizations on democratic outcomes in Nigeria through organizational factors that have facilitated the capacity of each organization to advance the struggle for democracy in Nigeria.

To link the activities of the organizations researched to the broader democratic transition that ensued, this book examines the political opportunity conditions. The method employed specifies the circumstances and confrontations that shape democratic outcomes by underscoring Nigerian state-society relations as the contingent historical element in the Nigerian case. In situating the study of the Nigerian pro-democracy movement against the backdrop of the Nigerian military's "transition-to-democracy" and neoliberal economic restructuring programs initiated in 1986, the book articulates the manner in which Nigerian state power is organized and how it relates to Nigerian social forces.

The selected period of Nigerian democratic struggles, 1986-1999, is understood within the context of the effects of the global economic crisis beginning in the mid-80s, as well as the liberalization of authoritarian regimes worldwide after the end of the Cold War. These two international variables are analyzed in terms of their impact on the democratic transition in Nigeria. My method recognizes the global tensions and contradictions of social change after the post-Cold War period and analyzes democratic struggles in Nigeria in relation to the historical relationship between the state and society, using a periodization that captures the contradictory and changing character of both forces.

During the 1986–1999 period in Nigeria, civil society sectors, expressed as social movement organizations, vigorously and continuously challenged authoritarian rule and pressured the Nigerian military state for immediate re-democratization. This period is further sub-categorized by key events marking the progress of the democratic movement. 1986 marks the initiation of the Babangida military regime, the establishment of the country's third "transition-to-democracy" project and the introduction of the Structural Adjustment Program, a neo-classical monetarist economic policy. This period set the stage for pro-democracy activity. 1993 marks the annulment of the presidential elections for the Third Republic, the vigorous activation and climax of the pro-democracy movement represented by the June 12 movement, and the anti-climatic termination of the Babangida military regime.

The period from 1994-1998, includes the termination of the Third Republic and the democratic transition project, the re-intervention of the military regime under General Abacha, the expansion of the pro-democracy movement to encompass broader middle class sectors and the international arena, and finally the growth of human rights abuses and political subversion by the military regime of pro-democracy activity. 1998-1999 represents the pro-democracy movement's victory, the replacement of the tyrannical Abacha regime with the liberalizing Abubakar regime, and the enactment of the 1999 Nigerian democratic state under the Fourth Republic.

CHAPTER 2

THE DEMOCRACY PARADOX IN HISTORICAL PERSPECTIVE

I. A History of Nigeria

As early as 1914 in its pre-independence period, Nigeria had a rich, vibrant civil society coexisting with a "soft"[46] authoritarian state. Both state and society interacted to forge political development and to generate and maintain democratic space in civil society. At the same time, a professional and increasingly politicized military developed, which remained tied to networks within civil society. However, over time the military began to erode the rich tradition of civil society and democratic space.

For its twenty-eight years of politicization, the Nigerian military has not stood autonomously above civil society. Alternatively, until recently the Nigerian military and civil society have experienced long-standing, inter-penetrative, and mutually interlocking relations (Oyovbaire and Olagunju, 1993). In fact, the rich and vibrant civil associational life and political pluralism practiced among Nigerian civil society has kept tyrannical military rule at bay. In historical perspective, the paradoxical relationship between the Nigerian state and society has led to the political opportunity structures that facilitated the activism of the "pro-democracy" movement in the 1990s.

II. The Development of a "Soft" State: 1861-1966

Western European powers created many of the contemporary nations of Africa with artificial borders. Nigeria was no exception. British colonialism was established in Nigeria between 1861, with the annexation of the southern coastal post of Lagos and in 1903 with the final conquest of the northern, Hausa-Fulani heartland, the Sokoto Caliphate. In 1900 the British established two separate colonies: the Northern (north of the River Niger) and the Southern (south of the Niger). These territories held enormous diversity of ethnic groups with three major ones dominating the territorial landscape.

Above the Niger, Fulani-ruled Hausa states interacted with one another and with their neighbors under the Caliph at Sokoto. The Northern Protectorate approximated the geographical extent of the Caliphate becoming Nigeria's strongest region with control of the political machinery of the Nigerian state.[47] South of the Niger, the Yoruba constitutional monarchies held the largest ethnic entity. The Edos operated within the Yoruba orbit because of their strong historical and cultural ties to the Yoruba. However, due to the Edos' coastal location, where they traded with the Portuguese, and then the British, they were positioned for prominence in later British colonial relations. East of the Niger, the decentralized and acephalous Igbos formed the largest group. However, the neighboring coastal Tivs and Igalas forged centuries of trading ties with the Europeans and so had relative importance in the initial British colonial equation.

In 1914, the British amalgamated the two protectorates to establish the single administrative unit of Nigeria with the country's first governor, Lord Lugard. Imposing a system of "indirect rule"[48] through the Native Authority System, the British sought to rule the separate ethnic regions through their existing authority structures. Where there were no traditional rulers, as in Igboland, the British created "red cap" rulers from within the group. In the Northern protectorate, the Sokoto Caliphate was given control over the Northern territories and peoples.

In 1939, Nigeria was divided into four administrative units: the colony of Lagos; and the Western, Eastern, and Northern provincces. Expanding upon "indirect rule" in 1946, the British further subdivided the nation into regions with the South transformed into the Eastern and Western regions and the Northern Protectorate transforming into the expansive Northern region. This enhanced the practice of ethnic competition and created the structural determinants for Northern hegemony.[49] The boundaries of these regions coincided with the prevailing ethnic division in the country: the Igbo were the dominant group in the East, the Yoruba in the West, and the Hausa-Fulani in the North.[50]

This system was formalized by the Richards Constitution of 1946, and five years later Governor Macpherson's constitution "federated" the three regions by creating a central assembly in addition to the regional ones, delegating effective executive power to the regionally constituted elite. Between 1946 and 1958, there existed a "bargaining pantomime" between the tripartite federation to find an equilibrium between the three regions. This process lead to the development of Nigeria's ethnic-oriented political parties: the Igbo-oriented National Council of Nigeria and the Cameroon (NCNC)[51] in 1944, the Yoruba-based Action Group(AG) formed from the pan-Yoruba ethnic association, Egbe Omo Oduduwa, in 1950, and the Northern Peoples Congress (NPC) in 1951, formed from Jam'iyyar Mutanen Arewa.

Elections in 1951 returned victories for the NPC, the AG, and the NCNC in their home regions and established a political system with a close identity between region, party, and ethnicity that remains to the present day. De-facto independence during the British experiment with self-rule from 1951 to the 1959 pre-independence elections created the pathway for the precipitate arrival of the military in Nigerian politics. Nigeria achieved independence on October 1st, 1960. Its parliament was led by the northern-dominated NPC in coalition with the NCNC.

The Western and Eastern regions perceived the NPC ruling party as making no effort to be a national party because of its absolute population majority. The Yoruba-dominated AG assumed the role of leading opposition party, the west became disgruntled over perceptions of governmental discrimination against the west. Moreover, despite the NPC-NCNC coalition, the Igbos in the east still felt that they were being systematically excluded from national affairs. The relationship between the political parties, regions, and party leaders became one of mutual distrust. Relations deteriorated with a series of crises in the western and eastern regions that lead to the January 15, 1966 military coup led by Major Chukwuma

Kaduna Nzeogwu.

The six majors coup, as it was dubbed, set the course for the first round of political violence in post-independence Nigeria with the killings of the nation's first Prime Minister, Sir Abubakar Tafawa Balewa, as well as the premiers of the Western and Northern regions Chief S.L. Akintola and Sir Ahmadu Bello. As a result of the country's first and most violent coup d'etat, the Nigerian military took the front seat in Nigerian politics.

III. The Nigerian State and Military Vanguardism

On January 16, 1966, the acting president of Nigeria's First Republic, Dr. Nwafor Orizu, announced to the nation that the Council of Ministers had unanimously decided to voluntarily hand over the administration of the country to the armed forces of the Republic "with immediate effect."[52] The failed but extremely violent coup attempt of Major Nzeogwu led to a crisis that the Nigerian army attempted to meet. The stage was set for the militarization of Nigerian politics. In his acceptance of the civilian offer, the commander of the Nigerian Army addressed the nation in these words. "The invitation has been accepted, and I, General Johnson Thomas Umunakewe Aguiyi-Ironsi, have been formally invested with authority as the Head of the National Military Government and Supreme Commander of the Nigerian Armed Forces." (Agedah, 1993).

The supposedly interim presence of the military in politics stretched from 1966 to 1999. It was almost three decades later on November 17, 1993, when a similar event occurred. The military, led by General Abacha, met with the ministers and state officials of the Interim National Government and asked its head, Chief Shonekan, to invite the armed forces to resume the governance of the country in order to safeguard the integrity of the Federal Republic of Nigeria. Chief Shonekan informed the military leaders that the armed forces should announce the removal of his government from office.

Since the military's first intervention into Nigerian democratic politics in 1966, the institution has enjoyed a legitimacy among Nigerian civil society. In fact, it is democratic regimes that have been perceived as more of an aberration.[53] Legitimization of the military was based on the idea that their regimes were to be short and corrective, intervening at moments of political crisis.

Militarization was best expressed by former Nigerian Head of State, General Babangida who saw the military as "historical missionaries" in politics (Babangida, 1989). As long as Nigerian military regimes temporarily intervened into democratic politics for the resolution of acute political crises and the re-organization of democratic structures and institutions, as well as for the organization of elections, they were legitimated by civil society. The military was seen as a force that prevented civilian corruption and corrosive ethnicity.

Despite this corrective mission, the military turned out to be no better equipped to handle the systemic political problems of ethnicity and corruption. Ethnic politics were so entrenched in the Nigerian political system that it was the military who lead the new nation to civil war in 1967. In July 1966, disgruntled by perceptions of Southern—particularly Igbo domination—Northern officers led a counter coup, killing General Ironsi and establishing the leadership of Lieutenant Colonel Yakubu Gowon, a northern Christian from a minority ethnic group. However, Gowon's regime was unable to bridge the bitter ethnic enmity among the disparate regions. In May 1967 Colonel Chukwuemeka Ojukwu, the military administrator of the Eastern Region announced the secession of the Eastern region as the Republic of Biafra. As a result of this decision, in July 1967 the Nigerian civil war began.

The Nigerian Civil War lasted until January 1970 when Biafra surrendered. The old political order of four regions was replaced with a twelve-state arrangement. The Gowon regime believed it had a mandate to forge Federal supremacy. His regime used the might of the military to facilitate a post-war oil boom. The Nigerian Civil War fostered the legitimization of the military by civil society and led to the institution's politicization, bearing a post-colonial feature of Nigerian politics.

After a decade of military rule under the Gowon regime,[54] civil society began to view the regime more negatively. General Gowon reneged on his promise to relinquish power in 1976 and announced an indefinite continuance of his military government. There were allegations that the general's ambition was to become "President-for-Life." Losing the moral claim to his leadership, General Gowon was overthrown in a coup in 1975 organized by General Murtala Muhammed.

The *Nigerian Tribune* of August 1, 1975 stated the causes of

General Gowon's fall as his inability to express the wishes of the people and the breaching of his own solemn pledge to the nation to re-democratize. Instead, he sought to impose a military dictatorship on Nigeria indefinitely with himself as dictator.[55] For Nigerian civil society, military de-legitimization set in as it began to be seen as the hegemonization of the military interest with the subordination of the civil society. (Momoh, Abubakar,1997) Murtala Mohammed stated that the immediate priority of his regime was to establish the return of the nation to civilian leadership in 1979. The agenda for the country's 'transition-to-civil-rule' was announced by General Mohammed in his 15th Independence Anniversary broadcast to the nation. The leader announced a five-stage program aimed at transferring power to civilians by October 1 1979. However, due to Mohammed's untimely death in an unsuccessful, but fatal, coup on February 13, 1976, led by Lt.Colonel Buka Suka Dimka, the liberalizing regime of Major General Murtala Mohammed came to an abrupt end.

Mohammed's second in command, General Olusegun Obasanjo was ushered in as Nigeria's fourth military head of state and commander in chief of the armed forces. Obasanjo sought a continuum of the administrative plans and policies of his predecessor, and therefore, immediately sought to continue Mohammed's five-stage transition to democracy program. This plan included the appointment of a constitutional drafting committee (CDC) in October 1975; election into a constituent assembly in October 1977; lifting of the 1966 ban on political parties in 1977; and state and federal elections by 1979. General Obasanjo implemented an elaborate military-organized, democratic transition program.[56] It drew extensively on civil society participation. This is one way in which the military and civil society have collaborated for the purpose of determining the development of a democratic culture and sustainable democratic institutions for the country.

October 1, 1979, saw the birth of the Second Republic, a political system based on the American presidential system. This model had been borne out of a debate by Nigerians to design a political system that would provide solutions for the political problems of the First Republic. General Obasanjo and armed services stood back to allow President Alhaji Shehu Shagari, a civilian, to become the new commander-in-chief of the armed forces. However, the

Second Republic lasted a mere four years.

The 1983 elections with their allegations of massive rigging reinforced the notion that President Shagari's National Party of Nigeria (NPN) was a northern-dominated party that would do anything to control the Western and Eastern regions. In addition the economy was failing as a result of drastic decline in oil production that Shagari could not seem to arrest. There was blatant corruption and profligacy by NPN ministers and other politicians. Because of this, a military coup led by General Muhammadu Buhari overthrew his administration on December 31, 1983.

Paradoxically the coup that ended Nigeria's second experiment with democratic government and returned the military to power sparked nationwide celebration. There had been much dissatisfaction with the Shagari administration. However, public jubilation was short-lived. Less than four months into its leadership, the Buhari regime incited animosity and disaffection from all sectors of Nigerian society. Buhari and his second in command, General Idiagbon, instituted a 'reign of terror'[57] supposedly to instill discipline and sanitize the decadence and chaos that pervaded civilian politics.

The glaring excesses, repression, high-handedness and political insensitivity of the Buhari regime, however, made Nigerians fear re-militarization. That created the conditions for the emergence of a new government under General Ibrahim Babangida , which came to power in a palace coup on August 25, 1985. The Babangida administration broke with the role of the military as "impartial arbiter," and instead embarked on personal military rule with General Babangida assuming for the first time in military history the title "President". General Babangida repealed the tyrannical military decrees officiated by his predecessors.

Moreover, General Babangida made a bold commitment to returning power to a democratically elected civilian government. He announced a five-year transition program, 1986-1990.[58] General Babangida's plan was the result of a vibrant exchange of ideas between state and civil society embodied in civilian committee known as the Political Bureau, which was to set the stage and the basis for this transition. The Political Bureau debàte offered opportunities to Nigerians to seek to improve control over their institutions. The bureau was especially remarkable for its varied, high quality composition of historians, educators, political scientists, psychologists, dramatists, journalists, labor leaders, women and others.[59]

The Political Bureau submitted the blueprint for a democratic model that was to become the Third Republic: a socialist-oriented economy within a liberal democratic institutional framework restricted to a two-party system. The bureau drew up a program of returning state power to a democratically elected government, recommending August 1992 as the terminal date, ending with presidential elections.[60] However, the scheduled hand-over to democratic rule never occurred. The transition program went into crisis on June 12, 1993 with the annulment of the presidential election results by General Babangida.

Much of the public thought the annulment reflected the Nigerian military's goal to perpetuate itself and General Babangida in power. Military rule was now almost completely de-legitimized. Civil society began to relentlessly try to reverse the attempt to revert the nation back to military politics. Despite uprisings from civil society, the Third Republic was officially abrogated by a military coup led by General Sani Abacha in November 1993. In 1994, General Abacha announced yet another "transition-to-democracy" program to culminate in democratic government in 1998. In an act reflecting a more modern and sophisticated means of military politicization, General Abacha, before his death in 1998, gave indications that he was orchestrating his own election as the sole presidential candidate in the impending 1998 democratic elections.

IV. The Decline of the Tri-Partite Alliance

As a result of the politicization of the Nigerian military and its fostering of political relations with the political elite among civil society, the dominant alignment of socio-political forces from January 1966 to 1990 has been aptly described as a "triangular elite alliance" of military, the civil service, and various business groupings. (Graff,1978) Within this constellation, the military were, and remained, the politically dominant elite group; however, the civilian political elite middle class including bureaucrats and local business sectors[61] were essential to the military government's goal of "corrective mission".

However, by 1993 the fall-out from the abortion of the Babangida transition-to-democracy program accelerated the erosion of the military's preeminent position in Nigerian politics. By the 1990s when it became clear to even the political class that the military's transition-to-democracy program was being used by the military to sustain itself in power, the civil-military alliance that had developed through the 70s and 80s became severely weakened and fractionalized. The alliance transformed itself into a civil-military paradox, whereby former mutual interests among civil and military sectors became competing interests of political contention.

With a growing national resentment against military rule as a whole, a resentment that the Babangida and Abacha administrations heightened, the notion of military vanguardism began to be replaced by an active campaign against military rule and an anti-militarist ideology. The 1993 political crisis resulted in the end of the Third Republic and the formal initiation of the pro-democracy struggle, the flip side of anti-militarism.[62]

CHAPTER 3

THE NIGERIAN STATE AND POLITICAL OPPORTUNITY 1986-1993

I. The Political Opportunity of the Mid-80s

The main incentives for social movement creation and diffusion are found in the structure of political opportunities. Increasing access to power, realignments in the political system, conflicts among the elite, and the availability of allies give early challengers the incentive to assault the power structure and create opportunities for others. [63] By 1993, all of these political opportunities existed so that the Nigerian pro-democracy movement could come into being.

At no time in Nigeria's history has there more social movement organizations advocating democracy than during 1986-1999. Although Nigeria had its national independence movement and episodic organized action against the state by professional associations and labor groups, the "democracy movement" did not exist until 1986-1999. Because the military has ruled Nigeria since 1966[64] and the democracy movement has emerged only two decades later, it is important to identify the conditions that led to emergence of this movement.

Both domestic and international events facilitated the growth of social movement organizations within Nigerian civil society that collectively challenged the Nigerian military state.[65] Three general distinguishing factors led to the political opportunity conditions[66] and to the emergence of the Nigerian pro-democracy movement. First, the historically and relatively "open" authoritarian Nigerian military state paradoxically became an increasingly "closed" system[67] during General Babangida's period of national governmental reorganization.[68] The subsequent "closure" during the Babangida regime manifested in the restriction of criticism against the political transition program and the repressive handling of the drastic social upheaval caused by a second feature—neo-liberal economic restructuring.[69] Both factors occurred at the same time as pro-democracy activism among a broader sector of civil society heightened as a result of the international support for democratization in the post-Cold War Era period. [70]

These conditions precipitated changes in political interests and identities as political networks, opportunities, and strategies shifted to create one of the strongest opposition movements ever to emerge against military rule in post-colonial Nigerian history. The national governmental and economic restructuring programs implemented by the Babangida military regime were "contingent"[71] political opportunity structures that facilitated a period of state/society contention that resulted in the emergence of the Nigerian democracy movement.

II. The Babangida Military Regime (1986-1993)

In August 1985, in what might be described as a counter-coup against the military junta that ousted the democratic regime of the Second Republic, [72] "President" Major General Ibrahim Babangida, urged in his maiden speech the need for the country to undergo a "controlled or guided opening of the country's economic and socio-political space." (Olagunju, Oyovbaire and Jinadu 1995). The Babangida coup was about leadership style, consultation, accountability, consensus, justice and human rights in so far as it was directed against the high-handed activities and the obnoxious leadership style of the previous Buhari military regime, which it replaced.[73] Like previous military regimes, in his administration's early years, General Babangida's was extremely popular during its earlier years. The first of Nigeria's seven military leaders to take on the title "President," General Babangida earned a reputation for political skill and decisiveness. Here, it seemed, was a military politician with an ear for public opinion, a liberal and populist bent, the wisdom and self-confidence to draw in an extraordinary range of expert professional and intellectual counsel. The general expressed a determination to carefully and deliberately restore democracy. Babangida repeatedly promised that his coup would be "the last in Nigerian history." [74]

In the first five months of his administration President Babangida took several significant measures to popularize himself with civil society. He revoked Decree 475 of 1984 and a number of other decrees; he released political detainees and began to reform the discredited chief intelligence institution, the National Security Organization (NSO). Other consolidation measures included the appointment of a number of prominent members of professional associations to the Federal Council of Ministers. Prince Bola Ajibola, the immediate past president of the Nigerian Bar Association (NBA), was appointed federal attorney-general and minister of justice, a popular move in view of the active role the NBA had played in opposing the excesses and human rights violations of the Buhari regime.

Similarly, a senior member of the Nigerian Medical Association (NMA), Professor Ransome-Kuti—also the elder brother of human rights campaigner, Dr. Beko Ransome-Kuti, was appointed federal minister of health. Finally, Prince Tony Momoh, a leading journalist and senior member of the Nigerian Union of Journalists (NUJ), two of whose members had been jailed under Decree 4, was appointed federal minister of information. Subsequently, the Babangida administration lifted the ban on the Nigerian Medical Association (NMA), the National Association of Resident Doctors (NARD), and the National Union of Nigerian Students.[76]

The most important landmark in the Babangida regime, however, was the implementation of the structural adjustment program, (SAP) and the transition-to-democracy program, (PTP)[77]. On October 1, 1985, the military president said that "intermittent bad government has left us a legacy of economic mismanagement and a chain of political instability... we must begin a most vigorous search for a new political order capable of ensuring sustained economic growth and social development."[78] The address conceptualized the regime's idea of transition in such a way as to link the issue of economic restructuring with that of political and social restructuring, portraying restructuring as a problem of social and political design or engineering.

The combination of economic and political crises that emerged from the implementation of these two programs provoked the emergence and proliferation of the pro-democracy movement by 1993. Both programs ended up as calamitous failures. First of all, the social contradictions that the economic crisis generated led to sporadic and varied popular resistance. As military repression intensified in the form of the regime's unwillingness to hand-over power to civilians, the counter-offensive mobilization for democracy was set in motion.

III. Structural Adjustment Program (SAP)

In 1989, the normally "open"[79] posture of the Nigerian military dramatically changed as a result of socio-economic restructuring triggered, ironically, by the military's economic restructuring program. A drastic drop in the standard of living for most Nigerians, led to a dynamic reconfiguration of social relations among the country's middle and working classes. The implementation of a neo-liberal monetarist economic model in the structural adjustment program (SAP) set the stage for pro-democracy activism.

The 1980s saw global economic recession, which especially affected Nigeria because of the dramatic decline in oil revenues.[80] This crisis manifested itself in the form of revenue falls, industrial decline, inflation, a payments crisis, rising unemployment and a debt service problem.[81] Supported by the International Monetary Fund (IMF)[82], and the World Bank in July 1986, the Babangida regime introduced a far-reaching and controversial economic program. The Babangida regime set itself the task, primarily with external support, of redressing the effects on the economy of, "...25 years of administrative controls, legal restrictions and bureaucratic regulations. The culture of controls is [having] in its place.....a new philosophy of economic liberalism and deregulation."[83]

The government program aimed to: devalue the *naira* in order to stimulate exports and discourage imports of nonessentials; combat inflation through a generalized liquidity and credit squeeze, including the minimizing of deficit budgeting and reducing public expenditures; liberalize the economy by removing exchange and trade restrictions and deregulating prices and interest rates; and: d) repay the huge foreign debt of the country. In a national broadcast announcing the commencement of the restructuring process, President Babangida removed 80 per cent of the "subsidy" on petroleum products, cut subventions to state parastatals, reduced public expenditure, reduced imports, and announced the intention to privatize public enterprises.

An important part of the case for structural adjustment-led economic liberalization was its claim that it would improve income distribution among lower and rural classes. The IMF and the World Bank attempted to link economic liberalization with democracy by arguing that marketization frees up agency from excessive state-ness, and thereby improves income distribution among non-state sectors.[84] However, in Nigeria, during this period, the link between economic liberalization, increased incomes, and democracy was weak; within a very short period after its introduction, the SAP unleashed an unprecedented inflationary pressure on the economy.

The devaluation of the *naira* meant reduction of real wages by at least 50 per cent since wages were frozen. The SAP, in fact, had a negative effect on Nigerians' well-being. The Nigerian middle classes, already badly hit by the economic crisis, suffered additional setbacks. The introduction of market reforms far from restoring their economic and social fortunes actually diminished them further. By 1989, after three years of the SAP, empirical research demonstrated that the changes in income caused by the implementation of SAP, were distributed relatively, and therefore differently among individuals, groups and sectors respectively (Ihonvbere, 1994).

In general, the perception by the masses regarding the SAP was that it undermined the living standards for most Nigerians and posed major livelihood challenges for others with more losers than winners in the reform process (Beckman, 1990; Olukoshi, 1991). Where "Democracy" for the World Bank/IMF, meant economic liberalization and the opportunity for individual Nigerians to make more market choices, but the SAP did not meet the democratic goals of the Nigerian populace in the realm of democratic governance and the ability of groups and sectors to participate in the choice of economic policies. Ironically, the effect of the SAP for most of Nigerians was a deterioration in their socio-economic conditions and concomitant civil and democratic rights.

Above all, economic restructuring resulted in a change in the traditional alignments between civil society and the military with the middle classes becoming especially impoverished and disgruntled in relation to the state. The dramatic emergence of a lower-middle class as a result of the readjustment of income levels and devaluation of the currency, led to the majority of the middle class's exclusion from access to state patronage and to the market. This led to break up of former military alignments and the formation of new ones. Given the drastic transformation of the Nigerian economy that accompanied economic liberalization with devaluation and reduced living standards, loss of jobs in the urban areas, and sky-rocketing inflation, anti-adjustment sentiments began to take the shape in the pro-democratic struggle. There developed a coalition of urban social groups that demanded inclusion and change (Ihonvbere, 1994).

The SAP came under attack from all sides with unions and professional associations leading the agitation for the lifting of the wage freeze and the scrapping of the program. In 1989, despite the glaring problems with the economic restructuring program, General Babangida declared, "there was no alternative to SAP." At the same time, anti-SAP discussion began to be suppressed as exemplified by the police raid in June 1989 when intellectuals, journalists, labor leaders, and lawyers, including Gani Fawehinmi,[85] Tai Solarin, and Micheal Imoudu were detained for discussing alternatives to SAP.

May 1989 produced anti-SAP riots, in which at least 58 people were killed in two weeks of mass protests organized by ASUU and NANS against SAP.[86] These organizations were dissolved and others, including the NLC, were persecuted. The "openness" of the early days of the Babangida military regime moved toward an increasingly "closed" system. The regime reversed its initial human rights posture of civil societal alignment and inclusion and instead began to employ authoritarian tactics to suppress the increasing anti-SAP sentiment.

The growing protest by various organizations over the adverse effects on their interests as a result of the market reforms began to translate into a political struggle between an increasingly repressive state and a traditionally active civil society.

IV. Political Transition Program (PTP)

Consistent with his initial 1986 military vanguardist, political strategy of civilian inclusion, President Babangida launched his January 1986 political transition program (PTP). In an address that announced a five year "attempt to attain national consensus on the content of the transition and the new national agenda through debate and consultations across the wide spectrum of

Nigerian society" [87] General Babangida established his political transition program (PTP). Thereafter, the government established the Political Bureau, which among other responsibilities, was to draw up a comprehensive timetable for a transition from military rule to a democratically elected government. The stated objective of the bureau was to shift the debate on the content and direction of the transition program away from in-house discussions and exchanges of memoranda to a publicly organized and populist-based discussion which would systematically elicit, sift and analyze the views of the "common man" on the program. General Babangida pointed out that the establishment of the Political Bureau was a "kick off", the "national debate on a viable future political ethos and structure for our dear country." (Babangida, 1989).

What emerged out of this intensive discussion was the draft report of the bureau submitted in 1987. The report synthesized the views of a sampling of the population on issues that ranged from the philosophy of government to a new political economy for Nigeria; from the form of government and legislative representation; and on local government and development. The Political Bureau drew up a program for returning power to a democratically elected legislature in early 1992 and with presidential elections in August 1992. The Political Bureau envisioned the transition to be, " a gradual, measured, and supervised process of military disengagement from governance....a period of some learning in democracy in which a set of reformed institutions, which are deemed critical to the development and sustenance of democracy, are consciously executed and tested."[88]

The Babangida administration, through its "White Paper Report on the Political Bureau", adopted 90% of the bureau's recommendations, summarizing the thrust of the transition-to-democracy program as the establishment or re-establishment of a number of critical political, social and technical institutions intended to enhance the democratic and development process; a number of actions and processes intended to eliminate anti-democratic forces and undue excesses in political culture and behavior; and the Armed Forces Ruling Council supervising the transition project including the gradual disengagement of the armed forces from governance.[90]

DIAGRAM I

THE THIRD REPUBLIC TRANSITION-TO-DEMOCRACY PROGRAM[89]

Schedule 1 —1987

Third Quarter	Establishment of the Directorate of Social Mobilization, National Electoral Commission, Constitution Drafting Committee
Fourth Quarter	Elections into local governments on non-party basis

Schedule 2 —1988

First Quarter	Establishment of National Population Commission, Code of Conduct Bureau, Code of Conduct Tribunal, Constituent Assembly, National Revenue Mobilization Commission
Second Quarter	Termination of Structural Adjustment Program (SAP)
Third Quarter	Consolidation of gains of Structural Adjustment Program (SAP)
Fourth Quarter	Consolidation of gains of Structural Adjustment Program (SAP)

Schedule 3 —1989

First Quarter	Promulgation of a new constitution. Release of new fiscal arrangements.
Second Quarter	Lift of ban on party politics.
Third Quarter	Announcement of two recognized and registered political parties.
Fourth Quarter	Election into local governments on political party basis

Schedule 4 —1990

First Quarter	Election into state legislatures and state executives
Second Quarter	Election into state legislatures and state executives
Third Quarter	Convening of state legislatures
Fourth Quarter	—Swearing-in of state executives

Schedule 5 —1991

First Quarter	Census
Second Quarter	Census
Third Quarter	Census
Fourth Quarter	Local government elections

Schedule 6 —1992

First & Second Quarters	Elections into federal legislatures and convening of National Assembly
Third & Fourth Quarters	Presidential election. Swearing-in of new president and final disengagement by Armed Forces.

However, initial enthusiasm for the transition-to-democracy program gave way to mounting skepticism, anger, and alienation as the military-president, General Babangida, repeatedly altered the transition timetable to reflect military interests. On too many occasions, the general subverted the initial widespread, grassroots participation of the Nigerian populace in the democratization process. The Babangida administration revised the program eight times. Gani Fawehinmi, then a Campaign for Democracy member, in an interview with a popular news magazine[91] asserted that the administration's "over 57 decrees with their 1,774 sections, including numerous amendments on and to the transition program, are highly indicative of a praetorian outfit unwilling to honor its promises to the nation."

The first change came through the Political Bureau, which extended the program's termination date from 1990 to 1992.[92] Next, on 23 September 1987, twelve weeks after announcing the two-year extension of the transition, General Babangida banned all principal politicians and cabinet officers from all previous administrations from seeking political or party office during the transition, thus clearing the decks for a "new breed" of politicians. In 1988, Babangida reversed himself on the policy of "new breeds" un-banning the previously banned political candidates. And then in a stunning speech on October 7,1989, the administration denied registration to all the political parties that applied, necessitating a whole new process for forming parties, and thereby pushing forward the early portions of the transition program.

Restructuring the original program, General Babangida created by fiat two new political parties:[93] the Social Democratic Party (SDP) and the National Republican Convention (NRC). Another revision—one which greatly eroded the credibility of the general's commitment to complete the transition—came in November 1992, when he disqualified all 23 presidential candidates. Then the 1992 presidential primaries were canceled because of protests over violence and fraud. The timetable moved to a 1993 termination date. The final blow in 1993 came with the annulment of the presidential election results, thereby aborting the entire five -year transition program.

By 1991, the transition-to-democracy program had already lost credibility not only among domestic forces, but also with the international community.[94] Actions between 1991 and 1993 culminating in the tumultuous events of June 12, 1993 confirmed civil society's suspicions that the Babangida administration had little intention of completing the transition program, which would terminate military control over Nigerian politics. By 1993, the Babangida administration's political transition program was clearly a dismal failure.[95] Strikes, including a month-long work stoppage by nearly one million state government workers demanding salary increases, seriously interrupted basic services. Believing that the Babangida regime was either unwilling or unable to save the country, Nigerians from all walks of life became increasingly vocal in calling for the government to leave office.

The growing arbitrariness of the political transition program and its over-regimentation were contested by various organizations. In fact, the politics of the transition generally fed into, and was reinforced by, the politics of the market reform process. The combination led civil society into a growing struggle for popular democracy and the state into an increasing disposition towards intolerance, authoritarianism and repression. Military rule of the Babangida regime was perceived as steadily drifting toward dictatorship—personal, indefinite, and increasingly arbitrary and abusive. The military state stood above any laws and standards of accountability. Organized groups in civil society and outspoken critics of the regime were subject to similarly harsh repression from a military regime that had promised a transition to democracy.[96]

The administration's pattern of subversion of civil societal groups made people doubt that the Babangida Regime would actually hand-over power. In January 1993, the general disbanded the Armed Forces Ruling Council (AFRC), which had been Nigeria's supreme authority since the military seized power in 1985. He replaced it with a National Defense and Security Council, but ultimate authority remained with him. Moreover, the National Assembly, whose members were elected in July 1992, was inaugurated on December 5, 1992. However, according to a decree promulgated on December 2, 1992, the National Assembly was prohibited from legislating on 29 out of the 38 subject areas over which it had power under the 1989 constitution. The remaining items on which it was allowed to legislate concerned relatively trivial matters such as national titles and cinematography.

The repeated actions taken by the administration to rearrange the transition program perpetuated the confusion that characterized the transition program from the beginning. The government's failure to live up to promises to leave power on schedule demonstrated the extent to which it heightened insecurity about its agenda. It was amidst this political climate that lead to the climactic events of 1993 when the Babangida administration annulled the presidential election results.

Despite the several previous delays in the implementation of the schedules of the transition program, all scheduled conditions had eventually been successfully fulfilled with only the last quarter of schedule 6 —the presidential elections—remaining. The political mix of ambition and calculation of the presidential race[97] introduced one of the country's wealthiest businessmen, Chief Moshood K.O Abiola as the candidate for SDP. His choice of a running-mate was former civil servant from the north of Nigeria, Babagana Kingibe. On June 12, 1993, in what has been described as Nigeria's freest and fairest election,[98] the SDP won a landslide victory.[99]

Events immediately prior to the elections were dramatic. In early April the military promulgated the Presidential Election Decree 13 of 1993, which empowered the Nigerian Electoral Council to call off elections if there appeared to be a threat of unrest. Following this promulgation came the campaign by a military-sponsored organization claiming membership of over 25 million civilians. It was led by General Babangida's confidante and business partner, Arthur Nzeribe. Nzeribe's Association of Better Nigeria (ABN) was an organization that promoted an anti-democracy ideology. The ABN urged General Babangida's military administration not to hand over power and to halt the June 12 election. On June 4, the Association of Better Nigeria went to court seeking an interim injunction to stop the presidential election under Decree 13. Two days before the election, the Abuja High Court granted the association's request for an injunction. Though, the military regime overruled the court action the next day.

On June 16, Radio Nigeria announced that the NEC was suspending the announcement of election results because of "developments and actions pending in courts." It cited a restraining order granted the day before by Chief Justice M.D Saleh, which prohibited the NEC from publishing the results. The order had been issued in response to a motion filed by Abimbola Davies of the ABN, who charged that the elections had been plagued by corruption.

In response, on June 23, the military announced its decision to suspend the NEC and annul the election results. In his national broadcast, the military president offered electoral malpractice, widespread use of money, conflict of interest between the government and the two presidential candidates, and the confusion of conflicting judicial rulings, as the government's reasons for annulling the Presidential elections (Rotimi and Ihonvbere, 1994). The effect of annulling Nigeria's fairest national election to date and the scuttling of the transition program plunged the country into a political crisis. Combined with the deteriorating economy that was worsened by structural economic liberalization, the political opportunity conditions were created for the emergence of the contemporary pro-democracy movement in 1993.

CHAPTER 4

THE NIGERIAN PRO-DEMOCRACY MOVEMENT

In many respects the organizations agitating for political change in the Nigerian political scene can trace their roots to the periods of pre-independence. Many of the same individuals reemerged in the 90s, and the contemporary organizations were founded upon the early ethno-cultural civic associations and political organizations of the 1950s and 60s. One of the most ardent pro-democracy activists against continued military rule in 1993 was Anthony Enahoro who was a pro-independence nationalist in the 1950s. The early ethnic associations such as the Egbe Omo Oduduwa and their political correlate of the 1960s , the Action Group were direct forbearers of NADECO in the 1990's. The Nigerian pro-democracy movement of the 1990s was Nigerian civil society re-constituted.[100]

This expansive social force changed the power equation of civil-military relations in Nigeria. Here we look at the movement's attributes and its contemporary features and boundaries. The Nigerian pro-democracy network was successful in dramatically transforming the content and context of political discourse and the pattern of political action in Nigeria by 1998. It was able to capitalize on its historical political opportunity, between 1990-1998 through social alignments, agent leadership, organization, ideology, actions and events. In this section, I examine the "emancipatory" character of Nigerian associational life, as well as its pro-democracy "agency" — actually-existing organizations directly involved in the democratic struggle. I identify pro-democracy agents among Nigerian civil society, by tracing their historical determinants and drawing out current conditions[101] and boundaries[102] among Nigeria's rich and dense associational life. Through unity, organization, mobilization, and collective action the Nigerian pro-democracy movement consistently challenged the power of Nigeria's military.

I. The Development of Nigerian Civil Society (1940–1998)

Africanist historian, Thomas Hodgkin wrote that African civil consciousness was expressed through the many sided, multi-purpose organizations that had come to dominate the social scene of most African towns by the early 1940s(Hodgkin, Thomas, 1961). In Nigeria, the pre-independence protectorates had their full share of the types of organizations described by Hodgkin. Since the 1920s, Nigeria has had a rich associational life at all levels of society, from village and community associations to specialized professional groups, including the associations of old-boys and girls from the most prestigious professional schools of the world. This early dynamism of trades, professional, and student bodies in Nigeria was one of the clearest signs of the democratic drive embedded in its civil society.[103]

Under the British colonial state, the creation of private space first emerged as a result of the sprouting up of associations formed due to ethnic migration to cities and non-native communities. Several cultural associations including the notable Jamiiyyar Mutanen Arewa, Egbe Omo Oduduwa, and the Igbo Union were born. These "progressive" or "improvement" unions were quite influential by the beginning of World War II and they developed close ties with regional parties, [104] forming in many cases the social bases of Nigeria's foundational political parties[105]

At the time of Nigerian independence in 1960, a welter of religious, peasant and communal, women's, student, and labor groups pervaded the Nigerian sociological landscape. Nigeria's most prominent professional associations, including the Nigerian Union of Teachers, the Nigerian Bar Association, the Nigerian Society of Engineers, the Nigerian Medical Association, and the Pharmaceutical Society of Nigeria, were all founded before independence and were patterned after similar European groups. After independence, during the First Republic, professional associations became firmly rooted in the country with the emergence of new associations, such as the Nigerian Union of Journalists (NUJ).

However, with the exception of the trade union movements, the nationalist movements, and many students organizations,[106] during the country's early period, most professional associations and ethnic unions were dormant regarding national intervention for democratic rights. Membership in a professional association was largely a status symbol granting admission into a privileged fraternity.[107] According to Attahiru Jega's[108] study of the period, most associations seemed to be pre-occupied with advancing and defending the particularistic interests of their members, especially in the area of private practice. They generally assumed a marked degree of indifference to national politics in the tradition of the aloofness and detached "professionalism" of their British counterparts.

By the 1970s, not only had many more professional associations emerged in Nigeria, but as education expanded the membership of the older associations grew. Development generated by Nigeria's 1970's oil boom also resulted in the proliferation of civil societal associations with populist and activist persuasions, some significant groups of which included the Movement for a Progressive Nigeria, the Nigerian Democratic Movement, Women In Nigeria, [109] and the more populist Market Women of Nigeria. The trade union movement came to play a prominent role in national affairs in the 70s, articulating a broad range of demands that affected several other groups. [110] Workers led the way in forcing policy makers to channel some of the new oil revenues to the poorer sections of the society. They worked with business groups and professionals in agitating for the indigenization of the economy. They were among the social forces that protested General Gowon's decision in 1974 to postpone indefinitely, the return to civilian rule (Bangura and Beckman, 1992).

By the early 1980s, the Nigerian Labor Congress (NLC), the National Association of Nigerian Students (NANS) and the Academic Staff Union of Universities (ASUU) spearheaded a democratic movement to improve living conditions of the populace and resist state repression. Other professional associations such as the Nigerian Bar Association (NBA), the National Association of Resident Doctors, and the Nigerian Medical Association, joined the struggle for improved social services. With the NLC's Worker's Charter of Demands in 1980 and NAN's Charter of Demands in 1982,[111] a consciousness began to grow among Nigerian civil society that specific economic and social demands could be met in

Nigeria if only the frontiers of democracy were broadened.

In the mid and late 80s, the post oil-boom period[112] the struggle for rights within Nigerian civil society began to assume a sharper organizational focus targeting human rights and democratic rights. The return of the military to power in 1983, brought in an unprecedented era of suffocating human rights abuses, including the sentencing to death of General Vatsa and others for alleged coup plotting, the massacre of students at Ahmadu Bello University, and the killings that followed the anti-SAP demonstrations of 1989.

From this period until to the early 90s, many organizations were established for the explicit purpose of defending civil rights and liberties in the country. The Nigerian Bar Association (NBA) became more openly assertive of its commitment to the rule of law and democratization when in 1984, it rose against the suspension of due process and the systemization of military tribunals to prosecute politicians. In 1985 the Association of Democratic Lawyers of Nigeria (ADLN) was set up by a younger generation of Nigerian lawyers, who represented a more radical element in advocating legal rights for the people.

In response to the growth of a more fundamental movement for human rights during this period, the Civil Liberties Organization emerged to coordinate the struggle for civil liberties. In 1989 the Committee for the Defense of Human Rights was set up under the chairmanship of the human rights crusader, Dr. Beko Ransome-Kuti. In 1990 another important human rights organization, the Constitutional Rights Project was formed.[113] In December 1990 the CLO published a report Human Rights Violations in Nigeria, as a working document to help in the fight against arbitrariness by the state and its agents. The activists of the 1980s set the stage for a struggle against social and political injustice in a context whose defining feature was an increasingly repressive and authoritarian military government.

The years between 1986 and 1994 saw the greatest proliferation of civil societal organizations in Nigerian history.[114] By the onset of the 90s, the social dimension of civil activism had dramatically transformed to correspond to the changing political landscape. In the 1990s, taking on the characteristics of social movement organizations, a different brand of civil association emerged, ones that had overt political reform objectives.[115]

Political reform movements arose essentially to mobilize Nigerians to "chase the military out of power" and to construct a basis for the institutionalization of genuine democracy in Nigeria. (Momoh Abubakar, 1997).

The formation of the Campaign for Democracy (CD)—the embodiment of this new type of social movement organization—saw human rights crusaders of the late 80s aligned with older professional and civil groups of the 60s and 70s in a movement whose central principle was the belief that the Nigerian military was the biggest obstacle to democratization. The founding organizations of the Campaign for Democracy were the CLO, Committee for the Defense of Human Rights, the National Association of Democratic Lawyers (NADL), the Gani Fawehinmi Solidarity Association (GFSA), National Associations of Nigerian Students (NANS), Women in Nigeria (WIN), and the Nigerian Union of Journalists (NUJ).

Following the formation of the CD and until the attainment of the 4th Republic in 1999, there emerged a proliferation of political reform movement organizations both at home and abroad. The subject of the present study, these organizations included the Campaign for Democracy (CD); the National Democratic Coalition (NADECO); the Movement for National Reformation (MNR), the Association for Democratic Governance (ADGN), the Universal Defenders of Democracy (UDD), the Association for Democracy (AD), the Democratic Alternative (DA), the United Association for Democracy (UAD), the National Liberation for Democracy (NALICON), the United Democratic Front of Nigeria (UDFN). Diagram II in the appendix illustrates the historical transformation and linkages among the pro-democracy movement.

II. The Pro-Democracy Network: Identifying Agents

Well-known, though controversial, pro-democracy activist, Ebenezer Babatope, is quoted to have said that, "All the ingredients of a revolution were present in Nigeria by June 12, 1993, when a popular election was annulled by the Babangida government." Babatope further writes that, "Dissatisfaction with the annulment was widespread among all classes of Nigerians. The armed forces became divided. The political class was awakened by the enthusiasm of the mass of the people in Nigeria. The university students were restless for power, and so were their ideologically committed lecturers. All working class organizations in Nigeria including market women and peasant farmers were unanimous in their demand for democratic justice." Babatope continues, "Although at the time, a mass movement that would direct and coordinate the determination of the mass of people in demanding justice and socio-economic changes in the country did not exist, the network that began to surge as a result of the "June 12,"[116] historical momentum, is what has become the pro-democracy movement today." (Ebenezer Babatope, 1995)

Rallying around what came to be known as the "sanctity of June 12,"[117] the pro-democracy movement, consisting of as many as a hundred non governmental, political organizations, with the goal of promoting democratic governance in Nigeria, became a mass social movement. It was made up of a network of activist professional organizations, popular civil rights organizations, political-reform movements, reconstituted ethnic political organizations, and international non-governmental organizations. In 1999, this pro-democracy movement was alive and thriving as a social force in contemporary Nigeria; representing the formal opposition movement against absolute military government in the country and the driving force mobilizing support for a sustainable democratic Nigerian government. One hundred of the pro-democracy organizations[118] that constitute the core of the Nigerian democratic movement here are identified and analyzed to clarify roles in the contemporary democratization process in Nigeria. The broad social movement driving Nigerian democratic struggles between 1993-1999 consisted of a loose, structure-less alliance among these diverse organizations and other sectors of civil society, where there existed a shared aim of democratization.

Despite the nationwide, "June 12" demonstrations, the persistent and extensive media campaigns advocating immediate democratization and the numerous pro-democracy conventions and conferences, as well as behind-the-scenes pro-democracy lobbying,[119] there are certain mobilizers of this consensus-building and collective action campaign that have provided the impetus.

The core agents of the Nigerian pro-democracy movement are its organizations whose main objective was the mobilization of the Nigerian democracy cause and to influence the cause for re-democratization and the termination of military rule. Core agents in this landscape include the "early riser" organizations, who have been in the forefront of mobilizing members by activating social networks and forging coalitions that have forced the state to react to the disorder around it. Through this activity, core agents represented by select movement organizations among the civil society arena provided incentive structures and created opportunities for other organizations and civil society sectors with similar claims. In so doing, these groups created a consensus and a spread of the pro-democracy claim to a larger constituent.

Although all involved organizations supported pro-democracy against the Nigerian military state, they differ substantially in their capacity to realize outcomes within the democratization movement. Organizations are driven by their social class, their ideological leanings, their ethno-regional and organizational social bases. Each organization's capacity to realize outcomes is also affected by the leadership dynamics of prominent leaders and the resources these organizations have been able to garner.

Moreover, the organizations utilized different methods of mobilization reflected in the range of collective actions that they became involved in. Although organizations frequently became allies in order to carry out collective action, each organization varied in its style and type of mobilization, with some organizations being characterized as effective organizers of mass demonstrations and strikes and others more effective at raising the level of political discourse through press events, conventions, and conferences.

The pro-democracy organizations are clustered into three convergent and distinguishing categories: claims-beliefs-values-ideology; internal leadership/structure and agency; events-actions carried out/alignments. Organizations that constitute the pro-democracy movement have been categorized into five groups A through E, according to the chart referenced diagrm III. Among the score of pro-democracy organizations, the most influential have been the CD collective, NADECO, and the UDFN abroad who because of their ideology, internal leadership, and actions are the hub of the pro-democracy movement.

The five categories of organizations summarized are the following:

Group A: New popular civil liberties organizations are non-governmental organizations that blossomed in the '80's. Through their advocacy for human rights, they set the foundation for pro-democracy activism. The main organizations in this cluster include the Civil Liberties Organization (CLO), the Committee of Defense Against Human Rights (CDHR), the Constitutional Rights Project (CRP), the National Association of Democratic Lawyers (NADL) and, due to its foundational roots in all these organizations, ands its significance as a pacesetter for the broader democracy movement, the Campaign for Democracy (CD). The organizations within this group cluster were the "early risers" of the Nigerian democracy movement and established the political opportunity for the expansion of the movement.

Group B: Political-ethnic organizations, while representative of select ethnic regions, had political advocacy for democracy as their goal. Organizations within this cluster are reconstituted from older ethnic unions, but as a result of the changing political opportunity became rather radicalized. Two organizations among this cluster stand out as symbols of the ethnicization of the democratic movement: Ken Saro-Wiwa's Movement of Survival of Ogoni People, (MOSOP) existed as a founding member of the CD and has been extremely active in linking democratic rights to environmental rights in the polluted Delta region, as well as the sectional rights of minority areas. More directly involved with the immediate collective action for democracy is the Yoruba Forum in Afenifere, an extremely active ethnic association, whose prior cultural objectives have been replaced by advocacy of political reform. Other organizations representative of this cluster are the Igbo Nation in Mbpoko Igbo, the Middle Belt Forum, and the Northern Elders Council.

Group C: Political reform movements that represent the post-Babangida organizations mobilized around pro-democracy advocacy and political reform. These groups are best reflected in the organization of the National Democratic Coalition (NADECO), the largest and most significant of this cluster. Although all these organizations mobilized around some objective for democracy, there are significant differences in the models of democracy each group advocated. Other organizations within this cluster included the Movement for National Reconciliation (MNR), the Association for Democracy and Good Governance in Nigeria (ADGGN), the Gani Fawehinmi Solidarity Association (GFSA), the Universal Defenders of Democracy (UDD), and all other political organizations formed around the crisis which emerged as a result of the "June 12" debacle and which became particularly prominent in the post-annulment period of General Abacha.

Group D: The traditional stalwarts include professional organizations that have been in existence since the pre-nationalist era. They have been in the vanguard of demanding sector-specific democratic rights. In the 1990's, these organizations have reactivated to form a significant coalition for the newer pro-democracy organizations to build on. Organizations in this category include the Nigerian Labor Congress (NLC), Academic Staff Union of Universities (ASUU), and the National Associations of Nigerian Students (NANS). Significant for their strike activities in support of the current pro-democracy struggle are the Petroleum and Natural Gas Senior Staff Association of Nigeria (PENGASSAN) and the Nigerian Union of Petroleum and Energy and Natural Gas Workers (NUPENG). This group cluster also includes the media in the Nigerian Union of Journalists (NUJ) and sectors within the clergy such as the Christian Association of Nigeria (CAN) Both organizations have strengthened alignments with pro-democracy organizers.

Group E: The International NGO's represent the globalization of the movement an effect of the transnational nature of Nigerian expatriate communities as well as NGO models and opportunities in specific regions of the world, especially the U.S and the U.K. which also became safe havens for exiled pro-democracy activists. The international movement focused initially focused around the activities of Randall Robinson's Trans-Africa, Chief Abiola's Washington lobbyist Randall Echols, the Nigerian Democratic Awareness Committee, the Nigerian Democratic Movement, NADECO-abroad, and Wole Soyinka's National Liberation Council of Nigeria (NALICON). Most of the Nigerian-based international pro-democracy groups later come under the umbrella of the Pittsburgh-based organization, the United Democratic Front of Nigeria (UDFN), which consolidated more than 100[120] Nigerian-based pro-democracy organizations for mobilization for Nigerian democracy on the international front.

The CD Collective and Popular Civil Liberties

There was not a single human rights group in Nigeria until 1987 when the Civil Liberties Organization (CLO) was founded by a number of young lawyers led by Olisa Agbakoba. A human rights philosophy emerged from the associations of the Nigerian left. In 1989, the Calabar Conference of the Nigerian left, which was attended by the Nigerian Labor Congress (NLC) and several other social and radical organizations, was faced with two formidable challenges. One was the forming of a political party to articulate and champion the cause of the Nigerian left and the working people, and the other was the forming of a broad-based, mass-oriented democratic forum. The conference split into ideological factions, one the Nigerian Labor Party (NLP), and the other the nucleus of the CLO and the CDHR.

The success of the CLO in its extensive documentation of Nigerian prison conditions, arbitrary arrests, and corruption among the military[121] spearheaded the formulation of splinter organizations, which dealt with more specific issues. Significant among these was the Constitutional Rights Project (CRP), led by Clement Nwankwo, which focused on constitutional and legal questions pertaining to mass civil rights. Similarly, the Nigerian Association of Democratic Lawyers (NADL) was formed in 1987 after the 1987 demonstrations against the Babangida military regime's arbitrary detention and curtailing of press freedom decrees.

The NADL also represented the newer and more impoverished lawyers whose profession had been hard hit by the declining economy. Identifying with the mass urban population whose basic civil rights had previously been subverted under the absolutist power of recurrent military regimes and the growing civilian elite, this new organization sprang from the urban populist classes. With the expansion of human rights advocacy came the particular notion of democracy as a basic human right. This sparked the way for the Campaign for Democracy (CD) the first social movement organization to be founded with the exclusive objective of the termination of military rule and the actualization of sustainable democratic governance.

The formation of the CD in 1991 under the radical leadership of Dr. Beko Ransome-Kuti was one of the most important social movement organizations of democratic mass mobilization in Nigeria. The initial sponsorship came from the Civil Rights Organization (CLO) and the Committee for the Defense of Human Rights (CDHR The CD became an umbrella organization for the following organizations: CLO, CDHR, MOSOP,[122] NADL, Women in Nigeria (WIN), the Gani Fahwehmi Solidarity Association (GFSA),[123] and the Nigerian Union of Journalists (NUJ).

Afenifere, MOSOP: Politico-Ethnic Organizations

Nigeria's volatile history with ethnicity led to laws and governmental policies and institutions aimed at dissolving and proscribing ethnic or cultural organizations that sought to promote ethnic differences. However, the anti-democratic characteristics of the Abacha military regime, including the treatment of Chief Abiola and the "June 12" debacle, the question of minorities, especially the execution of Ken Saro-Wiwa and other members of MOSOP, and above all the issues related to the military disengagement from politics forced the promotion of separatist concerns by way of the reemergence of scores of narrowly focused cultural organizations, often regionally based, which took an active role in the pro-democracy movement. Although ethnic unions are expressly political in their agenda, their ethnic social basis limits their broader legitimacy in national politics.

Organizations within this category include the newer Afenifere, a reconstitution of the Egbe Omo Oduduwa in the Southwest, a group which best represents the interrelationship between ethnic associations and political agency. The 1960s social-democratic Action Group led by Chief Obafemi Awolowo gave rise to the social bases of the powerful ethnic union, the Egbe Omo Oduduwa. The Action Group's association with the Egbe Omo Oduduwa caused its being labeled a sub-nationalist/ethnic party, which limited it in forming alliances with other ethnic groups. In the 1990s, the Afenifere held a similar relationship with the political opposition organization, NADECO—whose leader also led Afenifere.

Similar groups emerging from other ethnic regions include the Ohanze, the Mbpoko Igbo, the Eastern Mandate Union (EMU), and the Igbo Nation in the East, and the Northern Elements Coalition, the Northern Elders Forum, the Northern Consultative Forum, and the Turaki Committee in the North. Among the minority-represented regions are the Southern Minorities Forum, made up of leaders from the minority Delta states, and the Middle Belt Forum, representing the minorities in the middle belt area.

The New Political Reform Movements: NADECO, PDM, and ADGGN

If the CD symbolized the pro-democracy struggle during the Babangida military regime, the National Democratic Coalition (NADECO), formed in May 1994 as an opposition organization to the 'post-annulment' Abacha military regime, marked a significant expansion of pro-democracy collective action and the intensified the struggle between 1994 and 1999. In early May 1994, Chief Abiola announced his intention to form a "government of national unity." About a week later, the formation of NADECO was announced. Made up of politicians, retired military officials, and pro-democracy figures, the organization was formed in an effort to coordinate and focus the various pro-democracy organizations.

The formation of NADECO presented a very dangerous threat to the interests of the military because NADECO's declared goals included reinstating the "June 12 mandate", and especially because the formation of the organization signified that the civilian political elite[124] were ready to take on the military.[125] Membership in NADECO and other political-reform movements is significantly representative of a strong array of elite leaders who draw legitimacy from a cross-section of the Nigerian public. Moreover, because NADECO was formed in direct opposition to General Abacha's abolition of the successfully implemented Third Republic democratic institutions such as the National Senate, displaced Third Republic politicians flocked to join the NADECO membership.

NADECO's formation rested on the prior formation of pro-democracy organizations such as the ADGN, the MNR, and the GFSA. The foundational formation of these groups also led the way for the proliferation of many more political-reform movements, whose main objective focused on reinstating the election of Abiola and/or the advocacy of some form of democratic model. Other groups founded either before or after NADECO that similarly acted as pro-democracy forces included the Movement for National Reform (MNR) led by two well-known firebrand Zikist fighters, Anthony Enahoro (Chairman), Mokwugo Okoye, also a philosopher and social critic (Deputy Chairman), and activist constitutionalist, Dr Olu Onagoruwa. From its beginning, the MNR had espoused a radical philosophy rejecting any form of military rule for Nigeria.[126]

Former military head-of-state General Olusegun Obasanjo

formed the more moderate Association for Democracy and Good Government in Nigeria, (ADGGN). The position of Obasanjo reflected in ADGGN was characterized by a certain flexibility and pragmatism. As platform for the civilian political expression and ambitions of the general, the ADGGN, become prominent during the annulment crisis. He made several public calls for mediation urging civil society and the military to avoid a prolongation of the destructive crisis. The retired chief-of-staff Shehu Yar-Adua formed the moderate People's Democratic Movement (PDM). The Northern progressive (impeached) civilian politician Balarabe Musa formed the Movement for National Unity (MUP).[127]

Dozens more political reform movement organizations led by charismatic leaders propped up under the banner of democracy fortifying the pro-democracy movement in its opposition to continued military rule in Nigeria. Smaller organizations included the Association for the Protection of Democracy (APD), the Universal Defenders of Democracy (UDD) the Democratic Alternative (DA), and the African Democratic League (ADL). Moreover, in some instances political reform movement organizations were created or funded by the incumbent military regime in order to divert attention, generate crises within the pro-democratic community, or to stall the march toward democracy. The Association for Better Nigerian (ABN), led by millionaire businessman Arthur Nzeribe, was floated by General Babangida as part of his then hidden agenda to remain in power permanently.[128]

Finally, within the political reform movements category there also existed cultural organizations promoting intellectual political discourse. These groups, usually broad-based and national in orientation include the National Consultative Forum, which first launched the idea of convening a Sovereign National Convention, and which also spearheaded the foundation of the CD. Others are the National Unity Club (NUC), the Peoples Consultative Forum, the New Dimension, Club 95, Club 258, the Justice Forum, the Group of 34, and the Progressives Summit. Pro-democracy groups in this cluster differed from those in Groups A and B in that they were less involved in the organization of mass demonstrations, strikes, and other direct protest actions. Rather, they served more as friendship clubs and factions, raising the public dialogue on pro-democracy by way of the many widely covered pronouncements with respect to democratization by their prominent leaders.

Labor and Professionals The Old Social Movements

Older social movement organizations or the 'traditional stalwarts' [129] include the Nigerian Labor Congress (NLC) and its affiliates in the Academic Staff Union of Universities (ASUU),[130] the Nigerian Union of Petroleum and Natural Gas Workers (NUPENG) and the Petroleum and Natural Gas Senior Staff Association of Nigerian (PENGASSAN). All have been core agents contributing to the pro-democracy insurgency. As early as 1986 they acted fervently against the Structural Adjustment Program (SAP) and in the CD "Babangida-must-go" and anti-ING (Interim National Government) mass demonstrations during the peak of the movement in 1993.

Officially becoming part of the pro-democracy movement on July 9, 1993 under the controversial leadership of Pascal Bafyau, the Nigerian Labor Congress (NLC) issued a strike notice in which it gave the military government a 12-day ultimatum demanding an immediate cessation of political arrests and detentions. The NLC boldly demanded the immediate release of the winner of the "June 12" presidential election, Chief Abiola of the SDP. Following the NLC were the National Union of Petroleum and Natural Gas Workers (NUPENG) led by the union's Secretary General, Chief Frank Ovie Kokori and the PENGASSAN, which were traditionally less activist groups made up of senior-level oil and gas managers embarked upon a more radical campaign against the military's annulment of democracy.

Moreover, professional organizations such as ASUU continued to act as key agents in the democracy movement. In the military's determination to check the growing importance of the ASUU as a nationally recognized organization agitating for progressive changes in the educational sector as well as on such national issues as the economic structural adjustment and transition-to-democracy program, the military banned the association in February 1988. This ban was lifted in 1990, only to be restored recently in 1996 after the ASUU under Attahiru Jega became a significant pro-democracy advocate against the Abacha military regime.

The Nigerian press and the clergy represent professional sectors of civil society. The privately owned Nigerian press has come out boldly in support of the pro-democracy movement, contributing to the ideological critique of the military regime. The criticism of the government by papers such as Tell and Tempo was extremely virulent and effective. Moreover, press associations also participated in pro-democracy coalitions and alliances. For example, the Lagos chapter of the Nigerian Union of Journalists and the Journalists for Democratic Rights (JODER) are both members of significant pro-democracy umbrella organizations.

International NGOs: UDFN and Trans-Africa

Trans-Africa, under the leadership of Randall Robinson, was one of the first international nongovernmental organizations to raise the question of pro-democracy in Nigeria, thereby firmly establishing pro-democracy advocacy as a human rights question for American foreign policy on Nigeria. Trans-Africa's activism opened the space for the expansion of the pro-democracy movement for Nigerians abroad. One of the earliest organizations, with affiliate offices throughout the U. S., was the Washington DC—based Nigerian Democratic Awareness Committee (NDAC), headed by Edward Oparaoji. Other groups included the Nigerian Democratic Movement, (NDM), whose president is Mobolaji Aluko, a professor of chemical engineering at Howard University and son of professor Sam Aluko. Some domestic organizations founded exile movements abroad. For example, the NADECO—U.S. office headed by Ralph Obioha and the National Liberation Council of Nigeria (NALICON), led by exiled Nobel laureate Wole Soyinka, who became the exiled spokesperson for the pro-democracy movement abroad.

Most of the Nigerian international pro-democracy groups were later to come under the umbrella leadership of the Pittsburgh-based group, the United Democratic Front of Nigeria, (UDFN). The UDFN was also chaired by Wole Soyinka. It brought the myriad pro-democracy organizations together with a common platform in the United States and Western Europe, especially in England, Germany, and Norway.

III. Driving the Network: The CD, NADECO, and UDFN

The organizations aforementioned contain the core constituencies of the network that makes up the Nigerian pro-democracy movement. However, all the organizations discussed were not equal in the extent in which they influenced democratic outcomes in Nigeria's recent transition to democracy. Three organizations within the pro-democracy network stood out for their especially effective role in directing, sustaining, and expanding the movement. Their effective organization, their ability to forge extensive alliances, their ability to capitalize on political opportunity, and their ability to procure needed resources made the three organizations the largest and most influential in the movement[131]

These three are the Campaign for Democracy (CD), which as an early riser through its civil liberties foundations prepared the groundwork for collective action in support of democratization. The National Democratic Coalition (NADECO) through its social alignments with Afenifere sustained and expanded the movement into elite sectors, broader-based ethnic regions, and the international arena. The UDFN abroad provided a significant international dimension. Because it is a coalition, the UDFN has been able to consolidate the movement abroad in single front of more than 100 Nigerian pro-democracy organizations.

In the next chapters we will look at these organizations' make up, in particular their internal organization, alliances, political opportunity, and resources. We see that there exist concrete linkages between these select social movement organizations and a society-led democratic transition in Nigeria's democratization phase between 1993-1998.

CHAPTER 5

THE CAMPAIGN FOR DEMOCRACY (CD)

I. ORGANIZATION: THE LEFT IN OPPOSITION

In his study of Nigeria's political transitions and the future of democracy, Nigerian author and social critic Arthur Nwankwo alludes to a third democratic force emerging to realize true democracy in Nigeria "However, such a force is at the moment weak organizationally and ideologically immature to such a degree that it poses only a potential but not real threat to the designs of "military/elite" forces. It is at present scattered in a motley of civil, human rights and democratic organizations, chief among which is the Campaign for Democracy."[132]

The mid-1980s, coinciding with political and economic decline in Nigeria, led to a sharper organizational focus for the struggle for human and civil rights. Despite the country's rich tradition of activism by professional groups, a newer, more narrowly focused movement emerged to expose the human rights abuses of the military government. In 1985, the National Association of Democratic Lawyers was formed, and in 1987 the Civil Liberties Organization, the first of its kind, was founded to monitor "the mass violations of human rights occurrences by the Nigerian government."[133] Furthermore, in 1989, a Committee for the Defense of Human Rights (CDHR), under the chairmanship of Dr. Beko Ransome-Kuti, was created to broaden the struggle for human rights beyond the legal arena.

However, it was not until 1990 during the Babangida regime's Transition-to-Democracy Program, after the cancellation of the results of the presidential primaries in nine out of the thirty states and the disqualification of twelve controversial candidates, that these human rights groups began to organize around the already widespread discontent of Nigerians who had questioned the transition program's viability since its inception.

On November 11, 1991 Nigerian human rights organizations and other groups including the CDHR, CLO, NADL, the Gani Fawehinmi Solidarity Association, the National Consultative Forum, the National Association of Nigerian Students, the Lagos State Chapters of Women in Nigeria, and the Nigerian Union of Journalists held a press conference to announce the inauguration of the Campaign for Democracy movement in Nigeria. The press release announcing the CD's founding reads in part:

"The unilateral and reckless way the program, *Transition-to-Civil Rule,* has been tampered with. . . . the rules changed and the wish of the people, expressed through elections, disregarded, have not only perpetuated massive and gross abuses of human rights of the Nigerian people, but has created serious doubts as to the sincerity and capability of the present regime to see the program through and to hand over to a democratically elected Civilian Government on October 1, 1992. The fact must be emphasized that the Transition to Civil Rule Program of the Babangida administration is both politically and economically the most costly transition in the whole world. This cost would have been tolerable if the process were leading towards democracy."[134]

Formed as the political alternative to the more constitutional/legally based human rights groups that collaboratively founded it, the CD was the first organization founded on an exclusive objective of advocating for political democracy in direct opposition to the Nigerian military regime vis-a-vis Nigerian civil society. The objectives of the Campaign for Democracy were listed as follows:[135]

1. Restoration of the sovereignty of the Nigerian people to self-determination.
2. Right of people to form their own political parties without interference
3. Termination of military rule for all time.
4. The replacement of imposed transitional agencies by independent and impartial transitional agencies including the immediate establishment of impartial electoral bodies.
5. Respect of fundamental Human Rights, the Rule of Law and the abrogation of all decrees.
6. Termination of economic policies, which have caused the people hardship, poverty, disease, hunger, unemployment,

retrenchment and illiteracy.

7. To achieve all these, the Military does not have to be in power beyond October 1, 1992. All the processes for the restoration of Democracy must begin now!
8. Convening a Sovereign National Conference

Structured as an umbrella convention, the CD's membership allows for organizations, which include professional and civic organizations, and individual membership, which are organized as state branches. The Convention of the CD, the supreme authority, is made up of members of a National Implementation Committee, a National Coordinating Council and State branches. The National Coordinating Council is composed of members of the National Implementation Committee and representatives of affiliate organizations and state branches. The National Implementation Committee constitutes the leadership body for the CD, including its chairman, deputy chairman, six vice chairmen, general secretary, assistant general secretary, national treasurer, and three ex-officio members. Among the more prominent in the CD leadership are Dr. Beko Ransome-Kuti (chairman), Chima Ubani (general secretary) Sylvester Odion-Akhaine (general secretary), Chom Bagu (deputy chairman) Shehu Sani (vice-chairman) Femi Falana (ex-officio member); Ken Saro-Wiwa and Festus Iyayi, both zonal chairmen.[136]

Less than a year after its foundation, in May 1992, the CD had expanded to become an alliance of thirty-eight pro-democracy organizations cutting across the length and breadth of the country. At the first national convention of the CD held in Jos, Plateau State on May 2, 1992, more than 25 groups were represented. Delegates from the following organizations attended:

Attendance

1. Civil Liberties Organization (CLO)
2. Committee for Defense of Human Rights (CDHR)
3. Women in Nigeria (WIN)
4. Pan African Youth Congress (PAYCO)
5. National Association of Democratic Lawyers (NADL)
6. Ethnic Minority Rights Organization of Nigeria (EMIRON)
7. African Democratic Heritage
8. Mahmud Tukor Memorial Committee
9. Academic Staff Union of Universities (ASUU)

10. Nigerian Union of Journalists (NUJ)
11. National Association of Nigerian Students (NANS)
12. Uhuru Research Center (URC)
13. Iron and Steel Senior Staff Association, Lagos
14. Council for Public Education
15. Nigerian Tenants Association (NTA)
16. Democratic Action Committee (DACOM)
17. Gani Fawehinmi Solidarity Association (GFSA)
18. Nigerian Philosophy Association
19. Nigerian Labor Congress (NLC)
20. National Union of Air Transport Services Employees (NUATSE)
21. Medical and Health Workers Union of Nigeria
22. Democratic Forum
23. African Redemption Movement
24. National Consultative Forum

The organization's umbrella structure, which includes a coalition of progressive organizations ranging from labor unions to women's organizations, affords the Campaign for Democracy a membership base and an organizational network representative of the Nigerian left.[137] In addition to its varied professional representation, the CD's urban roots in such Nigerian cosmopolitan cities as Lagos also facilitated a broad-based ethnic membership, a factor which spearheaded strong cross-ethnic and regional mobilization. The CD has local chapters evenly distributed across the various regions of Nigeria. The organization's zonal branches were representative of the major ethnic areas, including Lagos, the Delta, Enugu, Kaduna, Bauchi, Benue, and Plateau zones.[138]

The CD's membership is representative of a wide range of progressive activists and intellectuals. For example, the organization's chairman was also an inspirational founder of the organization. Dr. Beko Ransome-Kuti has been one of Nigeria's longest-standing human rights defenders. Former secretary general of the Nigerian Medical Association (NMA) and the Commonwealth Medical Association's delegated member to the Commonwealth Human Rights Initiative (CHRI), since graduating a medical doctor from the University of Manchester in 1963, he has been neck-deep in activism.

Originally, his podium was the Nigerian Medical Association, which he led into conflicts with every military regime since General Yakubu Gowon. In the mid-1980s, Dr. Ransome Kuti was part of the dissident movement that emerged from the failure of the Nigerian progressive professional groups, including the NMA, to forge a labor party. That faction founded the human rights organizations that emerged in the mid-'80s. Ransome Kuti became the founding chairman of the Committee for the Defense of Human Rights (CDHR), before forming the Campaign for Democracy.

In its eight years, the Campaign for Democracy suffered internal leadership problems that have severely limited its expansion and mobilization effectiveness. Less than four years after its foundation, in 1994, the ranks of the CD split. Two significant breakaway organizations were formed, the Democratic Alternative led by Alao Aka-Bashorun and Femi Falana, and later in 1996, the United Action for Democracy (UAD) led by former CD member Chima Ubani.

II. Alliances: The Ideology of the Movement

The initial success of the CD in advancing the Nigerian pro-democracy struggle was due to its organization of popular resistance among a wide cross-section of Nigerian society. The organization's radical roots, which had origins in the left helped form its opposition strategy and thereby the organization's effectiveness in mobilizing broad-based support for its objectives.

The emergence of the CD coincided with the gradual shift in mainstream leftist opinion in Nigeria in favor of civil liberties and rights. Before the 1980s, many left activists had treated civil liberties as inconsequential or as essentially elitist. However, for a growing number of activists and leftist intellectuals, increasing state repression and the absence of real commitment in bourgeois political circles to resist authoritarianism meant they had to address the issues of civil liberties and human rights themselves. As early as 1986, the CD's founding members—especially Ala Aka-Bashorun and Beko Ransome-Kuti—as early as 1986 began to alert Nigerians to the "hidden agenda" that the Babangida regime had in its transition to democratic rule. The National Consultative Forum, led by Aka-Bashorun, began to put forward proposals for the establishment of genuine democracy in Nigeria via the establishment of a sovereign national conference.[139]

By 1990, the vigorous campaign for human rights and civil liberties became one of the most potent forms of struggle against the authoritarian, militarized state. The CD came to exemplify the new role that the left came to play in Nigerian politics, a role that had the explicit purpose of defending the rights of Nigerians and extending the frontiers of civil liberties. As a result of the Transition-to-Democracy Program, the left also became convinced that the Nigerian military had become the most important obstacle to democratization and that no democratic project would be complete that did not ensure that the military submit itself to the authority of elected civilian officials. The National Consultative Forum (NCF) led a national conference to discuss the establishment of genuine democracy in Nigeria and the national question. Through the NCF's efforts to make broader consultations with mass organizations, the CD was launched.

The program adopted by the CD had a lot to do with the organization's ability to mobilize not merely other civil associations in alliance but also collective activism through strikes and demonstrations in Nigerian cities. Though the CD's first press release pointed to the failure of the transition program as the organization's primary call to action, the CD's first convention in May 1992 reviewed the economic, political and human rights situation in the country. The meeting also noted with "sadness that 32 years after Nigerian independence, and despite abundant endowment in human and material resources, Nigeria was facing an unprecedented economic and political crisis."[140]

Three important resolutions to the country's political and economic problems emerged from the meeting. First was the "Campaign for the termination of the IMF/World Bank imposed Structural Adjustment Program (SAP) and its replacement with a humane alternative economic program that would promote the welfare of Nigerians and ensure steady economic growth and development."[141] This message reinforced the anti-SAP feelings that had already spread across the country. A second and more resonant message was the call for a Sovereign National Conference: "A Sovereign National Conference has become inevitable as a means of restoring the sovereignty of the Nigerian people to discuss and proffer solutions to the economic and political crisis and human rights abuses in the country."[142] Restating a recurrent theme Dr Ransome-Kuti insisted, "beyond this immediate struggle lies the inevitability of the sovereign national conference which we consider the ultimate democratic platform where popular and lasting solutions will be sought to the economic, political, ethnic, religious and other problems confronting our country."[143]

Third was the campaign to terminate the Babangida regime by highlighting criticisms against the transition program and calling for an interim national government to replace the Babangida administration. In a press conference on November 24, 1992, the CD made the following demands on the Babangida regime: a) setting up of a popular-based interim government drawn from the National Assembly, mass organizations of workers, youth, women, students, professional associations of journalist, lawyers, manufacturers; and b) that the Armed Forces primary mandate should be to organize a Sovereign National Conference, which was to discuss national problems and design a new transition program leading to free and fair multi-party elections.[144]

The CD political program reinforced its criticism of the Babangida military regime in general, but especially the military's transition-to-democracy programs. Chima Ubani, general secretary wrote, "It has long been the contention of the CD that the type of 'democracy' being forced on the people by General Babangida cannot endure, principally because the premises upon which it is based were faulty and shaky either in the undemocratic manner in which the two parties were created and their constitutions and manifestoes drafted by government or in the mutilation of the report of the Political Bureau, the unjustifiable disqualification of certain categories of people from participating in the transition program, deliberate monetization of political intolerance of critical and objective views"[145]

The CD launched a massive campaign against military rule and the Babangida administration through media and the widespread circulation of press-release pamphlets among popular-based urban communities. For example, on September 4, 1992, a communique entitled "IBB's Seven Years in Retrospect" remarked "Seven years of IBB regime has witnessed the greatest hardship fostered on the generality of Nigerians, destruction of all moral values and national institutions, and the widening of the gap between the rich and the poor masses of Nigeria since this country became independent." [146]

CD symposiums and resolutions always concluded with a call for all democratic organizations and all Nigerians in the country to band together and enroll with and rally round the CD to save Nigeria from "dictatorship, economic collapse, and national chaos."

III. Political Opportunity: The CD: Initiating Popular Resistance

The Campaign for Democracy's (CD) took advantage of the available political opportunity, which featured a military regime besieged by labor and professional protest against the economy, human rights protests against military authoritarianism, and pressure from the international arena to democratize during the late 1980s.[147] However, these previous agitators were able to extract only limited concessions from the regime.[148] The Campaign for Democracy, on the other hand, was the first social movement organization during this period to effectively advertise the vulnerability of the military regime, and present a significant threat to the regime in the arena of public opinion.[149] In fact no other organization during the ten year pro-democracy movement did as much as the CD through its "Babangida-Must-Go" campaign to advertise the vulnerability of the regime, resulting in the "voluntary", though temporary, termination of a military regime in 1993.[150] As a pioneer opposition movement, the Campaign for Democracy set the stage for the period that followed in which organizations like NADECO, UDFN-abroad, and the UAD[151] were to later take advantage of the cycle of political opportunity, which fostered a new type of "opening" and "access"[152] to the military regime regarding the transition-to-democracy process.

Moreover, because both the Babangida and the successor Abacha military regimes facilitated access and opening to sectors and organizations among civil society unevenly, the period of political opportunity set in motion by the CD was not to directly benefit the CD. The military tried to neutralize the organization through the arrest and conviction of many of its leaders and members. As a result, the CD's democracy advocacy accomplishments were brought to an early climax, limiting the organization's later efforts to bring about the conclusive termination of military rule.

The "Babangida-Must-Go" Campaign

The annulment of the June 12 election was seen as a fundamental contradiction between military and civilian interests. The annulment posed a sharp political question: 'Was the military really interested in disengaging from politics?' The CD appropriately articulated the public discontent through the series of nationwide protests that it organized as the "Babangida-Must-Go" Campaign.

On June 16, Radio Nigeria announced that NEC was suspending the announcement of election results because of "developments and actions pending in courts."[153] The annulment had occurred as a result of a restraining order that had been issued in response to a motion filed by Abimbola Davis of the Association for a Better Nigeria (ABN)[154] who charged that the elections had been plagued by corruption. In immediate response, on June 17, the CD held an emergency press conference denouncing the ABN as "faceless campaigners for the perpetuation of military rule."[155] Declaring the ABN's motion illegal, the CD used the occasion to remind the public that as early as April 21, 1993, the CD and four of its component organizations had obtained an injunction from Justice Dolapo Akinsanya of the Lagos High Court restraining "all members of the ABN...from carrying out all or any part of their program of action to campaign for or urge General Babangida to remain in power as President of Nigeria beyond 27/8/93."

At the conference, the CD demanded the following: a) That NEC should release, within 24 hours, the result of the June 12 presidential election, failing which the CD shall publish the comprehensive and authenticated results; b) That the military should hand over power NOW to the winner of the election; c) The convening of a Sovereign National Conference (SNC) thereafter to seek popular solutions to the numerous problems of the country; and d) in conclusion, the CD called on its various affiliate organizations, and patriotic forces, to be resolved, mobilized and ready to bring an end to military rule and to defend democracy at all costs.[156]

On June 23, the government made the announcement that the nation had feared: the election was annulled. According to General Babangida's statement, the election was annulled "to save our judiciary from being ridiculed and politicized locally and internationally."[157] The civil and international societies reacted swiftly, leading to mass protests and demonstrations throughout the country in which over 154 people lost their lives to gunshots by the police.[158] Thereafter, the CD set in stage a flurry of political resistance activities against the regime, which ultimately led to General Babangida's quitting office on August 27.

On June 18, in defiance of Decree 13's threat of a five-year jail sentence and fine for publishing unauthenticated voting figures, the CD published the annulled election results. The results showed that Chief Abiola had won a majority of the vote in nineteen of the thirty states, with a total of 58.4 percent.[159] Henceforth, setting-off the campaign for June 12, calls for recognition of the results came from individuals and organizations including unions, politicians, and prominent Nigerians such as the writer Wole Soyinka, who called "any further delay in making the people's verdict official *will result in* a deliberate cultivation of chaos."[160]

The Campaign for Democracy mobilized popular resistance to military rule by organizing protest demonstrations on July 5-7 and by the organization of a stay-at-home protest on August 12 —14 and again on August 25. The CD called for a three-day protest. [161] The first day was to be marked by the burning of General Babangida's draconian decrees; the second day by burning of the voters cards; and the third day was to be marked by rallies all over the country. The CD called for one week of nationwide protests to begin on July 5. CD chairman Dr. Ransome-Kuti urged workers to stay home, traders and market women to close stalls, and cars to stay off roads. Students and youth were urged to organize themselves into civil defense groups to man barricades and make bonfires. The CD called for the, "embarkment of Nigerians all over the country to enjoin in an act of protest until Babangida goes."[162]

On the first day of the protests, thousands of youth closed major roads in Lagos and the CD led thousands of marchers to Abiola's home compound. Protests were also held in other cities, including Ibadan, Ilorin, Akure, Jos, Kaduna and Kano. In a subsequent press conference held on July 8, 1993,[163] marking the end of the "week of protest," the CD commended the courage and resilience demonstrated by the people during the protests, but called for a continuation of the struggle, especially against the government proposal to put in place an interim national government.

On August 2, the CD said it would press on with its civil disobedience campaign despite the Babangida regime's announcement that it would quit office and replace the military regime with an interim national government.[164] The CD launched another round of protests in August, Urging Nigerians to "reaffirm their resolve to terminate military dictatorship and ethnic democracy."[165] It called for renewed nationwide protests on August 12-14 to oppose Babangida's manipulations to prolong military rule, the continued detention of pro-democracy leaders as well as to back democratic proposals. In a public statement, the CD announced "the Abiola government should be defended by the Nigerian people and should be allowed to *assume* office on 27 August."[166] This time the CD stressed the need for nonviolence and urged protestors to stay close to home to avoid bloodshed. Despite the fact that some of the CD's most important members—Beko Ransome-Kuti, Femi Falana, and Gani Fawehinmi—had been detained in connection with the first series of riots, because of the expanded involvement by communities in the east and north[167] the August protests were more successful than the first ones.

On August 12, the strike shut down business in Lagos, Ibadan and other southwestern cities as Nigerian workers stayed home. And again, on August 25, the CD organized another, though partially successful, stay-home strike. In an August 22 press release, the CD outlined the objectives of the August 25-27 national protest as a reminder to the regime that the people were committed to June 12, which was a vote for unity and democracy. The protest was also to begin the resistance against the interim national government, which the CD dubbed "Babangida's new trick."[168]

Despite the government's brutal repression against the CD as a result of its strike campaign,[169] the CD's relentless organization of popular resistance did result in General Babangida and the federal military government's quitting office on the scheduled date of August 26. However, as CD representative Wole Soyinka remarked "Democracy, as the common goal of the struggle, could not be reached except through June 12."[170] The CD regarded the quitting of the Babangida regime and its handing power over to a new interim national government as a mere "surrogate" action by General Babangida, and therefore, a reason to continue the popular resistance campaign for the realization of the June 12 mandate.

Continuing the Struggle

Yet again, the CD slated two more protests for September 29-October 1 and November 18-19, 1993. On September 29, a stay-at-home protest was accordingly organized against the Interim National Government soon after its birth. The CD pursued its opposition to the ING in a newspaper advertisement on November 3. The communique condemned the Review of the Voters' Register exercise organized by the ING from November 1-14 in preparation for the local government and presidential elections that the ING had proposed for February 1994. The CD denounced the planned election as "hollow rituals," a continuation of Babangida's unfinished agenda to impose a predetermined result on the country.[171] Calling for a boycott of the Review of the Voters' Register exercise and the elections, the CD further affirmed that, "There can be no new elections until the June 12 mandate is exercised."[172]

Demonstrations and mass mobilization efforts organized by the CD went on for several months. During this period, all working class organizations in Nigeria including market women and peasant farmers were unanimous in their demand for democratic justice.[173] The demonstrations only abated although they continued after the military coup d'etat on November 17, 1993 brought in the regime of General Sani Abacha. Before this overthrow by the only military official of the interim national government and a former chief of army defense under the Babangida regime, top members of the Campaign for Democracy, including the chair, Dr. Beko Ransome—Kuti, had met with the pro-June 12 supporters in the military,[174] who had promised that the government would be handed over to Chief Abiola soon after they took over. [175]

As a result, the CD redirected its campaign to begin to realize its original goals of establishing a broad-based national government headed by Chief Abiola, which would in turn convene a Sovereign National Conference. However, immediately upon taking-over office, General Abacha abrogated all remnants of the Third Republic by proscribing political activity; delimiting and ethnicizing the June 12 question; and consolidating his military regime in power. Thus, with the onset of the Abacha military regime, the CD albeit weakened continued the struggle to actualize the June 12 mandate, and was again a significant force in the events that led to the ultimate arrest of the president-elect, Chief

Abiola. However, the CD's organization efforts diverted from the mass mobilization demonstration activities to a critique of the regime through publications and pronouncements.

For example, a CD news bulletin, in a damning critique of the Abacha regime, had this to say: "When the Abacha dictatorship gunned itself into power nine months ago, the CD had no doubts as to its status as an ill—contrived continuation of the minority rule of the most backward and undemocratic section of the ruling elite. Its agenda thwarts the democratic advances of civil society, creating and sustaining a political atmosphere within which the settler colonialist ambitions and utterly parasitic existence of that clique could be consolidated. The Wednesday August 17 broadcast of General Sani Abacha invariably marks a consummation of that agenda and a full-scale return to the regime's unmistakably fascistic, war-mongering and subterfuge-ridden antecedents. The frustrated attempt at sustaining the impression of being "in charge," the predictable regularity of insults and laughable peddling of vainglory all remind us of Babangida before our people bravely ran him out of town."[176]

Some of the CD's activities during the initial stages of the Abacha regime in 1994 included the calling for the formation of the Popular National Democratic Government, (PNDG) with Chief Abiola as president to replace the Abacha military regime. On May 9, 1994, the CD organized one of its last mass mobilization efforts—a day of "National Sit-At-Home Protest"—against the "unpopular regime of General Sani Abacha, as well as against the backdrop of the government-inspired fuel scarcity".[177] On June 12, 1994, one year after the annulment, the CD in a press statement again expressed its solidarity with the custodian of the June 12 mandate, Chief Abiola, for his formal declaration of the Popular National Democratic Government. The CD enjoined Nigerians to give Chief Abiola full support. The CD also called on the patriotic rank and file members of the Nigerian armed forces to give their loyalty to the new Popular National Democratic Government in its avowed task of rebuilding the Nigerian state through a Sovereign National Conference.

As the Abacha military regime began to consolidate its power and strengthen its strangle hold over elements of Nigerian civil society, the Campaign for Democracy (CD) shifted its mobilization emphasis to the international arena. The CD's civil disobedience campaign had received unprecedented encouragement from abroad, with full backing from non-governmental organizations in the United States,[178] England, and Canada. The CD was the only body that called on the Organization of African Unity not to accord recognition to the Abacha regime. The CD was also one of the first organizations to call "for comprehensive international sanctions" against the Abacha-led government. The body specifically directed all CD overseas formations to call for the diplomatic isolation of the military junta, putting the proceeds of Nigerian crude oil in an escrow account, an embargo on importation of arms by the Nigerian army; and calling for the freezing of foreign accounts of all military personnel and their civilian accomplices. Furthermore, the CD wrote a letter to the German Embassy demanding the repatriation of General Ibrahim Babangida. The CD also initiated a letter-writing campaign to the European Union, deploring the harboring of General Babangida and others in Europe.[179]

IV. Resources

The first time in Nigeria's post-civil war history, the Nigerian military regime was openly challenged by millions who took a stand for democracy in urban and rural settings, across ethnic, regional, religious, class and gender lines.[180] The civil disobedience actions promoted and coordinated by the CD received unprecedented support from both internal and external resources. However, the strength and the success of the Campaign for Democracy derived from its capacity to mobilize urban communities across Nigeria as a result of the organization's structure, leadership effectiveness, and organizational strategy to mobilize at the grass-roots level.

Structurally, the CD's greatest asset seemed to be its antecedent linkages with the early human rights organizations, the CLO and the CDHR. There was overlapping membership between these groups and the CD. Many of the members of the CDHR, including, Dr. Beko Ransome-Kuti, diverted their energies to do work in the Campaign for Democracy. In fact, in the early years, both the CD and the CDHR were quartered in the same house (Enemuo and Momoh, 1994:11). Moreover, the umbrella structure of the Campaign for Democracy maximized membership enrollment via the recruitment of organizations rather than single members. As a result of affiliations with a broad sector of progressive professional organizations, the CD merely gave expression to the sentiment already existent among these organizations by promoting this sentiment in a broad-based and enduring organizational platform. During the "Babangida-Must-Go" campaigns, the CD's affiliate organizations mobilized their constituencies to come out in opposition against the Babangida regime.

The CD was not heavily funded during its early years. Most of its activities were underwritten by the personal resources of its most active members. The bulk of the CD's resources emerged from the personal contributions and energy of the CD membership, mainly young radical professionals who invested their time in a cause they believed in. For example, "pamphleteering"[181] was used to effect maximum popular participation in the nationwide strikes. Hundreds of thousands of leaflets were printed by the CD, the CLO, the NADL, and the CDHR combined, exposing corruption, lawlessness, and abuse of power by the military regimes.

The CD's roots in social activism and organizing the urban populace and students facilitated the organization's popular-based techniques. For example, the organization capitalized on the presence of over 80,000 soccer fans at the World Cup -qualifying match at the National Stadium to distribute leaflets on the nationwide strike. In its later years, after its successes from the civil disobedience campaigns gave it greater exposure, the CD began to receive more support and funding from external sources, especially from municipal governments in France and Germany and from NGOs in the United States.

The progressive, social activist leadership of the Campaign for Democracy strongly facilitated the organization's effectiveness in generating successful outcomes in the organization of events against the regime. However, by 1994, the military embarked upon a campaign to neutralize the resuscitated activism among civil society spearheaded by the CD by arresting its key members. Its most prominent leaders including Dr. Beko Ransome-Kuti, Shehu Shani, Chima Ubani, Sylvester Odione-Akhaine were all incarcerated as political prisoners for their pro-democracy activity. Though driven underground by the repressive Abacha regime, the CD continued to effect the democratic mobilization for Nigerians at home and abroad through publications, press releases, and especially through affiliated groups, calling for the same goals: the actualization of June 12, the immediate termination of military rule, and the convening of a Sovereign National Conference.

CHAPTER 6

THE NATIONAL DEMOCRATIC COALITION (NADECO)

I. Organization: The Elite in Opposition

In May 1994, a new pro-democracy organization was formed, the National Democratic Coalition (NADECO). NADECO released a "Lagos Declaration"[182] calling for the military to leave politics within two weeks; for Chief Abiola to be installed as president and form a government of national unity; and for the new military government to finally convene the long-advocated "Sovereign National Conference" to determine the future shape of the Nigerian federation. The declaration continued, "that if by the end of the 15-day ultimatum, the Abacha administration had failed to call on Chief Abiola to form the government of national reconciliation, the lovers of democracy in the country will not hesitate to make this country ungovernable."[183]

As a result of NADECO's formation, soon afterward, the members of the disbanded House of Representatives and Senate reconvened and declared the Abacha government illegal; and more significantly, on June 11, 1994, Chief Abiola declared himself president of a Popular National Democratic Government at a public rally in Lagos. Following this event, on June 23, Chief Abiola was arrested and later charged with "treasonable felony."[184]

Nationwide strikes demanding the restoration of "June 12" and the release of Chief Abiola were spearheaded by NADECO. The strikes gained momentum when NADECO was joined by the National Union of Petroleum and Natural Gas Workers (NUPENG), and the Petroleum and Natural Gas Senior Staff Association of Nigeria (PENGASSAN),whose strikes brought the country to a virtual standstill.[185] These events set the stage for renewed pro-democracy activity under the Abacha military regime, and NADECO was very much the galvanizing force behind this stage.

By June 1998, five years after the annulment of June 12, NADECO had become a household word among the Nigerian populace. NADECO had come to symbolize the most formidable opposition group in the continuing struggle for democratic government in Nigeria. Four years into the civil societal resurgence, the see-saw struggle between democracy and dictatorship in Nigeria played itself out with NADECO representing both the domestic and international organizations opposing General Abacha. A leading news magazine described the status of democratic struggle in the nation this way: " The fear of NADECO has eaten so deep that it has even permeated the forbidden walls of Aso Rock Villa.[186] Abacha's security handlers are so obsessed with the idea that NADECO is dominating the landscape that they seldom give their man permission to venture out of the fortress."[187]

Where the CD began to wane in its role as the foremost pro-democracy movement in Nigeria, NADECO stepped right in. Whereas the CD's historical significance in advancing the democratic struggle was to mobilize the Nigerian masses in pro-democracy struggle. NADECO made the campaign for democracy a force to be reckoned with by the Nigerian populace and the Nigerian military regime. Where the core of the CD's pro-democracy activity, 1990-1993, used General Babangida as the focus of its anti-military campaign, for NADECO, formed in 1994 with the consolidation of Babangida's successor regime by General Abacha,[188] the Abacha regime was the focus of the organization's pro-democracy activity.

NADECO emerged as the most significant coalition of various pro-democracy organizations, comprised of displaced politicians, labor unions, human rights organizations, and prominent activists demanding, at first, the immediate restoration of the political institutions of the Third Republic, but later the restoration of the mandate given to Chief M.K.O Abiola in the annulled presidential election of June 1993. By its own declaration,[189] NADECO brings together under one umbrella all the Nigerian democratic organizations, human rights campaigners, and progressive forces from all over Nigeria and abroad. "It is the culmination of a thorough review by leaders of democratic organizations, progressive forces and eminent Nigerians who held several meetings to review the state of the nation with a view to arresting its precipitate drift and to chart an appropriate course for economic revival and national reconciliation."[190]

NADECO's claim to umbrella democratic and human rights organizations around Nigeria and the world was more a loose assertion than a structural reality. Unlike the CD, whose foundation declaration was signed by at least 22 affiliated member organizations, NADECO's declaration contained no mention of the actual coalition member organizations that NADECO claimed to bring together. Rather, the statement included founding members who were affiliated with other pro-democracy organizations.[191]

NADECO's strongest foundational claim derives from its assertion that the organization is the culmination of a thorough review of the nation's most important political issues by leaders of democratic groups, progressive forces and eminent Nigerians. NADECO can trace its roots as far back as 1951. Through the leadership of the late premier of the western region, Chief Obafemi Awolowo, the Owo Meeting was initiated. What started as a series of meetings by the emerging elite of the Nigerian south-west transformed itself into the Action Group, a political party with a social democratic philosophy and a Yoruba ethnic base. However, after the termination of Nigeria's First Republic with the advent and consolidation of military rule, the Nigerian political class remained socially and politically active by continuing social gatherings like the Owo Meeting. During military regimes, through these meetings, the displaced political class would remain active in deliberating and debating national issues, as well as maintain direct access to the military government in influencing the national agenda.[192]

The Owo Meeting, however, had other significant functions. For example, the group had been largely instrumental in bringing together all progressive groups in the country to advance the struggle for the liberation of the oppressed in Nigeria (Babatope, 1996). In 1989, the group played a crucial role in the activities of the Social Democratic Party. Moreover, it has always been deeply involved in the CUU an affiliate political club made up of many significant progressive politicians in the country and a body set up by leaders of the East, West and the Middle Belt zone. In 1993, the Owo Meeting adopted the name Egbe Afenifere, meaning a political group that is committed to the struggle to make life better for the people. Continuing with its traditional role of representing the moving spirit behind the activities of the progressive political class in Nigeria, Afenifere and the Council for Unity and Understanding (CUU) spearheaded the formation of the National Democratic Coalition, NADECO on May 15, 1994.

In 1994, NADECO was formed to coordinate and focus the various pro-democracy factions and social forces around four main demands. (1) the military had to leave political office; (2) Chief Abiola had to be installed as president; (3) a sovereign national conference had to be held to debate the country's future; and (4) the country had to be restructured along truly federal lines. The coalition resolved to act as a nationwide, broad-based political platform for democratic and progressive forces. Recognizing the precarious state of Nigeria's fragile federalism, the coalition also demanded, as part of the restoration of Chief Abiola's mandate, the immediate convening of a Sovereign National Conference with a view to resolving Nigeria's multifarious problems of real and perceived domination by northern elements.

The following resolution published by NADECO outlines the organization's objective as follows: [193]

Whereas the Military as an institution is essentially authoritarian and cannot therefore, midwife true democracy in Nigeria.

Whereas the Nigerian political class which has been abused, subverted and humiliated in the past 10 years for co-operating with, and working within, the Military political agenda has now realized that there is not alternative to democracy in Nigeria.

Whereas, now therefore, the leaders of the major democratic and progressive organizations and eminent Nigerians hereby resolve to create a nation-wide, broad-based political platform where all democratic and progressive forces can find accommodation for a joint struggle for the restoration of democracy and true federalism in Nigeria.

It is hereby further resolved, therefore, to establish immediately a body to be known as the **National Democratic Coalition (NADECO)** and the body is hereby established.

II. Alliances

Nigerian scholar, Abubakar Momoh asserts that even though NADECO launched an offensive against the military by calling for mass protest, unlike the CD, it had no capacity to mobilize the people. Its affiliates were a mixed bag with contradictory tendencies and perspectives—ethnic, religious, economic and ideological.[194] NADECO's membership differs significantly from the CD's membership base, drawing clear distinctions between the two organization's social bases, including distinctions between each organization's ideology and strategy to democracy in Nigeria. NADECO clearly lacks the grassroots-populist, human-rights-cum democratic rights appeal of the Campaign for Democracy.

Rather, by drawing its membership base largely from displaced Third Republic politicians, former First and Second Republic politicians, former military politicians and former prominent civilians,[195] NADECO was less narrowly politically defined, thereby focusing its agenda on the immediate political process at hand, which evolved around the annulment of the June 12 Presidential elections, the reversal of the annulment, and the installation of Chief Abiola as president. Later, the organization mobilized around organizing the release of Chief M.K.O Abiola as Nigeria's foremost political detainee.

NADECO represents broad ethnic and ideological forces, built around the Nigerian "national" party model best represented by the Second Republic's National Party of Nigeria (NPN).[196] The most consistent feature of the organization is its political elite membership. Although spearheaded by the more progressive forces in Afenifere, the organization's broader affiliation with moderate think-tank groups like the CUU neutralized the foundational progressive philosophy rooted in the "Awoist" era. Moreover, the political activities leading to the Third Republic and resulting in the June 12 annulment reinvigorated the latent progressive spirit, which crystallized in NADECO.[197] The new progressive divide among civilians and former military politicians became one's position on June 12, with the June 12 advocates, regardless of previous ideological orientation, formulating the membership in NADECO.

To the extent that the 1993 political crisis in Nigeria resulting from the June 12 annulment was a crisis of ethnic and regional proportions, NADECO through its close and overlapping affiliation with Afenifere revealed the sectional and ethnic aspects of the pro-democracy struggle. Taking advantage of the ethnic makeup of the opposition movement, the Abacha military regime systematically ethnicized the June 12 question, turning it into a southwest/Yoruba affair. As a result, NADECO was erroneously labeled an ethnic organization linked primarily to the western, Yoruba states of Nigeria, as a result of the affiliation of NADECO's core founding members, including its leader, the late Pa Ajasin, and former governor Bola Ige with the Yoruba-based spin-off organization of the earlier Awolowo-led Action Group and Egbe Afenifere.

Nevertheless, though NADECO still has strong membership base within Afenifere, the organization also constitutes an ethnically diverse membership of prominent personalities from all over Nigeria as well as being affiliated with organizations representing all Nigerian regions. The organization's high-profile, broad-based elite membership afforded it significant coalition platforms with the CD and other prominent professional bodies—the Nigerian Labor Congress (NLC), NUPENG, and PENGASSAN during the movement's efforts to effectively mobilize direct action against the Abacha military regime.

NADECO's social bases reflected its organizational mobilization strategy. For example, because NADECO's membership includes a significant sector among the civilian political elite, the organization used its traditional access to the military regime to influence the regime through dialogue and negotiation. NADECO capitalized on its long-standing alliances with both military and civilian members of the Abacha regime in creating access to crucial spheres of decision-making within the military's executive unit, the Provisional Ruling Council.[198] Moreover, NADECO's high-profile membership gave the organization a consistent forum with the print media where major news magazines and journals consistently carried NADECO activities in their headlines.

III. Political Opportunity

Mobilizing Against the Abacha Regime

Before NADECO's entry onto the scene, the Nigerian military had undergone a one year period of agitation against the military state organized by the Campaign for Democracy (CD). The months of May, June, and July of 1994 were tumultuous months for the pro-democracy movement, and NADECO was at center stage of the pro-democracy movement's efforts to organize pro-democracy activity. The termination of the Interim National Government and the conclusive abrogation of the civilian political institutions of the Third Republic the already convened House, Senate, and gubernatorial governments by the Abacha regime provided a political climate for an expanded stage of pro-democracy struggle against the Nigerian military.

More specifically, however, two significant events served as a platform from which NADECO could expand its pro-democracy campaign: General Abacha's implementation of the controversial National Constitutional Conference (NCC) to launch the regime's "Transition-to-Democracy" Program: the return of Chief M.K.O Abiola from the United Kingdom and the United States of America where he had been launching an international campaign against the Nigerian military.

The military regime's launching of another elaborate Transition-to-Democracy program, whose cornerstone was a National Constitutional Conference tried the patience of the Nigerian people. After the arbitrary annulment of a presidential election born out of a long and elaborate military transition program, people had lost credibility in the military to guide them through yet another democratic process (Diamond, Kirke-Greene, Oyediran 1995). NADECO capitalized on these frustrations by shoring up a campaign to boycott the military's NCC and to call for a Sovereign National Conference to be organized by the Nigerian people independent of the military. [199]

The Abacha regime's National Constitutional Conference claimed to echo the long-standing calls of pro-democracy activists for the convening of a Sovereign National Conference. However, the regime's NCC fell short of the pro-democracy movements' demand for a Sovereign National Conference. Although, the NCC would be called to debate and draft a new constitution and set the stage for the holding of elections, but unlike the body called for by the pro-democracy movement, the NCC would have only consultative status and its members would not all be elected. Moreover, the NCC had a very limited mandate and its decisions were subject to the vetting and approval of the military executive branch the Provisional Ruling Council.

One of the core reasons NADECO was founded was to counteract the Abacha regime's National Constitutional Conference. Under the aegis of the CUU a meeting to plan the boycott of constitutional conference, was held in the residence of the later-to-become prominent NADECO leader, Major-General Adeyinka Adebayo (retired). NADECO emerged from this meeting as a political organization that dedicated a primary focus to the demand for a Sovereign National Conference, [200] as is cited in the following excerpt from the Charter of the National Democratic Coalition :

PREAMBLE

The Federal Republic of Nigeria shall be a State based on the principles of DEMOCRACY and SOCIAL JUSTICE

IT IS HEREBY ACCORDINGLY DECLARED THAT:

A Sovereign National Conference be convened. The conference shall produce a constitution which will be a supreme law of the land and shall only be amended by an Act of National Assembly, passed by at least two-thirds of the National Assembly and at least two-thirds of the number of the federating unit or states.

The constitution, which will be the outcome of this conference, shall be the basis of the existence of the Nigerian federation. Any violation of this constitution by way of a military coup d'etat or unconstitutional seizure of power shall be taken as the violation of the existence of the Nigerian Federation.

Following the organization's highly publicized launching, especially based around the critique of the regime's NCC, NADECO launched a massive campaign to boycott the local ward elections that would send representatives to the National Constitutional Conference. On Sunday, 22 May 1994, Chief Michael Adekunle Ajasin, the leader of NADECO, issued a statement urging the mass populace, especially the Yoruba South-western states, to stay away from the constitutional conference elections. (Ebenezer Babatope, 1995). The statement reads in full:[201]

> "This is to inform the general public that NADECO insists on a sovereign national conference whose decision will be final and binding. The type of conference which the government is now proposing and in which some traditional rulers are urging us to participate is not a sovereign national conference but rather a constitutional conference where decisions will be subject to changes and manipula-

tion by the military government.

Furthermore, the decisions of government to appoint 96 delegates who will represent nobody but themselves is an attempt to pack the conference with government nominees and frustrate the aspirations of the people of Nigeria. NADECO regrets this type of rubber stamp conference.

It is important to note that up till now, the enabling legislation that will govern the conduct of the elections and deliberations of the Conference does not exist. It is an indication of the contempt with which the Abacha government holds the people and their leaders that they can expect political leaders to stand for an election, which is not governed by any law and participate in the conference whose scope and powers remain undefined.

As soon as the government addresses the objection raised by NADECO and the various interest groups and nationalities in a satisfactory manner NADECO will be prepared to reconsider its stand. Since however, there is no evidence that government is reconsidering the specific and weighty objections already raised, the boycott will continue.

We appeal to all Nigerians who want peace, stability and justice in our dear country not to have anything to do with the so-called Constitutional Conference and the election scheduled for tomorrow 23 May, 1994."

The call for a boycott of the NCC caused a flurry of counter reactions, stirring up a debate over the wisdom of boycotting the conference. Through nationwide contacts and consultations towards influencing the boycott, NADECO mobilized resentment of the military regime throughout Nigeria. However, the mobilization had the greatest impact in the south-west, among the Yoruba where several Yoruba traditional leaders endorsed NADECO's boycott call.[202] NADECO's stand was strengthened by a statement issued after the meeting with some Yoruba traditional rulers. The Obas (traditional leaders) supported the recommendations of

NADECO to 'boycott the proposed National Constitutional Conference Election." "The Yoruba consultative committee agrees to call all Yoruba leaders to reject participation and urge candidates that have indicated their intention to participate in the election to withdraw forthwith from further participation."

Even though the elections to the constitutional conference were held, which were moderately successful nationwide, the elections were boycotted in significant communities of the southwest, Lagos and Ondo.[203] The military regime, however, insisted that there was no boycott, maintaining that the election recorded turn out in the East, the Middle Belt and the North. Nevertheless, despite the attempt by the Abacha regime to affiliate NADECO's boycott campaign with exclusive support in the Yoruba states, twelve democratic organizations and leaders from important regional zones supported the NADECO boycott. The Middle Belt Forum and the South-South Forum comprising leaders from the eastern minority states also supported the NADECO stand. [204] Moreover, significantly, in Rivers State, the chief whip of the reconvened Rivers State House of Assembly signed a statement rejecting "any move designed by the junta to perpetuate itself in office by whatever means or guise, and thus calling on Nigerians to boycott the constitutional conference for an alternative government of national unity presided over by Chief Abiola."[205]

However, even though NADECO was able to gain support for its boycott campaign from non Yoruba pro-democracy organizations, because of minimal mobilization efforts, the non Yoruba high-profile members of the organization, such as Ebite Ukiwe, Dan Suleiman and Ndubuisi Kanu, were unable to stop elections into the Constitutional Conference in their regions. Declarations from non Yoruba pro-democracy organizations were a far cry from grassroots mobilization that NADECO, through Afenifere, had conducted in the Yoruba states. As a result of this one-sided success of the NCC boycott and, therefore, the looming reality that the National Constitutional Conference would be held, NADECO began to withdraw from its focus on mobilizing against the NCC by adopting a more pro-active, but compromising, position in pressing for a Government of National Unity presided over by Chief Abiola.

The Popular National Democratic Government

Chief Abiola renewed his campaign for the immediate return to democracy on the platform of NADECO.[206] In turn, NADECO attempted to recapture its losses in galvanizing a boycott of the NCC by renewing its pro-democracy campaign around the winner of the June 12 elections. In the formative months of NADECO, and during the initial activism era of Chief Abiola after his return from the United States and Britain, NADECO and the annulled presidential aspirant worked hand in hand to deepen the pro-democracy struggle. Chief Abiola's activism occurred as a result of consultations with his Afenifere and CUU allies, who advised him to begin to take stronger measures to ensure the fulfillment of his mandate.[207] Encouraged by NADECO's successful launching, Chief Abiola renewed his struggle for recognition and acceptance of the June 12 presidential polls. NADECO called on President M.K.O Abiola to announce publicly, the structure of his government of national unity.[208] The general secretary of NADECO, Ayo Opadokun, declared, "This is no time for parochial or sectional rationalization. It is time for action. Nigerians want democracy now; Nigerians must act now in defense of democracy."[209] The CUU encouraged Chief Abiola not to let the group down in the fight for the realization of his June 12 mandate.

As a result of these consultations with the opposition-in-formation, Chief Abiola made his presidential proclamation on June 11 at Epetedo in Lagos Island, where he declared himself president in the presence of over 3,000 supporters. In a speech titled, "The Way Forward," which he delivered as president and commander-in-chief of the armed forces of Nigeria, Abiola promised to resume the federal system of government, to provide free education for all children, to improve housing and welfare provision, and to establish a Sovereign National Conference within 100 days of his inauguration. The presidential hopeful concluded by assuring the crowd of his determination to ensure that the "nightmare of military dictatorship is finally over."[210]

On the same day, the Nigerian police declared Chief Abiola wanted and offered a $2,000 reward for information leading to his arrest. Chief Abiola was accused of causing disorder and intending "to overthrow the government."[211] On June 23, 1994, Chief Abiola went public again, addressing a rally at the Lagos State

Sports Complex. Again, Abiola declared himself as President of the Federal Republic of Nigeria. In his famous 'Enough is Enough' address at the Sports Complex, Chief Abiola declared his "Government of National Unity" and declared the Abacha regime a "usurper" government.[212] Chief Abiola was arrested on June 23 and held incommunicado until his first court appearance July 5.

To protest against Chief Abiola's arrest, NADECO, the CD, and other civil society organizations called for a one-week stay-at-home protest against the regime on July 6. A flurry of pro-democracy protests occurred around the country, all over Lagos, and especially in the western states. Demonstrations were staged to back the demands of NADECO. One Nigerian magazine,[213] described the protests as follows:

> "Indeed, many Nigerians went out last week to vote for democracy with their feet. In many cities across the country, there were demonstrations by people calling for the installation of Abiola as President. In Lagos, protesters battled with the police in Ketu, and Agege. There were also protests in Ilorin, Abeokuta, Ibadan, Akure, Osogbo and Ile-Ife. Protesters in Akure, taking their cues from the CD, had taken over the major streets, chanting songs condemning Abacha and extolling Abiola."

Following NADECO's renewed civil—disobedience campaign, Nigerian trade unions joined the opposition coalition. The Nigerian Labor Congress and 22 progressive affiliate unions around the country embarked on a general strike to actualize June 12.[214] The unions in the crucial oil and transport sectors, the National Union of Petroleum and Natural Gas Workers (NUPENG) and Petroleum and Natural Gas Senior Staff Association (PENGASSAN) were the foremost participants escalating the protest. The NLC came out with a communique stating:

> "The military should restore all the dismantled democratic/political structures that were in place in 1993 and call on the acclaimed winner of the 12th June, 1993, presidential election to negotiate a peaceful handover of the reins of government to satisfy the yearnings of the teeming millions of Nigerians, who voluntarily gave him that historic mandate."[215]

The leader of the NUPENG, Mr. Frank Kokori, insisted that the oil workers would not go back to work until the Federal Military Government bowed to the demands for the installation of M.K.O Abiola as president of Nigeria in total respect of the June 12, 1993 electoral mandate. This pro-democracy activity coordinated and sparked by NADECO in May and June, and later in August when joined by the NLC and ASUU, seriously threatened the stability of the military government because of its effect on domestic fuel supplies and oil export earnings. [216] The Abacha regime was so vulnerable that it launched a counter-offensive against the pro-democracy organization. The regime carried out its campaign on the public relations end by sectionalizing the June 12 struggle, as well as by attempting to co-opt non-opposition,[217] civil society sectors to participate in the regime's constitutional conference.[218] The regime responded by persecuting and harassing the pro-democracy activists and strikers, with police and soldiers attacking demonstrators with teargas and live ammunition.

Capitalizing on Civil-Militarism: and NADECO-Abroad

As a result of the boycott campaign and the renewed actualization of the June 12 struggle around Chief Abiola both activities highly publicized by the Nigerian press NADECO became the foremost opposition organization. One news magazine summarized the state of affairs as follows: "That month, the two belligerents, the embattled Abacha regime and the pro-June 12 forces under the auspices of NADECO, became more bellicose."[219]

However, while sustaining the more activist campaign of civil disobedience, and the boycott, NADECO conducted a behind-the-scenes dialogue with the Abacha regime capitalizing on its traditional access to the Nigerian military.[220] Though encouraged by its diplomatic and propaganda successes against the regime, and remaining adamant in its support for June 12, NADECO and Afenifere began to entertain a gradual shift from the earlier "June 12-or-nothing" position to the acceptance of an interim arrangement that would accommodate Chief Abiola under an Abacha presidency.[221] The later-to-become prominent idea of a government of national unity[222] presided over by Chief Abiola with General Abacha as Chief of Defense Staff was initiated during this stage of the democratic struggle.[223]

As a continuation of its policy of holding discussions with all shades of civil society, including the opposition, the Abacha regime held several negotiation meetings between its executive council members and NADECO on Chief Abiola's release as well as on issues to be discussed at the constitutional conference. These meetings set the conditions of Chief Abiola's release. Two crucial meetings, for example, had been held in Lagos between May 23 and May 27 1995 between Lieutenant General Oladipo Diya and NADECO leaders, where the government acknowledged strong points raised in the NADECO memorandum on the constitutional conference. [224]

Moreover, the "progressive ministers"[225] became very active in trying to bring together NADECO and General Abacha. For example, the "progressive ministers" urged the Abacha Regime to meet with NADECO leaders with the view to resolving the June 12 crisis. On July 24, 1994, such a meeting was held to negotiate Chief Abiola's release, and was coordinated by Mr. Alex Ibru, a Minister for Internal Affairs and a member of the Provisional Ruling Council, with NADECO leaders in Lagos, led by Chief Anthony Enahoro. Dialogue sessions of this sort [226] eventually led to the planned release of Chief Abiola through the legalistic setting of bail conditions. However, demonstrating its support for the sanctity of June 12 and the principle of democracy, NADECO leaders denounced the conditions set by the Abacha regime for Chief Abiola's release. Chief Abiola was advised by NADECO leaders to reject the release conditions describing them as a "fraudulent contrivance by the *military* government to buy peace by foul means." Chief Abiola did so accusing the Abacha regime of forcing him to "abandon the mandate overwhelmingly given to him by Nigerians."[227]

By 1995, with the putative success of the strike leading to the proscription of labor unions and the growing trend of violence against NADECO activists, the pro-democracy momentum initiated by NADECO in early May 1994 began to wane, with many newspaper reports stating that General Abacha's regime had won the battle. Emboldened by the success of the constitutional conference, which was held despite the strident opposition by NADECO and the Egbe Afenifere, General Abacha began to feel that he had, "won the battle for the streets against NADECO and had pulverized labor and scared many NADECO members into exile."[228] Moreover, NADECO's mixed bag of Yoruba irredentists, political opportunists, careerists, pseudo-intellectuals and military renegades created obstacles against the organization's ability to build popular institutions of power, and thereby being able to more forcefully contend with the power of the Nigerian military state.

However, despite a temporary decline of the earlier momentum, NADECO had been able to re-boot the pro-democracy struggle in 1994, and the continued detention of Chief Abiola kept June 12 and pro-democracy on the front burner of national discourse in Nigeria. Furthermore, the violent anti-opposition environment had hounded into exile many prominent NADECO members, where they were to launch a concerted propaganda war against the Abacha military administration. Although they were no longer in a position to organize mass protests and strikes, NADECO sustained the cold war, while Afenifere remained firmly in control of the Southwest, despite efforts by the regime to prop up rival groups and personalities in this region. [229]

Similar to the CD, which had also been severely demobilized by the military regime's persecution and subversion, NADECO shifted its forces to the international arena and founded NADECO-abroad. Founded by exiled members of NADECO in February 1996 in Washington D.C. and London an international diplomatic campaign against the Nigerian military administration was launched. Charismatic members of NADECO[230] mobilized Nigerian communities abroad, U.S. and European communities, and foreign governments on the June 12 annulment and the struggle for democracy in Nigeria.

One of NADECO's international successes included the launching in June 1997, of Radio NADECO, a short-wave radio broadcast to the international community, including Nigeria. Through it NADECO was to not only influence and mobilize the international communities about the Nigerian pro-democracy struggle, but because the station could be picked up in Nigeria, it kept the home struggle going as well. Radio NADECO's maiden broadcast began as follows:

> Radio NADECO: The voice of Free Nigerian is made possible by free Nigerians who wish to create and uncensored medium to remind the Nigerian people the values of

> democracy and human rights. This voice shall be unequivocal in denouncing the evils of dictatorship, the brutality of military rule and the absence of the rule of law in Nigeria.
>
> Radio NADECO shall champion the cause all Nigerians illegally detained by the whims of the Abacha regime, especially those like Bashorun Abiola, Frank Kokori, General Olusegun Obasanjo, General Shehu Yar'Adua, Mrs. Chris Anyanwu, Dr. Beko Ransome-Kuti, victims of kangaroo court justice.
>
> The primary objective of Radio NADECO will be to mobilize Nigerians to stop the military clique from ruling Nigeria by force. No armed power is greater than the sovereign will of the people.[231]

IV. Resources

Because NADECO was based upon a 40-year social network, which dated back to the establishment of Nigerian politics as early as 1959, and because its membership was largely upper-middle class and wealthy, financial resources needed to carry out the pro-democracy campaign were acquired with little difficulty. The organization's charismatic leader, Chief Abiola was a self-made millionaire who funded the Council for Unity and Understanding and later the SDP progressive coalition through his M.K.O Abiola Presidential Campaign Foundation. Other wealthy donors included former economic minister and SDP presidential candidate Chief Olu Falae, and wealthy NADECO member, Chief Rewane, later assassinated. The organization set up an Economic and Revenue Allocation Committee under the chairmanship of Chief Olu Falae. The committee was charged with recommending ways by which the organization could raise money for its operations.

NADECO-abroad capitalized on the sophisticated fund-raising techniques used for acquiring funds for human rights causes in the United States, Great Britain, and Canada. Aside from fund raising campaigns to Nigerian communities and other human rights advocates, the body via Chief Alani Akinriade was able to secured a grant for its activities from the National Endowment for

Democracy.[232] As a result of this external funding, NADECO was able to publish promotional newsletters, develop a website, and operate an underground radio broadcast in the effort to promote Nigerian democratization.

On the domestic front, due to the high-profile status of most of its members, NADECO was virtually afforded free press in Nigerian news magazines and newspapers on any of its pro-democracy activities. In fact, between 1994 and 1998, NADECO was formally and exclusively associated with the opposition to the military.

CHAPTER 7

NIGERIAN PRO-DEMOCRACY MOVEMENT ABROAD (UDFN)

I. ORGANIZATION

By 1995, with the opportunity for protest inside Nigeria steadily decreasing much of the dynamic of the pro-democracy struggle, the movement expanded to the international arena. As with the anti-apartheid movement in the 1960s and 1970s, the Nigerian pro-democracy international movement was built on the efforts of exiled Nigerian pro-democracy activists, Nigerian immigrant communities abroad, and a wide range of international human rights organizations and foreign governments. Particularly, scores of pro-democracy organizations emerged among the large Nigerian expatriate population in the U.S. and other Western European cities.

The international pro-democracy movement was overall organized by Nigerians living abroad, but it also drew in international NGOs, environmentalists, domestic human rights activists, trade unionists, church groups, students, and many others, in addition to African advocacy groups. Though spearheaded by Nigerian pro-democracy exiles, the international pro-democracy organizations were primarily made up of experienced professionals, including lawyers, doctors, architects, and educators, who knew the ins and outs of advocacy politics.

Initially heavily influenced by the exiled leadership of NADECO-abroad,[233] most of the organizations aligned their objectives with those of the domestic movement, demanding the immediate termination of military rule, the reversal of the annulment of the June 12 elections, and the release of pro-democracy activists. However, as the international movement matured, it began to adopt its own objectives, especially leading the call for international sanctions against the Nigerian military regime.

Typical issue campaigns conducted by the foreign-based, Nigerian pro-democracy organizations have included: getting foreign governments and institutions particularly the United States, the United Kingdom, the UN and the Commonwealth to "reject Abacha's transition-to-democracy program and demand the release of all 100-odd Nigerian political prisoners/detainees; freeze the bank accounts and assets of members of the Abacha regime, as well as ban visas to Nigerian military personnel, their appointees, families, and business associates; boycott Nigerian oil and lead sanctions against Nigerian goods and products, especially petroleum products and companies; ban Nigeria from international sporting events, including the 1996 Olympics and the 1998 FIFA World Cup; expel Nigeria from international bodies, especially the Commonwealth."[234]

By the latter part of 1995, so many independent pro-democracy organizations abroad had sprung up advocating the Nigerian pro-democracy cause that some political organizations began to see the necessity of creating a coalition of sixty or more organizations with a single platform and a single agenda. The most significant umbrella organization abroad,[235] the United Democratic Front of Nigeria (UDFN), took on this job in 1996. The U.S.-based UDFN's steering committee included professor Sola Adeyeye, the Texas-based Organization of Nigerians Abroad (ONA), scholar, Julius Ihonvbere, and NALICON president/NADECO member, Wole Soyinka.

Following the founding of NADECO-abroad, scores of local organizations[236] were founded after the June 12 1993 crisis. The international movement started when concerned Nigerian professionals in major cities around the world began to forge transnational linkages especially through the usage of global information technology. To recruit new members, the movement's founders made use of the dense civil societal networks already existing in most foreign Nigerian communities.

On March 31 1996, under the umbrella of the UDFN, about forty of the international organizations joined together with a common platform to restore democracy in Nigeria on the basis of the popular mandate of June 12, 1993.[237] The UDFN adopted many of the resolutions already adopted by prominent home-grown pro-democracy organizations including a resolution to "reject in its entirety the three-year transition program of the Abacha dictatorship in Nigeria; to respect the mandate of the Nigerian people as expressed in elections prior to and including the June 12, 1993 presidential election; to demand that all political prisoners in Nigeria be released immediately and without conditions; and that president-elect M.K.O Abiola be released to form a broad-based government of national unity."[238] They also resolved to, "call on the international community to impose an oil embargo and full economic, cultural and sporting isolation of Nigeria until democracy is restored; to freeze all the assets of members of the military junta and their civilian collaborators."[239]

The UDFN served as the Nigerian pro-democracy, external opposition abroad representing all other organizations at public appearances and issuing policy statements on their behalf. The umbrella organization also serves as a congress or parliament, giving equal representation to all pro-democracy movements in and outside of Nigeria. Significantly, on September 29, 1996, the congress resolved to establish a parliament-in-exile agreeing that the parliament be, " a unified legislative organ of all Nigerian pro-democracy groups and will serve as the primary voice of the alternative to General Abacha and military dictatorship."[240] Consistent with the objectives of the domestic movement, the parliament also resolved to, "draw up proposals for a sovereign national conference in Nigeria and a model civilian constitution for Nigeria to replace unitary constitutions that have, since 1966, been foisted on Nigeria by military dictatorships." In addition, the parliament resolved to "set up an international panel of jurists to draw up an indictment against generals Babangida and Abacha for crimes against humanity during past and present military regimes under their command."[241]

The strongest feature of the organizational structure of the UDFN alliance stems from a team-oriented, steering committee of fewer than ten members, who represent a wide range of opinion among the Nigerian democratic community abroad. They participate in significant international events, including the Commonwealth Heads of Government Meeting (CHOGM), the United Nations, the U.S. Congress, and other G7 parliaments. At the same time, the independent status of the scores of local organizations affiliated with the UDFN has provided a great deal of grassroots mobilization for the Nigerian democracy movement. A typical local affiliate, the Nigerian Democratic Front, describes its organization as the UDFN chapter of the state of Michigan, and is active in four major areas: Organizes lectures, symposia, seminars, teach-ins, rallies, protests, demonstrations; issues public statements, press releases, write up articles, electronic media, websites; makes public appearances on radio, TV, in academic forums; organizes fund-raisers

Not all UDFN affiliates are so tightly aligned to the umbrella organization. For example, in the same state of Michigan, the Nigerian Forum for Democracy, also an affiliate member of the UDFN, focuses on environmental concerns, acting as the vanguard for boycotting Shell Oil in the area. Moreover, an organization based in Boston, the Nigerian Democratic Awareness Committee (NDAC), also a UDFN affiliate—led the international movement long before the UDFN came on the scene and still considers itself an umbrella organization. [242] As early as 1995, the NDAC had built an impressive network of support that gained direct access to the White House.[243]

An organization that maintained its independence as a pro-democracy movement organization in the Washington D.C. region, preferring to be loosely affiliated to the UDFN, was the Nigerian Democratic Movement (NDM). Its president is Mobolaji Aluko, a professor of chemical engineering at Howard University and son of the then chairman of the National Economic Intelligence Committee, professor Sam Aluko. Other well-known independent affiliate organizations included NADECO-abroad. Moreover, the National Liberation Council (NALICON), operating from London, and initiated as a wing of NADECO, stresses its independence as a pro-democracy organization. However, NALICON's founder, professor Wole Soyinka, was a steering committee member and chair of the UDFN. Finally, the Voice Forum, a small pro-democracy movement organization and UDFN affiliate based in Germany and funded by the local German council, organized exclusively around the release of Dr. Ransome-Kuti.

II. Alliances

UDFN alliances are transcontinental and represent ideologies that range from liberal to radical. Diagram V (134 A) schematically describes these organizations. The UDFN, attempts to organize common fronts in the implementation of uniform pro-democracy agendas both abroad and domestically. They have organized summits in Oslo, Norway; Johannesburg, South Africa; Dakar, Senegal; and Pittsburgh, USA for this purpose.

A significant feature of the Nigerian pro-democracy movement abroad was its ability to forge even greater alliances with international non-governmental organizations sympathetic to the Nigerian cause. This publicized the human rights question in Nigeria where a great number of Nigerian pro-democracy activists were incarcerated for their political activities. The UDFN has worked with Human Rights Watch, Africa Watch, the Sierra Club, Amnesty International, and the British Parliamentary Human Rights Group among others. Thus international NGOs have campaigned to free Nigerian political dissidents such as Beko Ransome-Kuti, M.K.O Abiola, Olusegun Obasanjo, and Shehu Yar'Adua. Some of these international campaigns include the Norwegian Nigeria Campaign, the Free Beko Campaign in Weimar, Germany, the Sierra Club's campaign in support of the MOSOP activists.

As a rule, the UDFN and its affiliate organizations extended their coalition umbrella to non-Nigerian pro-democracy organizations. Sometimes described as Friends of Nigeria (FON), these organizations fall into two categories: in the U.S. African-American-based organizations; and international human rights organizations. The center of the agitation to democratize Nigeria by non-Nigerian international NGO's and American lobbyist groups was Washington DC. The organizations began with an effort to de-annul the June 12, 1993 election and install M.K.O Abiola, as president, through the efforts of Randall Echols, a Washington-based lobbyist and Abiola's executive assistant for U.S. affairs.

Echols' initiative resulted in a flurry of support by the U.S. African-American congressional organization, the Black Caucus. On June 27, 1995, Randall Robinson, executive director of Trans Africa, a U. S.-based Africa-oriented, international human rights organization joined Nigerians in a daily demonstration in front of the Nigerian Embassy on 16th Street in Washington D.C. Robinson's activism made the Nigerian pro-democracy question a human rights issue in the United States.

Furthermore, Robinson regularly briefed members of the

Clinton administration's National Security Council and the Congressional Black Caucus on events in Nigeria. On June 28, 1995 Robinson hosted the cream of the American press in his office, thus beginning a flurry of anti-military editorials and articles on Nigeria, which appeared in such influential American newspapers as the *New York Times* and the *Washington Post.* As a result of Robinson's activities on June 29, 1995, the International Round Table on Nigeria, a coalition of human rights and pro-democracy organizations in the Washington D.C. area, sponsored a demonstration against Shell and Chevron. This event drew attention to the plight of the Ogoni people and asked Shell and Chevron to fight for an oil embargo against Nigeria.

The UDFN was led by seasoned Nigerian charismatic leaders, the most well-known of whom was Nobel Prize winner and radical pro-democracy activist, Wole Soyinka. The movement's ideology, however, ranges from radical intellectualism (NALICON—Soyinka, Ihonvbere) to moderate liberal (NDM—Aluko), and included some southwest Yoruba irredentism. The ideology expressed by the affiliate members of the UDFN tended to be reflective of the umbrella organization, with affiliate organizations exhibiting various strains of progressivism and radical-grassroots philosophy. Despite differences, all the pro-democracy organizations stressed the need to contribute to Nigerian democratic advancement through collaborative and sustained international activism to raise awareness of the tyrannical military regime.[244]

III. Political Opportunity

Unlike the domestic movement, the international Nigerian pro-democracy movement sought to agitate the Nigerian military regime by influencing international bodies and institutions, as well as foreign governments. Free from the oppressive environment against pro-democracy organizers inside of Nigeria, the Nigerian activists mobilizing the movement abroad enjoyed relatively open access to "friendly" host foreign governments and international institutions. They could capitalize on the activist organizational model practiced by a tradition of social movement organization in most Western cities.

In November 1995, after the Nigerian military regime hanged Nigerian pro-democracy and environmental activist Ken Saro-

Wiwa and eight other Ogoni activists—despite an urgent international appeal to the Abacha regime to reverse the decision[245]—the international campaign against the Nigerian military government's human rights abuses and refusal to establish a democratic government was initiated.[246] Two international bodies launched direct campaigns against the Nigerian government: the Commonwealth Heads of Government Meeting (CHOGM) and the United Nations. In addition, several G7 parliaments, including the U.S. Congress conducted direct campaigns against the Nigerian military. Though not directly leading these international campaigns, the UDFN and its affiliate bodies enjoyed significant access to the decision-making spheres of these campaigns, thereby influencing their direction. The UDFN-through its affiliate bodies-directly mobilized municipal and regional governments in Western European, U.S., and Canadian cities in support of the Nigerian democracy cause.

The UDFN and International Campaigns: The Commonwealth and the UN

The Commonwealth Heads of Government Meeting (CHOGM), an international organization of former British colonies, played a significant role in directing the international community against the Nigerian military regime. The first international institution to demonstrate its outrage against the Nigerian regime, the organization supported an unprecedented vote by its members to suspend Nigeria from the Commonwealth body. Nigeria was given two years within which to comply with the terms of the Commonwealth Harare Declaration, which commits Commonwealth members to democratic governance, failing which they face expulsion.[247]

The Commonwealth specified the conditions Nigeria must satisfy to reverse the suspension, stating that unless the conditions were met within two years Nigeria would be expelled from the Commonwealth. The conditions were: Immediate and unconditional release of all political prisoners, including the forty three jailed for an alleged coup plot and Chief Abiola; demonstrable progress towards the restoration of the liberty of the individual and the law; demonstrable progress towards the restoration of democracy within two years.

A Commonwealth Ministerial Action Group (CMAG) was appointed to deal with persistent violations in Nigeria. On April 23, 1996, the group recommended various sanctions against Nigeria, including visa restrictions on and denial of educational facilities to members of the Nigerian regime and their families, the withdrawal of military attaches and cessation of military training, an embargo on the export of arms, a visa-based ban on sporting contacts, and the downgrading of diplomatic and cultural links. It was also recommended that there be a ban on air links and additional economic measures, including freezing the financial assets and bank accounts in foreign countries of members of the military regime.

Pro-democracy international campaigns by the UDFN and its affiliate organizations, including the U.K.-based NALICON and the Canadian-based, Canadians in Defense of Democracy and Human Rights in Nigeria (CODHN) centered on creating linkages with Commonwealth members to influence the course for democratization in Africa. For example, in October 1997, two years after Nigeria's suspension, the Commonwealth was due to reassess the case and vote on either reversal of the suspension or expulsion. The international alliance of Nigerian pro-democracy organizations under the aegis of the UDFN organized to influence an aggressive two-year campaign to influence the impending reevaluation in favor of expulsion of Nigeria from the Commonwealth if the country did not reverse the June 12 annulment of the Nigerian presidential elections.

To achieve its goals, the UDFN held regular demonstrations outside of the Edinburgh CHOGM headquarters. Because no demonstrable progress had been made by the Nigerian military regime regarding human rights and restorations of individual liberties toward democracy. The UDFN presented a 16 page memorandum,[248] recommending that the CHOGM take the following measures against Nigeria:

- Expulsion of Nigeria at the Edinburgh meeting of the Heads of Government.
- Implementation of all measures agreed by the CMAG in London of April 23.
- Commitment to a major program of democratic assistance and solidarity with organizations engaged in facilitating the emergence of democratic governance and ensuring peaceful change.

Although the CHOGM did not vote to expel Nigeria from the Commonwealth, it did agree to continue the suspension of Nigeria from the Commonwealth, thereby acknowledging the non-compliance issues raised by the UDFN memorandum.

The United Nations also played a significant, though limited, role in international efforts to pressure the Nigerian military regime to respect human rights and democracy in that country. Professor Wole Soyinka president of the UDFN's National Liberation Council (NALICON), and Chairman of the United Democratic Front of Nigeria (UDFN), addressed the United Nations General Assembly on the question of Nigerian democracy and human rights abuses by the military regimes. Professor Soyinka urged the international body to enact sanctions against the Nigerian military regime in concert with the demands of the Nigerian pro-democracy movement abroad.

The UN General Assembly adopted a resolution on Nigeria on December 22, 1995. The resolution condemned the executions of Ken Saro-Wiwa and the others, welcomed the steps taken by the Commonwealth, and expressed the hope that these and other actions by other States would encourage Nigeria to restore democratic rule.[249] The following year, on April 22, 1996, the UN Commission on Human Rights adopted a resolution in which it requested report on the independence of judges and lawyers and on extra-judicial, summary or arbitrary executions in Nigeria. On July 29, 1996 the commission's rapporteur, Mr. Param Cumaraswamy, consulted with UDFN-affiliate, Nigerian pro-democracy and human rights organizations in London in regard to the situation in Nigeria. Among other conclusions and recommendations, the Human Rights Committee recommended that, "immediate steps should be taken to restore democracy and full constitutional rights in Nigeria without delay."[250]

Influencing American Foreign Policy and Local Public Awareness

UDFN pro-democracy affiliate organizations, such as the Howard University-based World Congress of Free Nigerians, the Nigerian Democratic Movement (NDM), and the Organization of Nigerians Abroad (ONA), were successful in influencing the U.S Congress and the British and Canadian parliaments.[251] Working in concert with Washington D.C.-based international bodies and NGOs, such as the International Roundtable on Nigeria (IRN), the Washington Office on Africa (WOA), and the Congressional Black Caucus, the UDFN and its affiliate organizations have successfully launched bills in the U.S. Senate introduced by Senator Kassebaum (R. Kansas) and in the House by Representative Donald Payne (D. New Jersey) Both Donald Payne and William Jefferson, who initiated a special task force in the Congressional Black Caucus on Democratization in Nigeria, directly lobbied Secretary of State Warren Christopher to intervene in the annulment of the June 12 elections.[252]

Continued lobbying resulted in some Congressional action, including additional American sanctions against Nigeria, including a ban on all new U.S. investment in Nigeria and a freeze on the personal assets of top officials of the Nigerian regime. The Payne Bill, titled "The Nigerian Democracy Act" (HR 1786) was by far the most comprehensive list of sanctions against the Nigerian military regime. The bill's official title stated its purpose as follows: "A bill to impose sanctions against Nigeria, and for other purposes."[253]

Through the UDFN and its affiliates, the international-based Nigerian pro-democracy movement has been successful in creating several local public awareness campaigns on Nigerian pro-democracy advocacy, including the mobilization of local communities in U.S. cities to pass laws and resolutions against Nigeria. Other successful campaigns included the setting up of clandestine radio broadcasts such as the successful Radio Kudirat organized by NALICON and the UDFN.[254] Radio Kudirat Nigeria was conceived of and implemented as a means for empowering the people of Nigeria and helping to counter the daily dose of regime propaganda in the country. Since June 12, 1996, Radio Kudirat Nigeria (RKN), broadcasted daily uncensored, pro-democratic information to Nigeria on the short wave. The popularity of the broadcast continued to grow. The response of the Abacha administration was to charge professor Soyinka and Chief Enahoro[255] with "levying war against the Federal Military Government of Nigeria." In addition, the military regime committed huge sums of money to intercept RKN's broadcasts.[256]

Haphzat Abiola, Chief Abiola's daughter and a prominent Nigerian pro-democracy activist in the U.S., launched a successful campaign-through the Kudirat Institute for Nigerian

Democracy (KIND) and NADECO-abroad to rename New York City's 43rd Street (the location of the Nigerian Embassy) Kudirat Avenue after the slain pro-democracy activist and wife of Chief M.K.O Abiola. After mobilization in New York City, the resolution was adopted by the municipal New York City Council in October 1997. Testifying at the hearings in favor of the resolution were UDFN chair, professor Wole Soyinka; former U.S. Ambassador to Nigeria, Walter Carrington; Anthony Enahoro speaking on behalf of NADECO, and Dr. Edward Oparaoji of the Washington-based Democratic Awareness.

In addition, the California branch of the National Conscience Party in Oakland, California—a Nigerian-based pro-democracy organization, and a UDFN affiliate campaigned for and got an ordinance setting forth a policy for the city of Oakland restricting the deposit, investment, or use of city funds with banks, financial institutions, investment firms, or professional service firms who do business with either the public or private sector of Nigeria.[257] A similar resolution was implemented in the Massachusetts town of Amherst, an effort mobilized by Haphzat Abiola's KIND—a UDFN affiliate organization. The local residents introduced into their city charter a by-law to promote human rights and democracy in Nigeria. Similarly, the Michigan-based Nigerian Forum for Democracy—also a UDFN affiliate organization-organized to get the city of Detroit to pass a resolution condemning the Nigerian military government.

The movement also forged platform coalitions with international NGOs, such as Human Rights Watch, Amnesty International, and the Sierra Club, whose organizations have worked to push the Nigerian democracy crises to the international forefront. Through the efforts of the Sierra Club and local Nigerian pro-democracy organizations in New York City, Resolution 1002-A was passed, "commending the Nigerian people for their courageous struggle against repression and tyranny, condemning the Nigerian military dictatorship, calling for the immediate release from prison of Chief Moshood Abiola, calling upon the United States government to take all practical steps, including economic measures, to effect the release of all unjustly detained political prisoners and the restoration of a free press and civilian democratic government in Nigeria."[258]

Human Rights Watch launched an international campaign with

UDFN affiliate bodies to free all Nigerian political prisoners and detainees under the Abacha regime's secret treason trials of 1995, where forty -three pro-democracy activists were convicted for allegedly trying to overthrow the Abacha regime. In Weimar city, Germany, the Nigerian Voice Forum, a German affiliate body of the UDFN, was successful in organizing the award-winning human rights prize, the Weimar City Human Rights Prize, to Dr. Beko Ransome Kuti, the jailed human rights and pro-democracy activist. The event mobilized German citizens towards the release of political detainees and the establishment of democracy in Nigeria.

Randall Robinson's daily protest against the Abacha military regime outside of the Nigerian Embassy in Washington D. C. brought out allies in the Nigerian pro-democracy movement abroad, and Trans Africa's model efforts were continued by local UDFN affiliate organizations. In 1996, the NDM organized a Martin Luther King-style march on Washington against the Abacha regime. The Indiana-based Free Nigeria Movement, (FNM) was successful in initiating and drawing wide support for several international campaigns against Nigeria including the Nigerian boycott of FIFA,[259] and a boycott of multi-nationals that invest in Nigeria, especially Shell and Coca-Cola.

IV. Resources

Funds utilized for the events and campaigns organized by the Nigerian pro-democracy movement came from three major sources: grants and sponsorship by international institutions, NGOs and non profits, such as the American National Endowment for Democracy; local affiliate organizational fund raising efforts, such as the organizing of conferences, seminars and fund raising events; and volunteer membership dues and personal contributions.

The UDFN umbrella organization with a steering committee of no more than ten active members was funded primarily by the volunteer services of its prominent members, especially Wole Soyinka and University of Pittsburgh professor, Sola Adeyeye. Basic services for the organization were covered through global fund-raising events, such as the democracy conferences held in Dakar, Oslo, and Pittsburgh, where steering committee members usually successfully aggressively solicited funds from UDFN affiliate member organizations.

Although the UDFN organization requested several grants, competition for funds for Nigerian pro-democracy was high with the UDFN losing out to NADECO-abroad for a National Endowment for Democracy grant.[260] Several UDFN affiliate bodies demonstrated greater success in receiving competitive grants for their activities than the umbrella UDFN. Several of the local affiliates, including the National Democratic Forum, Kudirat Institute for Democracy, and the Nigerian Democratic Movement, either received sponsorship from NGOs or small grants to support selected campaigns.

Most of the fund raising for the international campaigns was performed by UDFN affiliate organizations. Volunteer membership and personal contributions were the most consistent means of raising funds. Some mounted broader money producing events. For example, most organizations held elaborate launching events and annual fund raising awareness events. Many organizations also published newsletters for sale and developed commercial websites. However, despite several fund-raising successes, acquiring funds remained a challenge for the movement abroad and was often discussed at UDFN conferences.[261]

The limited resources available to the Nigerian pro-democracy movement abroad tended to be adequate for realizing their minimal objectives of influencing the Nigerian campaign abroad. The movement consistently furthered its cause despite limited funding because it was in a political environment that provided several models for effective resistance and organization. Not only did the Nigerian movement adopt strategies used by NGOs and social movement organizations in the West, it also aligned with these organizations to further their pro-democracy objectives.

CHAPTER 8

WINNING THE FOURTH REPUBLIC

Deepening and Expanding Democratic Space

The death of General Sani Abacha in June 1998 resulted in the reversal of all dictatorial and anti-democratic policies associated with his regime by the successor Abubakar regime.[262] However, even before the general's death, Abacha's discredited self-succession bid through his contrived transition-to-democracy program had come up against intense resistance even from the mainstream military; and it is believed that the military leader was seeking an abandonment of his self-succession bid as a result of overwhelming criticism.[263]

As its main objective, *People Power* links General Abacha's softening of policy on his transition bid and the ultimate emergence of the soft-liner military faction in the Abubakar regime to the collective efforts and achievements of the pro-democracy movement.[264] By 1998, the pro-democracy movement had nurtured a self-conscious, politically active civil society that had defined and established legitimate political authority. The movement had first been initiated by human rights organizations emerging from the Left, the CD collective, reconstituted in the United Action for Democracy (UAD); propelled into the forefront of democratic struggle by the pro-democracy organization network, forged through the efforts of NADECO; expanded into the broader network of the Joint Action Committee of Nigeria (JACON) launched in 1998; as well as even more broadly expanded by the entry of newly formed elite groups—significantly the 18 Northern Elite and the Group of 34; the media under the platform of JODER; and the international arena fortified by the UDFN with its newly formed international-domestic partnership organization, JACOM.

All became the collective voice representing fairness, equity, justice and democracy in Nigeria. General Abacha's self-succession bid represented the thorn that united these forces into cross-ethnic, regional and ideological coalitions in their efforts to resist Nigerian military-state power. Via this platform, virulent, consistent and comprehensive pro-democracy mobilization and opposition to the military government transformed itself into the wider movement for national rebirth and democracy in Nigeria.

I. Discrediting Military Vanguardism (1990-1998): Revealing the Vulnerability of the Military Regime

A recurring feature in the struggle for democratization in Nigeria has been the contradictory disposition of even the most informed citizens toward the military. There has existed a congenital aversion for military dictatorship and yet a momentary relapse into romance with the institution at the slightest disaffection with democratic governance (Aaron Gana, 1996). Moreover, Nigerian political culture has always believed that Nigerian civil society has been able to check tyrannical and extreme dictatorial tendencies within their military regimes (Oyovbaire, Olagunju &Agbaje, 1995) as a result of the interwoven alliances with the civilian class, creating civil-military class sectors(William Graff, 1988). These alliances have acted as checks and balances ensuring the civilianization of Nigerian military regimes.

How and to what extent did the pro-democracy movement advertise the vulnerability of the Nigerian military regime between 1990-1999? Was the movement collectively able to create a threat perception, compelling the military regime to democratize? This section demonstrates how the pro-democracy movement progressively became a threat to the military and gradually undermined the institution's credibility in Nigerian politics. In addition to the 1998 victory and the emergence of the Abubakar-led "soft-liners", the main indicators of this threat to the military were demonstrated by the institution's violent response to the democracy movement. By challenging military vanguardism and legitimacy in Nigerian politics, the pro-democracy organizations laid the foundation for the decline of military rule.

By 1990 because of the proliferation of Nigerian human rights organizations exposing military authoritarianism,[265] and a worsening economy due to the imposition of the Structural Adjustment Program, military vanguardism[266] was increasingly becoming discredited. The Babangida regime's topsy-turvy transition-to-democracy program became a symbol of the ineffectiveness of the military in politics. The 1993 annulment of the presidential elections accelerated the delegitimization of the Nigerian military in politics and military vanguardism took a nose-dive, a process that continued until 1999. This chapter describes the role of the Nigerian pro-democracy movement in facilitating the delegitimation of the Nigerian military among the general populace.

In 1993, as a result of the annulment of the presidential elections, the pro-democracy movement capitalized on the military's declining legitimacy among the populace and spearheaded a successful campaign to discredit military government once-and-for-all, and seek to terminate military rule in Nigerian politics.[267] The termination of military rule was identified as the foremost objective by most pro-democracy organizations, which popularized the idea that military rule was a human rights question for the country. [268] For these organizations, the Nigerian military had become the single most important obstacle to democratization; no democratic project would be complete that did not ensure that the military submit itself to the authority of elected civilian officials.

The June 12 annulment of the presidential elections by the Babangida military regime brought the pro-democracy movement further political opportunities. It was further evidence of the waning legitimacy of military dominance over politics and civilian alliances in Nigeria. Thus, unlike previous transition-to-democracy programs and military interventions through coup-d'etat, for the first time, through the organized platform of the pro-democracy movement, civil society demanded that the military regime reverse the annulment decision and mobilized the Nigerian populace around the reinstatement of the elected winner of that election, Chief Moshood Abiola.

The Campaign for Democracy (CD) set forth the "June 12 mandate"[269] as the foundation of the pro-democracy movement.[270] In a 1993 *Guardian* newspaper article, the CD announced, "June 12 is a historic expression of popular will. The CD stands for the democratic resolution of June 12 as a basis for the democratic advancement of the country."[271] As a result of the campaign by the CD to discredit military rule by mobilizing civil society to demand immediate democratization, a tumultuous expression of civil society activism occurred in 1993 with the anti-Babangida—military regime demonstrations. These demonstrations represented the highest expression of mass mobilization by urban popular sectors throughout the pro-democracy movement's activism between 1990-1999. The most successful day of protests was July 5, 1993 when the CD lead thousands of protests in cities across the country. The flurry of resistance activities organized by the CD resulted in the stepping down from power of the Babangida military regime and the installation of an Interim National Government headed by a civilian.

The period between August and November represented a unique and ambiguous time with the nagging question lingering as to whether the Nigerian military had quit politics once and for all. The pro-democracy movement continued its campaign against military politicization with the CD organizing more successful nationwide protest strikes against the Interim National Government. However, in November, 1994, through a coup d'etat organized by General Sani Abacha, the Nigerian military reentered Nigerian politics, abrogating all remaining democratic structures developed during the previous transition. The five-year, 1993-1998, military regime of General Abacha consolidated its power over the Nigerian state, but was defined as the most repressive regime in Nigerian history.[272]

Replacing the CD's role of agitator, the pro-democracy movement organized under the aegis of NADECO, which, by 1994, after the mass boycott of the Abacha regime's National Constitutional Conference, became the official authority against military authority. The height of NADECO's success came in 1994 when it called for mass protest and an immediate end to the Abacha regime. This seriously undermined the power and authority of the Abacha regime, which was just beginning to recreate the role of the Nigerian military in politics.

NADECO advertised the vulnerability of the Nigerian military regime, especially among political elite circles, where influence tended to have more impact. As a result of civil-military alliances that facilitated access to the executive branches of the Nigerian military, NADECO was particularly influential in fermenting factionalism in the military which contributed to the emergence of the Abubakar liberalizing faction.

The early links who served as liaisons between the pro-democracy movement and the military government included the "progressive ministers" especially Chief Walter Ofanagoro, who, as a June 12 advocate-turned Abacha appointee as Minister of Justice, for a short time maintained a fluctuating role among the civil-military network. Walter Ofanagoro eventually resigned from the regime on principle, citing its impending tyranny. This action marked the beginning of the discrediting by the civilian elite of tyrannical military authority. Alex Ibru and Lateef Jakande, also Abacha civilian appointees, mediated between civil society and the military, but experienced the same brutal treatment by the regime when the military leader's power felt threatened.

Also discrediting military vanguardism was the criticism of the regime by the former military political elite. In part this resulted from the disgraceful treatment meted out to General Obasanjo for his political activism supporting democratization, to General Shehu Yar'Adua, who was to die a political prisoner, and later to General Diya, who had been General Abacha's second in command and had played a crucial role in canvassing support for the Abacha regime from the civilian opposition. As a result of what has been described by a group of retired military officers as the desecration of the elite corps in the army, an eighteen-page petition was drawn-up against the expanding tyranny of continued military rule.[273] Reacting to General Abacha's attempted purge of military officers, especially those that were suspected to be June 12 supporters or "NADECO" officers, opposition against military rule within the military expanded.

Reaction by significant civil society sectors, including the northern political establishment represented by the Turaki Committee and the Northern Elders Forum, to General Abacha's 1997 self-succession bid, symbolized the extent of military delegitimization.[274] Key leaders from the North, as well as other prominent political elite leaders represented by the G-34, all followed NADECO in denouncing Abacha's transition program as a "sham" and calling for the general's immediate stepping-down from power.

The pro-democracy movement abroad was also successful in

discrediting the Abacha regime. The UDFN and its affiliates succeeded in advertising the vulnerability of the Nigerian military regime by promoting the former "Giant of Africa" as a "pariah state" in the international arena. Nigeria was now seen as a nation with a human rights record comparable to apartheid South Africa and with a corrupt military junta comparable to Latin American states in the 70s.[275] While also pursuing the pro-democracy movement's domestic agenda of immediate termination of military rule and a reversal of the "June 12" annulment, the movement abroad lobbied international bodies and foreign governments around the world to enact a comprehensive set of sanctions against the Nigerian military regime. For example, in an unprecedented move, the Commonwealth Heads of Government suspended Nigeria from the organization of former British colonies, citing the nation for its anti-democratic position and its human rights abuses.

Tyrannical Rule No Longer at Bay?

In response to the waning of its credibility, the military responded to what it considered an onslaught on its over two decades of dominance of Nigerian politics by launching a counter offensive against the promoters of anti-militarism, an offensive that combined political manipulation and cooptation of civil society sectors with the violent repression of military opponents. This counter offensive during the Abacha regime relegated the traditional non-tyrannical quality of Nigerian military leadership to a thing of the past.

The Nigerian military regime launched a counter-campaign to divide, discredit and subvert the Nigerian pro-democracy movement. Both the Babangida and the Abacha regimes employed energetic and purposeful state-led and tightly contrived democratic transition programs, which were attributable primarily to the manipulation of ethnic and ideological divisions among pro-democracy organizations, the co-optation and conscription of professional organizations involved in the struggle, and the regimes' ability to gain support among—and facilitate the organization of a coalition of pro-military organizations.[276]

However, while launching its diplomatic campaign to reassert military vanguardism and the legitimacy of the military in politics, the Nigerian military especially under General Abacha also subverted the pro-democracy movement by political detentions, incarcerations, forced exiles, and sometimes by para-military assassinations. By 1998, General Sanni Abacha was being described by most of the Nigerian media[277] as the most hated ruler in Nigerian history, his path since his usurpation of power in 1993 having been littered with executions, assassinations, imprisonment without trials and intimidation of opponents. One magazine put it this way, "Abacha escalates a nationwide war on all his opponents in a brutal bid to whip an entire country into embracing his ambition to stay in power."[278] By 1995, at least 100 Nigerians had been arrested and detained for being associated with the Nigerian pro-democracy movement.[279] On the unprecedented human rights record of the Abacha military regime, one magazine article had this to say, " Perhaps no regime in Nigerian history has more blood on its hand than this one."[280] In a war against the pro-democracy movement, the regime summoned up all its resources, including a security budget that runs into millions of budgetary expenditure allocations.

The Campaign for Democracy's success in organizing Nigerians in mass movements around pro-democracy activism resulted in that organization's early identification as a threat to the Nigerian military regime. Military repression of human rights and pro-democracy activism began immediately after the mass demonstrations in 1993, thereby crippling the continued effectiveness of the Campaign for Democracy. As the affiliate organizations in the CD collective became more involved in pro-democracy activities and more vocal in their calls for a hand over of power, the military government became harsher in its response.

The CD faced ongoing harassment during the Babangida administration. On January 1, 1992, the State Security Service (SSS) arrested Dr. Beko Ransome-Kuti and detained the CD chair without charge for three days. In January, the SSS sponsored a report that appeared on the front page of the Concord newspaper, that the Constitutional Rights Project (CRP), was involved with the U.S. government in an attempt to destabilize Nigeria. Also in January, the government claimed that a member of the CD had confessed to a plan to assassinate specific members of the military. On March 9, Femi Falana, president of the National Association of Democratic Lawyers (NADL) and CD member, was arrested over an alleged plan to overthrow the military government. On March 27, Dr. Beko-Kuti was arrested again and taken to SSS headquarters where he was questioned about his pro-democracy activities. On April 16, 2,000 CD leaflets were confiscated by about 50 police and SSS agents, who invaded the CD headquarters and mistreated staff members.[281]

By 1994, with the advent of the Abacha regime, attacks on the CD and other pro-democracy activists worsened. Many activists were killed; others had their homes and offices bombed. The offices of the more outspoken human rights organizations like the CD and NADECO were subjected to forcible police entry and the seizure of materials. Moreover, hundreds of activists had been detained for periods ranging from several hours to several months. Beginning in late August 1994, a new trend in the increased level of lawlessness and terror appeared in the southwest with firebomb attacks on the homes of dissidents.[282]

Continued social mobilization by the CD, despite violent repression by the military state, further aggravated the Abacha military regime. Dr. Ransome-Kuti, the CD chair, and many other pro-democracy activists were repeatedly arrested and released during 1995. However, in 1995 under the ill-famed Aziza Tribunal, the leader of the CD was convicted of being an accessory to treason and sentenced to life imprisonment, later commuted to 15 years imprisonment. In addition to Beko Ransome-Kuti, Shehu Sani, vice-president of the Northern branch of the CD was also sentenced to seven years on trumped-up charges. A CD statement on Kuti's incarceration had this to say, "We believe Ransome-Kuti's arrest and frame-up is a vindication of his earlier warning that leaders of the CD and some of its human rights affiliates are primary targets of this deadly plan of the junta."[283] The capacity of the CD became severely weakened as a result of the government's imposition of even harsher repression measures against the organization's activities.

By 1994, with NADECO taking over the CD's role of organizing the pro-democracy movement, the military government began to target NADECO as its prime object of repression. Reacting to the NADECO demand to install Chief Abiola as the rightful president[284] the regime detained the winner of the elections without trial after accusing him of treason. Chief Abiola incarcerated for four years until his death in prison in July 1998. Moreover, the Abacha regime was allegedly tied to the assassinations of two prominent NADECO leaders: Kudirat, senior wife of

Chief Abiola, and Alfred Rewane, 79-year-old financier of the coalition. Also, Olubiyi Durojaiye, a NADECO chieftain and former presidential aspirant, was abducted from his home by security agents, and Frederick Faseun, a leading Lagos physician and NADECO member, was detained for having criticized a military governor.

Other assassination attempts against NADECO members linked to the military include attempts against Abraham Adesanya, Alani Akinrinade, Wole Soyinka, Anthony Enahoro and others causing these top opposition leaders to flee the country.[285] Other NADECO members, including many university teachers, journalists and top politicians became exiles in the United Kingdom and the United States.[286] Moreover, General Abacha's regime was responsible for the execution of Ken Saro-Wiwa and eight other Ogoni leaders.

Also, in its war against NADECO, the military dismissed many military officers for allegedly harboring pro-NADECO sentiments. There existed an unwritten decree that people from the Southwest[287] were not to be entrusted with any sensitive governmental position due to a general belief by General Abacha's close advisors that such officers were NADECO officers.[288] In late December 1997, Abacha's second-in-command and the highest ranking military officer from the Southwest, Major-General Oladipo Diya, was arrested for his involvement in a coup attempt against the regime. It is believed that the administration had perceived Major-General Diya as being sensitive to the NADECO opposition and therefore a threat to the Abacha administration.[289]

General Abacha's war on the opposition was not limited to CD and NADECO membership. Since the NADECO-inspired uprising of 1994, Abacha has dealt ruthlessly with members of other pro-democracy organizations, especially with his own colleagues within the military. For example, General Abacha dethroned Ibrahim Dasuki as Sultan of Sokoto, who was known to be sympathetic to the pro-democracy cause. He jailed General Olusegun Obasanjo, former military head of state and chairman of his own pro-democracy organization, the Association for Democracy and Government in Nigeria (ADGN). In the same "trumped-up" trial conducted by the Aziza Tribunal,[290] former deputy head-of-state, General Yar'Adua was similarly sentenced and jailed for life. Moreover, the Nigerian military responded to the international movement's discrediting of its regime by persecuting exiled leaders. Wole Soyinka, chair of the UDFN and NALICON, and Chief Alani Akinriade, NADECO-abroad member, were both accused of treason and ordered to be arrested on arrival in Nigeria.

Throughout 1993-1998, the Nigerian military regime expressed its vulnerability to agitation against military rule by severely repressing the agitators of pro-democracy, thereby testifying to the threat that the Nigerian pro-democracy movement posed to the military. The Abacha military regime succumbed in 1998 with the death of General Abacha and the establishment of the successor Abubakar regime.[291] Marking the end of the Abacha regime's reign of terror, in 1998 the military regime headed by General Abubakar released all pro-democracy prisoners and repealed the controversial Decree Number Two, which had provided for the administrative detention of political opponents and critics of the military government for renewable periods of three months. Moreover, the new military regime abrogated the undemocratic transition-to-democracy program contrived by the Abacha regime and set the stage for a new, more democratic transition-to-democracy.

II. Mobilizing Democratic Consciousness

In addition to revealing military vulnerability and discrediting militarism, a significant accomplishment of the pro-democracy movement was the establishment of a broadened, democratically conscious, and activist civil society that by the mid '90s acted as a viable counterweight to authoritarian military rule in Nigeria. The pro-democracy movement was increasingly able to promote the principles of democratization to a wide range of civil society sectors, thereby deepening democratic space in Nigeria. The movement also was successful in empowering diverse civil society communities toward democratic awareness.

Nigeria has a history of pluralism and associational activity, which has been a long-standing feature of Nigerian civil society. However, the concerted, sustained and expansive campaign against state repression, human rights abuses and military rule by the Nigerian pro-democracy movement was a recent occurrence, emerging in the 1990's and fortifying as a result of the annulment of the 1993 June 12 elections. Despite its limited organizational achievements in driving-out the Nigerian military government, the emergence, growth and sustenance of the pro-democracy movement promoting democratic ideology to a wide cross-section of Nigerians was the movement's greatest achievement.

Through its social mobilization activities, which served to promote democratic ideology at home and abroad, the pro-democracy movement maintained the long-standing and rich democratic space for Nigerian civil society. More importantly, however, the movement also widened and deepened that space, especially by reestablishing a political focal point for civil society activity, enhancing civil society's ability to influence the nation's political agenda. By its intense and ardent social mobilization for democratic government, the pro-democracy movement is credited for keeping the question of democratization on the agenda, and compelling the military regime to make policy or structural adjustments.

Positioning civil society to leverage more intense demands for democratic government, the pro-democracy movement broadened social mobilization for democracy. The movement's activism facilitated social mobilization for democracy among broader elements of civil society, creating an increased environment of democratic awareness and therefore a sense of empowerment among expanded civil society sectors.

The ensuing section on the democracy movement's social mobilization efforts provides evidence demonstrating the effectiveness of the dominant pro-democracy organizations, the CD, NADECO, and the UDFN-abroad. Specifically, through the distinct characteristics of each organization's strategic mobilization activities and techniques used, collectively the pro-democracy movement mobilized a wide and cross-cutting section of the Nigerian populace into pro-democracy agitation, including the urban and youth populace, elite sectors, distinct ethnic regions, and other civil society sectors, such as the media and the clergy.

The effectiveness of social mobilization of democratic consciousness by the pro-democracy movement will be assessed by examining two important aspects of social mobilization: a) the movement's effectiveness in generating democratic consciousness and empowerment in grassroots communities, including cities and ethnic village communities, as well as the movement's influence in agitating violent pro-democracy struggles; and b) the movement's ability to mobilize alliances with other civil society sectors,[292] including elite sectors of the Nigerian populace.

The CD: Mobilizing Civil Disobedience among Urban and Youth Populace

The Campaign for Democracy changed the content and context of political discourse and the pattern of political action in Nigeria. It convinced most Nigerians that the most powerful military junta could be challenged and defeated through unity, organization, mobilization and collective action.[293] With its foundations in trade unions, student unions, human rights organizations, and progressive factions of political parties, the CD capitalized on its affiliate bodies' radical roots in mobilizing Nigerian workers to agitate against deteriorating economic conditions.

The Campaign for Democracy gave political expression and contested under a broader based and enduring organizational platform the pro-democracy agenda for the 1990's.[294] For the first time in Nigeria's post-civil war history, the military dictators were openly challenged by millions who took a stand for democracy in urban and rural settings, across ethnic, regional, religious, class, and gender lines.[295]

The epitome of the Campaign for Democracy's organizational and mobilization success was the organization's "Babangida-Must-Go" civil disobedience rallies organized between July and October of 1993. The CD mobilized popular resistance among ethnically diverse urban communities throughout Nigeria. Though these protests occurred throughout the country, including Kwara, Kano, Kaduna, Jos, Delta and especially in Lagos and other states in the Southwest,[296] the protests were concentrated in cities and participants especially included urban workers, university students and youth.

The CD embarked upon a grassroots but sophisticated campaign of direct action to encourage an already disgruntled Nigerian populace to take to the streets to advocate democracy. It decided to make the country ungovernable and to force the military regime out of power by the previously agreed date of 27 August 1993. The tone of the civil disobedience campaign, though always calling for peaceful rallies, took on a certain radicalism. For example, when the presidential election results were annulled by the military regime, despite the military government's complete censoring of the results, the CD boldly compiled and publicized the results based on data from the National Electoral Commission and the various voting and counting centers, showing that Chief Abiola had won an overwhelming victory.

In addition, for the first set of protests organized by the CD the "Babangida -Must-Go Rallies" the CD released a Bulletin that called for a three-day protest, which was to be marked on the first day by the burning of Babangida's decrees by lawyers and democratic organizations. Day two was to be marked by burning of voters cards and day three by general rallies all over the country. In addition to regular press release bulletins distributed to CD affiliate member organizations, members and the general public, over one million pamphlets and leaflets were directly circulated and distributed to the populace by CD members as well as through the efforts of the CD affiliate organizations. The leaflets all exposed the corruption, lawlessness, and abuse of power by the regime, urging Nigerians to take a final stand against military dictatorship and against the subversion of the popular will.

Strategically, the CD capitalized on the presence of over 80,000 soccer fans at the World Cup qualifying match at the National Stadium in Lagos on July 3, 1993, distributing leaflets calling on all Nigerians to embark on one week of national protest to force General Babangida to quit office and to enforce the result of the June 12 election. Appealing directly to the popular classes, CD agitators prepared for the protest rallies by having meetings and enlisting the support of meat sellers, market women, shopkeepers, students, trade unions, and road transport workers. Workers were asked to stay away from work; market women were asked to close their shops; and taxi/lorry drivers were advised to keep their vehicles off the road. Other participants were instructed to bock roads with barricades and burn tires on the roads and streets.[297]

The CD's mobilization message strove to galvanize the populace purely on ideological grounds, taking care to avoid ethnic and religious divisions. For instance, the CD leaflets pointed out that the national protest had not been organized for Chief Abiola as an individual, but because he represented the democratic desires of those Nigerians who had given him a popular mandate. Moreover, people were advised by the CD that the struggle was not between North or South,[298] or between ethnic or religious groups or political parties, and thereby people were advised not to attack fellow Nigerians from other parts of the country.[299]

The CD's efforts to mobilize urban communities against the Nigerian military regime were successful. As a result of the five days of mass demonstrations, on July 5-9, 1993, Nigeria became paralyzed as banks, markets, schools, and government offices were closed, while many streets in the major cities were deserted. The boycott of courts by the Bar Association in Lagos and Ikeja, Ibadan, Ijebu Ode, Ondo and Edo State led to a serious pile up of cases. Moreover, civil societal sectors strongly supported the civil disobedience campaigns.

The National Association of Nigerian Students, the Nigerian Bar Association, the Nigerian Union of Journalists, Women in Nigeria, and the Nigerian Labor Congress all came out in opposition to the Nigerian military government. The National Union of Petroleum and Natural Gas Workers called out its members on strike to protest against the annulment of the elections. SDP state governors favored the popular action, and finally traditional leaders and prominent politicians in the East and North all openly backed the demonstrations and the need to uphold democracy in Nigeria. As a result of the CD's mobilization activities, the Babangida military regime stepped down from office, a decision widely believe to have resulted from the general's realization that his regime no longer had legitimacy with the Nigerian populace.

Five years of pro-democracy activity raised the stakes for new challengers against Nigerian military-state power. Capitalizing on the level of state/society contention by 1995, these new challengers, particularly militant pro-democracy movements, aligned with the ideological platform advocating an end to state militarism, human rights abuse, and a call for democratic government—all cornerstone issues of the pro-democracy movement. Thus, in an environment of severe state repression of the pro-democracy movement, the political climate in Nigeria produced an expanded pro-democracy movement,[300] including a variant of that movement that was willing to use violence to attain its goals.

By 1996, terror had become an instrument of public discourse in Nigeria with violence emanating from both a repressive state and the outbursts of resistance from civil society. Bomb explosions and assassinations became a regular feature occurrence in Nigerian cities causing one writer to heed the warning that Nigeria was beginning to exhibit features of societal violence and guerilla activity similar to Latin America (Arthur-Nwankwo, 1994). One magazine described conditions during this period in the following way, "The emerging scenario is that of two armed groups holding the nation to ransom. One group is in power, the beneficiary of a coup, the other group,[301] faceless, vicious is countering with mindless force."[302]

In December 1996, the Liberation Organization of Nigeria (LON), claimed responsibility for two bomb attacks in Lagos. The organization made the following statement: " In the past few years, Nigerians have witnessed the sight of military dictatorship and it's sickening. Nowhere in the world have tyrannical juntas been removed without hitting them where it hurts. Nigeria cannot be different. We, in the Liberation Organization of Nigeria, together with some bright and professionally patriotic officers in military barracks across the country, have now come to the conclusion that force would be necessary to emancipate our people from the clutches of a narrow clique, who hijacked state's power to loot the treasury, and subject the populace to dehumanizing circumstances."[303] The group demanded that: All political detainees must be released at once; all those convicted of the framed coup plot including Generals Obasanjo and Yar'Adua be released immediately; The army of occupation in Ogoniland must be removed.

Another organization also taking responsibility for bomb attacks called itself the Association for True Nigeria. In a letter sent to General Abacha, the organization declared: "We wish to state that the bomb attacks were targeted against the military. We are civilians who have taken our destiny into our hands. Nnamdi Azikiwe, Tafawa Balewa and Obafemi Awolowo cannot fight for independence for us again. We have to do it. NADECO is too inactive to be reckoned with."[304]

Also, in January 1996, General Abacha lost his first son in a plane accident. The Movement to Advance Democracy (MAD) claimed responsibility. This organization was also suspected of the involvement in the hijacking of a Nigeria Airways plane in January 1994. Moreover, the organization claimed it was in possession of information implicating top officials of the Nigerian military regime in corrupt practices.[305]

NADECO and Elite Social Mobilization: Promoting the Progressive Coalition

Expansive social mobilization and deepening the awareness of the need for democratic change through the efforts of the pro-democracy movement has not been limited to popular urban sectors. The Nigerian elite sector, including civilian and military politicians, have also been significantly mobilized toward a reorientation of this sector's thinking about democratic ideology, and NADECO has been in the forefront of expanding pro-democracy ideology to the elite sectors. The creation of the National Democratic Coalition (NADECO) by retired generals, experienced politicians, and businessmen to join the struggle against military rule was clear evidence that diverse interests in civil society were beginning to converge to establish democracy in Nigeria.[306]

By forging stronger political and social alignments and facilitating dialogue and ideological platform building, through NADECO, civilian elite and former civil-military coalition members, such as former military politicians, have promoted an increased awareness of democratic ideology among middle class and elite sectors of Nigerian civil society.[307] More than any other pro-democracy organization, NADECO has the largest number of prominent[308] personalities as members of the movement. Furthermore, despite the organization's close affiliation with the Southwest. NADECO membership is equally reflective of its cross-cutting membership, with membership fairly dispersed among charismatic personalities native of the Southwest, northern, and eastern regions of the country.[309]

For example, out of the twenty-three NADECO founders at least ten members are non-Yoruba.[310] This leadership has contributed to the organization's visibility and legitimacy as an opposition force. With former military politicians and civilian advisors to the military, such as Omo Omoruyi a former Babangida advisor, former minister of communications Brigadier-General David Mark, former military governor of Kaduna State Abubakar Umar, former defense minister, General Akinriade and a host of others involved in NADECO, the military regime became ever more fearful of the opposition movement. NADECO was also able to successfully employ its ethnically broad-based and politically high-profile membership base as a mobilization technique, especially in forging a strengthened opposition force among the political elite based on a pro-democratic, progressive agenda.

The pro-democracy organizations in this period, especially the membership of NADECO, trace their roots back to the formation of elite social forces and their alliances forged in previous democratic eras as early as the pre-colonial era. In the 1990s struggle, these old alignments attempt to redefine themselves: by reviving old organizational coalitions and alliances to advocate democracy; through democracy summits and seminars, which fostered expanded dialogue; and through outreach to the press, which served as the informational liaison to the popular sectors. The demand by the pro-democracy movement for a Sovereign National Conference [311] and a Government of National Unity; the movement's rejection of the military-sponsored National Constitutional Conference; the debate over the June 12 principle; and other key national mobilizing issues were consistent issues of national debate during the five-year period. In a deliberate strategy to facilitate the mobilization of pro-democracy dialogue among the Nigerian populace, NADECO sponsored several regional and nationwide conferences, seminars, public town meetings, and press statements, activities, which were all disseminated to the populace by the Nigerian press in the nation's daily headline news.[312]

NADECO was very successful in broadening the democratic prospects for Nigeria through such activities. For example, the pro-democracy movement undermined the National Constitutional Conference[313] through its campaign for a public boycott of the Conference, which sought to discourage civilian participation in the military contrived transition program.[314] NADECO forged a series of sustained coalitions with other pro-democracy forces, especially as a result of its position as the locus of the pro-democracy network for civilian politicians. NADECO aligned with long-standing discourse and 'think-tank' groups like the Afenifere, the People's Consultative Forum (PCF),[315] the National Unity Club, (NUC) and the All Nigeria Congress (ANC).[316] By so doing NADECO resuscitated the progressive coalition movement, particularly sharpening and refocusing the progressive ideology[317] toward a truly progressive agenda of democracy and human rights for the Nigerian citizen.[318] Such groups formed the underlying social bases of NADECO and the continued alliance and loose coalition with these organizations fostered increased outreach and greater facilitation of cross-cutting coalitions with an even broader sector of elite social forces. This expanded the membership of NADECO, and therefore pro-democracy awareness, to diverse regions of the country.

Significantly, NADECO's role in revitalizing the progressive coalition[319] became a strong factor in the organization's ability to facilitate national debate on pro-democracy, especially among political elite sectors. As an umbrella pro-democracy organization[320] NADECO was able to recruit members from the old civil-military alliance, forging such alliances across ethnicity, region and social class.[321] For example, in 1993, before NADECO was founded, the progressive coalition promoted and informed the social basis of the Social Democratic Party platform that advocated the continuance of governmental social programs and an end to IMF Structural Adjustment Programs. The progressive coalition of the SDP also promoted as candidate for president controversial millionaire businessman, Moshood Abiola. On the SDP progressive ticket, as a Southerner, Abiola won an unprecedented and massive electoral victory in core Northern states during the presidential elections for the Third Republic.[322]

Between 1994-1998, NADECO strengthened the progressive coalition network with Afenifere, and other social clubs—the PCF, the ANC[323] and the NUC—by actively organizing democracy summits, conferences and meetings to deliberate on the on-going political crisis in the country. For example in December 1995, Afenifere, NADECO and the PCF organized a summit bringing together all three ideological forces including the conservative ANC to develop a consensual response to Abacha's transition program. Among the moderate camp, NADECO has forged alliances with the National Unity Club, an association of leading progressives in the Middle Belt, the far North and the East, who held at least nine summits of which "June 12" and national reconciliation were the main subjects of deliberation.

The NADECO network has also played a role in mobilizing moderate forces, such as General Olusegun Obasanjo's National Unity Organization (NUO)[324] and General Yar' Adua's[325] Peoples Democratic Movement(PDM). Both groups have played a significant role in forging democratic alliances and promoting platform issues among broader sectors of civil society. Through his NUO, for example, Obasanjo worked hard to bring about an east-west alliance, which could stand up to the North in any election. Obasanjo also used the NUO and his Association for Democratic Governance in Nigeria (ADGN) to criticize the Abacha military regime. Yar'Adua, through his PDM, also courted the regime's opposition by placing himself at the forefront of the faction at the National Constitutional Conference that passed the resolution calling on Abacha's military regime to quit by January 1, 1996 after a two-year period of transition.[326]

In addition to the forging of an ideological platform, during the five-year aggressive Nigerian pro-democracy struggle ethnic politics also played a dominant role with ethnic political organizations springing up for the sole purpose of participating in the struggle for democratization.[327] NADECO, for example, draws its foundational membership from Afenifere in the Southwest region. Afenifere, an organization that has its roots in the Yoruba Egbe Omo Oduduwa political force, symbolized the dual and mutually overlapping influence that ethnic political organizations and pro-democracy organizations had in mobilizing ethnic and regional communities. Afenifere dominates pro-democracy activity in the Southwest Yoruba regions. Firmly committed to the June 12 principle, Afenifere established NADECO as a pro-democracy political organization during Afenifere's fervent activism around Chief Abiola's return from the United States in 1994.

With its foundations in progressive social activism since its Owo Meetings and the Action Party opposition in the 1960s, Afenifere also has a tradition of organizing progressive forces across ethnicity and region. For example, during the current crisis, 1993-1998, Afenifere has held several summits with the National Unity Club (NUC) to find a new basis for unity. It also flirted with the idea of forging an alliance with Northern conservatives on the premise that Northern members of this pro-democracy force have shown sympathy for the June 12 cause.[328]

As an umbrella organization, NADECO also draws broad organizational membership and coalition membership from pro-democracy organizations in non-Yoruba regions. Broader alliances of this type include NADECO's loose coalition with Balarabe Musa's National Unity Club and other pro-democracy organizations, such as the Movement of Unity and Progress, organizations that dominate the crucial Northern middle-belt region. Other ethnic coalitions include the umbrella organization's alliance with the

Igbo-based Eastern Mandate Union, coalitions based on the mutual commitment to stand firm in their support for "June 12".

Emerging from these ideological organizations and ethnic political associations came many pro-democracy organizations with NADECO emerging as the most prominent, largest and ethnically diverse pro-democracy organization. As a result of NADECO's prominence both as a facilitator for the progressive agenda, and its "national" character, the pro-democracy movement succeeded in promoting pro-democracy discourse among the Nigerian elite sector.

One outcome of NADECO's intense social mobilization for democracy was the incipient steps toward forming an alternative political platform based on pro-democracy ideology and progressive democratic attitudes. A platform initiated by the Nigerian left via the Campaign for Democracy, the new focus on human rights, constitutional rights and anti-militarism were issues informing the national political debate in the post-Abacha transition-to-democracy. This progressive dialogue reflected the national political stage with the progressive forces mobilized through the NADECO network reshuffling to forge political parties.

In mobilizing elite communities, NADECO also precipitated the mobilization of new pro-democracy allies and challengers against the military regime. A prominent ally and challenger against the Nigerian military, the non-governmental Nigerian mass media[329] played a crucial role in facilitating pro-democracy discourse and thereby fostering mobilization for democracy among Nigerian popular and elite sectors in civil society during the period between 1993 and 1998. The Nigerian print media performed the role of liaison between the pro-democracy forces and the mass public, by publicizing the activities and events organized by the pro-democracy organizations, as well as by keeping public statements issued by pro-democracy leaders and issues in the news headlines.

As with other sectors within Nigerian civil society, the media has had a long and rich history, especially with commercial journalism, which developed as an instrument of political agitation during the colonial era. [330] In the 1990s a divided but vociferous press acted as a vanguard for pro-democracy activism. This has been demonstrated by the commercial press' regularity and extent of focus on issues pertaining to pro-democracy activism and critique of the military regime. According to the degree to which the media was committed to the campaign for the June 12 mandate, the following daily journals and weekly news magazines were in the forefront of the pro-democracy struggle: *the Nigerian Tribune, African Concord,* [331] *The Guardian, Newswatch, Tell Magazine, The News, Meridian, Today, Tempo,* and *This Week.*

Many media outlets came out boldly against the military regime after cancellation of the June 12 elections, as a result of which five media organizations were closed while a host of journalists were detained. Drawing upon the press's tradition of pamphleteering,[332] many of the press members that escaped arrest decided to continue publishing and distributing their papers illegally, publishing them underground by "unknown" printer companies.[333] The media's criticism of the military regime, however, became extremely virulent and effective, and the military became virtually powerless in containing them, except by detaining vendors and seizing copies of publications.[334]

By 1997, the commercial media's role in pro-democracy activism became so threatening to the military that media sectors that promoted the pro-democracy movement were considered part of the movement, and therefore were included as part of the military opposition. Like other pro-democracy activists, journalists began to fill the jails as political prisoners. During 1993-1998, at least fourteen prominent journalists [335] were detained for their role in publishing articles that criticized the military regime under General Abacha.

As a result of the connections among Nigerian pro-democracy organizations and other elite sectors[336] of civil society, such as the commercial media, a deepening of democratic awareness and consciousness occurred among the broader civil society. A well-known Nigerian social scientist, Oyeleye Oyediran, wrote, "The positive side of the coin, regarding the future of Nigeria, is that Nigerians now know who the enemies of democracy are. They are *now* aware of the manipulations of military-led democratic transitions. They *now* know that the resolution of the National Question, the relations of Nigeria's constituent groups, has to be done through dialogue, negotiation, consensus and democracy. Increasing numbers of Nigerians *now* also believe in consonance with the global trend that military rule has outlived its usefulness and must be replaced with democracy."[337]

The UDFN: Mobilizing International Communities

Strategies for social mobilization advocating Nigerian pro-democracy in the international arena have focused on the mobilization of international governmental communities, such as foreign embassies and governments, the United Nations, Commonwealth Heads of Government through the network of the United Democratic Front of Nigeria (UDFN) and its affiliate bodies. As a result of these ventures, NADECOs[338] strength on the home-front was partly attributable to the UDFN's [339] success as a viable pro-democracy movement mobilizing international and transnational Nigerian communities abroad. The UDFN coalition's core membership[340] primarily comprises of a continuance of the progressive camp abroad with most pro-democracy organizations abroad standing firmly behind the June 12 mandate.

The foreign-based Nigeria democracy movement waged an effective campaign in favor of the restoration of democracy in Nigeria in the international arena. The effects of the international campaign cannot be minimized when assessing the successes of the pro-democracy movement's impact upon social mobilization and democratic awareness among broadened segments of civil society beyond the domestic arena. Social mobilization among Nigerian communities in Western Europe, the United States of America, and Canada, for the single purpose of democratic change in Nigeria has been unprecedented as reflected in the sheer volume of civil associations who identify themselves as Nigerian pro-democracy organizations abroad. Though frustrated by their inability to effectively exert pressure on Western governments to enact bold and comprehensive policies against Nigeria in support of the demands of the pro-democracy movement, like the domestic movement, the international movement through the efforts of the UDFN has created an environment of international awareness on the Nigerian democracy crisis.

UDFN affiliate organizations have successfully organized several 'march-on-Washington' public awareness campaigns and other demonstrations at the United Nations headquarters in NY, the Nigerian consulate in New York City, the Commonwealth Heads of Governments headquarters in London. Nigerian communities abroad have been significantly mobilized through the World Wide Web, with more than seventy percent of the Nigerian pro-democracy organizations abroad and the UDFN affiliates maintaining web sites. Nigerian pro-democracy organizations abroad used the Internet to effectively disseminate and promote the Nigerian pro-democracy cause among middle-class Nigerian communities abroad. Most of the Nigerian pro-democracy web sites maintain links with domestic Nigerian pro-democracy organizations and media publications.

Social mobilization among international and Nigerian communities abroad resulted in subtle influences upon the Nigerian military governments' vulnerability in the international community. For example, through demonstrations and witness reports by the UDFN against the decision to renew Nigeria's membership with the Commonwealth, the international body maintained Nigeria's suspension status pending the Nigerian military government's more sincere efforts to implement democratic government.

CHAPTER 9

LOSING THE FOURTH REPUBLIC

The Nigerian Democracy Paradox

I. Limiting Democratic Outcomes

The period between 1990 —1999 demonstrated that associational activity and pro-democracy activism by Nigerian civil society was expressed at its highest level of agency. As a result, as the previous section demonstrated, the pro-democracy movement had unprecedented success in advertising the vulnerability of the Nigerian military state as well as in raising democratic consciousness among proliferate levels of Nigerian civil society.

Yet by March 1998, neither the combined forces of the formidable combination of adversaries called the pro-democracy movement, nor the efforts of the Commonwealth, the European Union, South Africa, and the United States were able to compel General Abacha's military regime to cede power to its domestic opponents, or even to a coalition of civilians controlled by its supporters. During this climatic period, Nigeria stood at a cross-roads of power-balancing between and among forces of state and society with the military-dominant, civil-military alliance crystallized in the Abacha regime. The civil-military alliance embedded the nexus of anti-democratic forces, portending to perpetuate itself in power by promoting its Transition-to-Democracy Program as a model for an ideal framework for democratic government for the future of Nigeria.[341]

By early 1998, after five years of strident opposition against the Nigerian military, especially against the repressive Abacha Regime, despite cumulative accomplishments, the pro-democracy movement was in a weakened position. Having been disqualified from participating in the general's interminable transition-to-democracy program because of its opposition stance,[342] increased military repression of pro-democracy activists resulted in heavy losses for the movement's members. Many of the leading members had been detained, convicted of treason, were in hiding or exile, or were living in daily fear of any of the afore-mentioned happening to them. In addition, many of the professional alliances, including the labor movement, had been penetrated, discredited, and weakened by the military as a potent source of opposition. While many new political organizations, lacking a united democratic goal, studied the unfolding scenario, and thus continued to organize civil disobedience campaigns. Meanwhile the populace had become weary from long periods of crisis (Oyeleye, Oyediran, and Kirke-Greene, 1997).

At no other time did the weaknesses of the pro-democracy movement crystallize as much as this period. This exposed a culmination of five years of organizational limitations among the movement deriving from the inability of some organizations to separate from problems associated with internal democracy and the embodiment of elite and personal politics within their organizations. Despite the movement's successes, already outlined in the previous chapter, the movement was constrained from complete success in ousting the Nigerian military regime and replacing it with a democratic regime embodying the consciousness of civil society.[343]

These mitigating factors derive from a combination of socio-historical conditions manifested in the internal organizational limitations of novice activists, employing the skills of direct political action for the first time, both which further derive from implications emerging from long-standing civil-military relations embodied in the democracy paradox. This hypothesis was presented earlier to establish a theoretical framework for understanding the unique historical determinants of Nigerian democratization. This final section argues that the long-standing and mutually interactive state-society relationships contributed to the pro-democracy network's limitation in realizing a more effective, popular-based democratic transition. For example, for the third time [344] in Nigeria's political development, democratic transition was realized from the top by a state, military-led transition program. Although the transition was led by a liberalizing military faction, the popular democratic demands of civil society, including the call for the reversal of the June 12 annulment and for the convening of a Sovereign National Conference, were never met.

Even though it was the constant agitation by the pro-democracy movement that precipitated conditions for the liberalizing forces within the military to emerge as successful in the institution's internal struggles, it is especially noted by the present study that this achievement was a manifestation of the Nigerian democracy—paradox. In earlier chapters, the democracy paradox was defined as a culturally-imposed paradox arising from the interlocking cultural, economic, political, social and clientele networks which organizations in civil society created and which Nigerian military regimes drew from to legitimize its dominance in Nigerian politics. The paradoxical relationship noted here was that the very close and sometimes non-distinguishable alliances and coalitions forged between civil society and the military state provided, on one level, a check on the excesses of authoritarian military regimes in Nigeria, but on the other level, fostered the Nigerian military's expanded politicization, thereby undercutting the development of a sustainable democratic polity.

During the 1990's democratic transition, in its traditional fashion, Nigerian civil society acted as a "check" on the excessive, arbitrary power of the tyrannical tendencies of the Abacha regime. The, however, paradox is more significant: Nigerian civil society through the pro-democracy network was unable to act as more than a mere "check" on the balance of power in Nigerian politics. Despite the sustained struggle by the pro-democracy network, the movement faced significant limitations in achieving a popular-based democratic transition in 1999.

The pro-democracy movement's limitations in realizing a sovereign national conference and a popular-based democracy was a demonstration of the forcefulness of the paradox of civil-military relations defined as the democracy paradox by this study. The most important limitations concern the problems associated with the features of civil-militarism, with civil society exhibiting entrenched social cleavages embodied in personal rule, ethnic politics, and class. These features, associated with long-standing inter-penetrative civil-military relations were manifested in the internal organization of the pro-democracy network, especially in leadership issues pertaining to each group.

This study's final sections assess the outcomes of Nigeria's pro-democracy struggle by unraveling the paradox of democratization, anti-politics, and civil-militarism[345] in Nigeria, and by demonstrating the manner in which the paradox limited the pro-democracy movement's ability to generate more progressive democratic outcomes. The democracy paradox[346] limited the emergence of a stronger unifying coalition among diverse civil society sectors and pro-democracy agents, who might otherwise have been able to generate a more democratic, popular-based regime transition.

The movements' limitations resulting from the longstanding practice of civil militarism are reflected in the fact that the paradox has been embodied in the internal organization of the pro-democracy movement as a whole, as well as in each organization's ability to reflect the principles of democratic consciousness in its leadership methods. These problems of internal democracy especially relate to internal organizational behavior, ranging from issues of elite and personal politics, including ethnic politics. These influences have translated into factionalism and division, leading to the fracturing and the diverse proliferation of the movement, factors that have limited stronger unification among pro-democracy organizations and have implications for more successful democratic outcomes.

In sum, this chapter demonstrates that as a result of civil-militarism, personal elite politics, and ethnic competition—all aspects of the paradox the pro-democracy movement—were susceptible to military infiltration and the co-option of its members by military interests. This led to a weakening of the movement's credibility as a pro-democracy agent,[347] affecting the overall goal of generating a democratic regime that embodies a democratic consciousness.

The Pro-Democracy Paradox

Longstanding and mutually interlocking relations between military state sectors and the civilian elite have had significant implications for the internal organization of pro-democracy groups, which have affected the performance of the Nigerian pro-democracy movement. Nonetheless, such relations are not new. Civil militarism has complicated Nigerian politics in the past. All successful coups and attempted coups in the country's long transition to and from military dictatorship have had civilian support if not prompting.[348] As a result, civil-military alliance politics has been adept at manipulating divisions among pro-democracy and other civil societal sectors, and in its traditional style of strategically exploiting civilian interests, both General Babangida and General Abacha were adept at manipulating the flux of competing forces among civil society.

Particularly consequential for the derailment of pro-democracy movement struggles during the period studied, 1990-1999, was the role that civil-military alliance politics played in the Babangida military regime's manipulation of civilian actors during the regime's transition-to-democracy, which resulted in the annulment of the June 12 elections. Observations of military manipulation were manifested in the pro-democracy struggle, in 1993. At the time, the Babangida regime successfully floated and funded shadowy anti-democracy organizations, which had emerged from civil society, such as the Association for Better Nigeria (ABN) and Third Eye, to disrupt the transition program. The ABN had openly expressed its commitment to keeping the military in power. It had also demonstrated its willingness to do anything to sabotage the transition program. Eventually, the ABN's court action against the presidential elections of 1993 resulted in the annulment of the June 12 elections and the abortion of the Third Republic.[349]

However, it was General Abacha who raised civil-military alliance politics to unprecedented proportions when in early 1998 after several non-governmental organizations including Youth Earnestly Ask for Abacha (YEAA) and National Movement for Vision 2010 and all five political parties agreed to adopt the general as their consensus presidential candidate for the October elections in his ambitious self-succession bid. As a result of the general's manipulations of civil society despite the repressiveness of his regime, the regime was able to sustain an energetic and purposeful public policy backed by a political coalition from civil society that was stronger than the active domestic opposition.[350]

Civil-militarism also underscored the importance of personal leadership in the political actions of the pro-democracy organizations. Defined as the organization's leaders' ability to govern their movement organizations in a democratic style and the extent to which the organizations contained the requisite consciousness to pursue, practice, and preserve democracy, personal politics associated with problems of internal democracy help in explaining performance outcomes among the pro-democracy organizations. In the Nigerian case, personal politics dominated pro-democracy governance, with persons leading the pro-democracy organizations becoming most identifiable with the opposition movement;[351] whereas the organizations themselves provided platforms to propel diverse political agendas, sometimes not always directed toward sincere democratic ideology. For example, by 1998, it had become evident that personal and elite politics had infiltrated the pro-democracy movement due to the expansiveness of the movement's reach and its lack of unified coordination.

The Campaign for Democracy was the first organization to succumb to the problem of internal democracy. A split at its National Convention in February 1994 resulted in the decimation of the organization. The central issue in dispute was that the leadership of Dr. Beko Ransome-Kuti had met with the military to discuss the political future of Nigeria without any mandate from the organization's National Executive Council. The CD general secretary, Chima Ubani and deputy chairman, Chom Bagu parted ways with the CD, charging Ransome-Kuti with collaborating with the Abacha junta and submitting a list of names to the regime for appointment to the National Constitutional Conference. The breakaway faction of the CD formed a new organization called the "Democratic Alternative".

Prompted as much by problems of internal democracy and personality clashes as by differences over tactics and strategy, the CD crisis led to new debates over what the left should do and how it should deploy its national influence. The view which seemed to predominate insisted that the left must move beyond pressure group politics and actively make a bid for power on the basis of a solid program and an equally formidable national presence. Hence, in 1995, Chima Ubani, formed the United Action for Democracy (UAD), which sought to unite all the pro-democracy organizations in the country including the CD and NADECO, for the purpose of building a national democratic platform. Yet, the formation of splinter organizations in the Democratic Alternative and the United Action for Democracy fractured the pro-democracy movement on the whole.

Despite the organization's successes, NADECO embodied personal and elite politics more than any other pro-democracy organization. Founded as a body based on the continued alliance of elite politicians from the defunct Third Republic, NADECO applied the traits of personal and elite politics to the internal organization of the movement. For example, NADECO stalwart Bolaji Akinyemi, who was a former external affairs minister under General Babangida, invited General Abacha to displace the civilian-led Interim National Government headed by Ernest Shonekan (Ebenezer Babatope, 1996). In two open letters to Abacha on 29 October and 12 November, 1993, Akinyemi called on the military to intervene so as to save the country from disintegration.[352]

Moreover, Chief Abiola, the symbolic leader of NADECO, is known to have recommended members of his winning Social Democratic Party (SDP) ticket to General Abacha's executive cabinet. According to Essien-Ibok, a member of the SDP caucus, who was among the most implacable advocates of the actualization of the June 12 mandate, the majority of the leading members of the party who attended a meeting in Abiola's residence shortly after General Abacha's coup voted for participation in the regime on grounds that, "unless they participated, they would be treated as the opposition group and consequently they would not be able to carry the gains of June 12 to the post-military era."[353]

Whereas NADECO's internal democracy problems did not cause the break -up of the organization, they did affect the organization's ability to facilitate more positive democratic outcomes. The organization's close association with establishment figures diminished its capacity to organize direct political action. By secretly persuading the military to eliminate the Interim National Government without a clear agenda, NADECO members, representative of the Nigerian civilian elite, were again outwitted by their wily alliance partners in the Nigerian military. When the public was informed about the secret meetings between the general and Chief Abiola, the organization gained a reputation as a mixed bag of career politicians and opportunists with contradictory tendencies. As a result, NADECO had little capacity to mobilize the people. [354]

The weaknesses of the opposition internally were also reflected in the pro-democracy movement abroad where personal politics and internal democracy dominated. In 1996, a crisis brokered by leadership squabbles engulfed the movement abroad, which led to its severe weakening of legitimacy among the Nigerian communities abroad. Taking over from the embattled World Congress for Nigerian Democracy (WCND),[355] the UDFN emerged as a titular head of the voluminous pro-democracy community abroad, spread over the United States and Western Europe. However, despite the UDFN's attempt to consolidate the movement, most organizations chose to function autonomously from each other and especially of any monolithic force.

International supporters of Nigeria's pro-democracy cause expressed their preference to fund and deal with a single organization rather than many. As a result of the limited strength of the pro-democracy movement abroad, in the international arena the Abacha regime again sustained a tactical foreign policy attributable primarily to skillful diplomacy and its ability to be supported by a coalition of transnational corporations, thereby withstanding the assault mounted by leading Western powers and their allies.

Related to personal politics and internal democracy problems, other factors that constrained a more complete successes of the pro-democracy movement were the challenges of forging broader ethnic bridges and developing deeper cross-cutting coalitions with and among ethnic communities across the nation. In Nigeria, ethnic politics has always interfaced with personal politics with civilian and military politicians both using ethnicity as the basis for Nigerian politics. More than the CD and the UDFN-abroad, NADECO embodied ethnic politics in its internal organization.

Unlike the human rights crusaders and intellectuals of the left in the CD, members of NADECO lacked the same kind of ideological coherence and vision toward democracy. The organization had emerged from the annulment of the June 12 elections and the abrogation of the Third Republic's democratic institutions. Therefore, only a few NADECO members could seriously be looked upon as sincere democrats. Instead many were aggrieved politicians who carried over elite politics into the pro-democracy struggle.

With a membership base from the Middle-belt, North, East, West and Southern parts of Nigeria, NADECO appeared to have a national character; however, NADECO failed woefully in transferring its national character into a solid, observable presence all over the country. The political clout and following of most of NADECO supporters came from the Southwest and Lagos. Having taken root in Lagos, NADECO did not spread to other parts of the country, nor did the organization set up administrative structures and/or even parallel state structures, which could have enhanced its regional presence and bargaining power with the military.[356]

Continued civilian engagement in military-dominated civilian-military alliance politics meant that despite the accomplishments of the pro-democracy movement, as outlined political agents in Nigerian civil society remained divided over the means for effecting democratization. As has been shown, members of the pro-democracy movement and other crucial civil society sectors oftentimes compromised the principles of the movement's objectives by, on occasion, continuing to align with and solicit the military in Nigerian politics. Moreover, internal division leading to ideological and personal disputes among pro-democracy organizations led to the splintering of the movement, thereby raising questions about the movements' unity in the face of the critical issues facing the nation.

The aforementioned findings support Stephen Ndegwa's similar conclusion in *Two Faces of Civil Society* where the author asserts that the progressive tendencies of some civil society organizations should not mislead analysts into thinking that such organizations are naturally predisposed to democratic government or that all of civil society is progressive.[357] Alternatively, Ndegwa concluded that it is the sway of leadership and personal politics that directed the political actions of the pro-democracy organizations. The present study demonstrated that some elite-based organizations represented the contradictions of civil society in their efforts to democratize the Nigerian state. The Nigerian pro-democracy movement's accomplishments were mitigated by the limitations of personal and elite politics, as well as by other non-democratic missteps by pro-democracy forces.

Moreover, similar to Kenya, organizations among Nigerian civil society conducted impressive organizing among the urban populace. However, whereas popular-based mobilization had implications for the "promise of democracy,"[358] the extent to which democratization was to be advanced in Nigeria was to depend on the success of the organizational features exhibited by the pro-democracy organizations. Whereas the CD, NADECO and the UDFN-abroad appeared to demonstrate successful attributes in their organization, alliances, resources and their political opportunity, a closer more detailed analysis demonstrated that these groups' organizational weaknesses relating to internal democracy and personal leadership limited the democracy movement's ability to effect a popular-based democratic transition.

Because of the pro-democracy movement's poor regional links to the rest of society beyond ethnic home-bases and its extremely limited resource base, there have been few avenues for cross-fertilization of ideas and concerns among pro-democracy organizations and other civil society sectors. These limitations affected the movement's ability to forge greater organizational unity among the pro-democracy organizations in the domestic and international arenas.[359] The pro-democracy movement was engulfed by problems of disconnection and poor organization, which has contributed to its weakened struggle against Nigerian military rule.

II. Providing a Model for Future Organization

The effectiveness of the pro-democracy movement over the eight-year period of democratic struggles may be assessed in the context of the following question: To what extent does each organization and the movement as a whole provide a model for effective resistance and future organization? Asked another way, has the Nigerian political landscape changed as a result of the 1993-1999 pro-democracy struggle?

The pro-democracy struggle has created changes in the Nigerian political landscape, with civilian party political alignments having been significantly changed to include a broader participation of civil society communities as well as to accommodate new political issues, including human rights, Northern dominance of government, and the accountability of Nigerian political leadership. In the post-Abacha political terrain, the creation of a sustainable human rights opposition movement by the CD, and the elevation and serious discussion of issues pertaining to constitutional rights and the democratic structure of Nigeria by NADECO and the UDFN-abroad are important gains.

Due to the unexpected turn of events in June 1998 with the death of General Sani Abacha, 1998 represented an important test-case year to assess the future of democratic government in Nigeria. General Abubakar's liberalizing military regime set the stage for yet another activation of civilian party politics, preparing for a civilian regime in May 1999. Observing the pro-democracy movement reconstitute itself into party politics provided an indicator of the future model of political organization, highlighting the role that this movement will play in an anticipated Nigerian democratic regime.

In the 1998 transition, the Campaign for Democracy expanded into a more forceful radical human rights opposition party, the Joint Action Committee of Nigeria (JACON). The National Democratic Opposition transformed itself into a progressive political party, the Alliance for Democracy (AD). Other important organizations within the pro-democracy network participated in status-quo "career politics" Nigerian-style, such as the emergence of the G-34 and General Obasanjo's ADGN into the powerful Peoples Democratic Party (PDP) Wasting no time after the abrupt termination of an unprecedented era of repressive dictatorship in the country, the Nigerian pro-democracy movement and civil society organized politically. In October 1998, the new Independent Nigerian Electoral Commission (INEC), registered nine political parties, the most critical of which are the People's Democratic Party (PDP), the All People's Party (APP), the Alliance for Democracy (AD), and the Joint Action Committee of Nigeria (JACON). All four parties constituted social re-alignments carried over from the Nigerian pro-democracy movement.

Positioned to become the most successful party is the PDP, whose presidential aspirants include former military ruler and jailed pro-democracy activist, General Olusegun Obasanjo,[360] who also led the Association of Democracy and Good Governance (ADGN), a moderate-liberal pro-democracy movement organization. Also a heavy weight presidential aspirant for the PDP was the former vice-president in the Second Republic, Dr. Alex Ekwueme. Ekwueme's pro-democracy group, the G-34, a coalition of politicians cutting across six geopolitical zones of the country, on May 9, 1998 wrote a 10-page memo pointing out reasons why General Abacha should not run for the presidential elections. The PDP was established on the foundation of the G-34 membership. A centrist party, strongly supported by Northern interests, the PDP is increasingly gaining the reputation of representing status-quo elite politics in Nigeria. Dubbed the Party of Generals, the PDP was rocked by scandals over campaign finance donations with General Obasanjo, who had been released from a three—year jail term less than six months earlier, donating 130 million naira to the party.[361]

The All People's Party (APP) was nicknamed the "Abacha People's Party" by its detractors, due to the fact that the APP included many politicians who took part in Abacha's discredited democracy plan. Its strength is built around wealthy political strongmen who are able to assure the party of votes in their home regions, among who are Emeka Ojukwu, defeated civil war leader of break away Biafra. Founded on August 28, the APP was initially predicted to become the most formidable political force in the country.[362] However, with the withdrawal of its alliance with the Southern Leaders Forum (SLF), the APP lost its formidable position.

The break away faction of the APP, represented in the Southern Leaders Forum the foundations of which are Afenifere and NADECO—founded the Alliance for Democracy (AD). The ADs strength is concentrated in the traditional bastion of opposition to military rule, especially reflected in the ethnic Yoruba Southwest. Most of its leaders backed the presidential claim of Moshood Abiola. Championed as being the only ideologically-based party, the AD represents the leadership of NADECO and stands on the "side of truth, equity, justice, and democracy."[363] Avoiding opportunistic political alliances with the APP and the PDP, the Alliance for Democracy has propelled to the forefront the question of restructuring Nigerian politics and of holding the Nigerian political elite, which pandered to the Abacha regime, accountable for corrupt leadership.[364]

The Joint Action Committee of Nigeria (JACON) is led by radical pro-democracy activist Gani Fawehinmi. Comprised of the coalition of human rights organizations and radical pro-democracy organizations, including the Campaign for Democracy (CD), JACON has promised to boycott the election and demands a sovereign national conference, which would establish a popular-based return of democracy. Through JACON, the human-rights oriented pro-democracy network has transformed itself into a radical political party, maintaining its strategy of direct political action in its advocacy of a sustainable Nigerian democracy.

Consisting of 62 pro-democracy organizations, including the Campaign for Democracy (CD), the Committee for Defense of Human Rights (CDHR), the Gani Fahwehinmi Solidarity Association (GFSA), and the Constitutional Rights Project (CRP), JACON regards the Abubakar military regime as a continuance of the Abacha military regime.[365] The human rights community continues to advocate the sanctity of June 12 and the illegality of military regimes and military transitions. The expanded and transformed movement[366] continues to call for a sovereign national conference and for a for continued strategies for critically evaluating Nigerian government.[367] Finally, in March 1998, the UDFN-abroad established a joint commission (JACOM), with NADECO in an effort to link the international movement to the domestic pro-democracy movement.

The Future of Democracy in Nigeria

In May 2000, former military head of state, international statesman, and pro-democracy activist, fourth republic President Olusegun Obasanjo, declared May 29 of every year a public holiday, Democracy Day, in honor of Nigeria's achievement of a democratic government. The next day, two human rights lawyers and pro-democracy activists, following a flurry of criticism from the reconstituted pro-democracy movement, filed an action before a federal high court in Lagos, challenging the constitutional competence of President Olusegun Obasanjo to unilaterally declare May 29 a public holiday.

The future of democracy in Nigeria remains ambivalent. Whereas it was highly likely that in May 1999, a democratic polity governed by civilian politicians would be established, it was less clear what the character and the consciousness of a civilian elected democratic government would look like. Despite the Abubakar regime's repeated proclamations that his regime would merely in transition, and that the Nigerian military would exit from politics once and for all,[368] similar pronouncements by previous military regimes[369] reminded the Nigerian public that the military would remain a viable entity within the newly democratic government.

The Nigerian military adopted more sophisticated and subtle forms of "vanguardism" in its effort to remain a viable force in the Nigerian political scene. The Abubakar military regime strategically canvassed the candidacy of former Nigerian military head of state, General Olusegun Obasanjo. Opponents of the general's candidacy claimed that he was "hand-picked" by the military, and therefore represented a tool to serve military interests. In accepting his presidential-bid victory, in March '99, the general announced that once in power his government would not purge the military on corruption charges. With military politicians remaining prominently behind the scenes, and elite politicians maintaining interpenetrative relations with the military, predictions for the future of Nigerian politics may fulfill Robert Kaplan's concept of semi-democracy or neo-authoritarianism.[370]

On the other hand, the future of pro-democracy and civil societal activism in Nigeria is optimistic, though its path is paved with several challenges. As a result of the pro-democracy struggle, many gains have been achieved in terms of promoting the rights of civil and human rights to Nigerian citizens, which has widened the space in which popular mobilization for future change can take place.

Nevertheless, as the 1999 election victories demonstrated, civilian democratic politics will continue to be pervaded by "money politics" with career-oriented elites contesting for power. However, progressive sectors among civil society will continue to be active in advancing democratic consciousness in Nigeria. Having maintained and expanded its democratic space, which has always facilitated active political discourse and socio-political alignment, the Nigerian pro-democracy movement has positioned the Nigerian political landscape for a more participatory democracy.

For example, the pro-democracy movement via JACON will replace its current issues of pro-democracy and the struggle against authoritarian rule, with more intensified human rights advocacy, including greater demands for constitutional reform and demands for political accountability among democratic regimes. Moreover, the ideology of pro-democracy, a characteristic initiated by the pro-democracy movement, will be sustained into the Third Republic and beyond by an activist opposition party in the Alliance for Democracy (AD).

As the introductory paragraph of this section demonstrated with the May 2000 declaration of "Democracy Day," the Nigerian pro-democracy movement will continue to embed pro-democratic values more deeply in communities in civil society, empowering the populace and expanding awareness about national politics. Pro-democracy ideology will be used as the standard by which civil society continues to check the future anti-democr atic regimes that emerge.

Bibliography

Abrams, Philip. *Historical Sociology.* (New York: Cornell University Press, 1982).

Abrahamsen, Rita. "The Victory of Popular Forces or Passive Revolution? A Neo-Gramscian Perspective on Democratization," *The Journal of Modern African Studies,* 35.1, 1997, page 129-152.

Adedeji, Adebayo. *Nigeria: renewal from the roots?: the struggle for democratic development.* (London: Zed Books, 1997).

Agedah, Dickson. *The Military in Politics: from Ironsi to Babangida.*(Lagos: Perception Communications Limited, 1993).

Agbese, Pita Ogaba. "Nigeria: How to Derail a Transition Program," in *Multiparty Democracy and Political Change in Africa* (New York: Bookfield USA, 1998).

Agbese, Pita Ogaba. *Journal of Asian and African Studies* Volume 31, Issue 1-2, June 1996, page.82-98.

Ake, Claude. "Rethinking African Democracy," *Journal of Democracy* 2, Winter, 1992.

Ake Claude. *The Nigerian State.* (London: Longman, 1985).

Ake, Claude. *The Political Economy of Nigeria.* (London: Longman, 1978).

Ake, Claude. *Revolutionary Pressures in Africa.* (London: Zed Press, 1978).

Akinola and Agbaje. "Two-partyism and Democratic Transition in Nigeria" in *The Journal of Modern African Studies,* 1991.

Alvarez, Sonia. *Engendering Democracy in Brazil: The Women's Movement in Transitional Politics.* (Princeton: Princeton University Press, 1990).

Allen, Chris. "Who Needs Civil Society?" in *Review of African Political Economy.* Number 73, 1997.

Ames, Barry *Political Survival: Politicians and Public Policy in Latin America.* (Berkeley: University of California Press, 1987).

Ananaba, Wogu. *The Trade Union Movement in Nigeria.* (Lagos: Africana Publishing Corporation, 1969).

Anonymous. "The Countdown Continues, To Democracy or Confusion", in *The Economist,* Volume 324, July 1992, page 37.

Arato, Andrew. "Civil Society vs. the State" Telos, Number 47, page 23-47.

Arrighi and, Saul. *Essays on the Political Economy of Africa.* (New York: Monthly Review Press, 1984).

Mahmood Mamdani "Conceptualizing State and Civil Society Relations: Towards a Methodological Critique of Contemporary Africanism" in Auroi, Claude. *The Role of the State in Development Processes* (London: Frank Cass Publications, 1992)

(London: Frank Cass Publications, 1992)

Babatope, Ebenezer. *The Abacha Regime and the June 12 Crisis,* (Lagos: Ebino Topsy, 1995).

Babangida. Ibrahim, *Portrait of a New Nigeria: Selected Speeches of IBB,* Vol.1 (Lagos: Precision Press, 1989).

Bangura, Yusuf & Beckman, Bjorn. "African Workers and Structural Adjustments," in *The Politics of Strucutral Adjustment in Nigeria.* (Portsmouth: Heinemann, 1993).

Bangura Yusuf, Gibbon and Ofstad. *Authoritarianism Democracy and Adjustment,* (Upsala: Nordiska Africaninstitutet, 1992).

Bangura,Yusuf. "Structural Adjustment and the Political Question". *Review of African Political Economy,* Number 55, 1986.

Bates, Robert. "Socio-economic Bases of Democratization in Africa" in *African Governance in the 1990s.* (Atlanta: Emory University Press, 1990).

Beckett and Young. *Dilemmas of Democracy in Nigeria.* (Rochester: University of Rochester Press, 1997).

Beckman, Bjorn. *Expanding Democratic Space.* (Enugu: Fourth Dimension.1998).

Beckman, Bjorn. "Peasants and Democratic Struggles in Nigeria." *Review of African Political Economy,* Number 60, 1988.

Beckman, Bjorn. "Whose Democracy?" *Review of African Political Economy*, Number 71,1989.

Beckman, Bjorn. "The Military as Revolutionary Vanguard: a Critique," *Review of African Political Economy*, Number 54. 1986.

Beckman, Bjorn and Attahiru Jega. "Scholars and Democratic Politics in Nigeria," in *Review of African Political Economy,* Number 64:167-181, 1995.

Bianchi, Robert. "Interest Group Politics," in *Third World Quarterly,* Volume 8, No.2, April 1986.

Bratton, Michael and Nicolas van de Walle, "Popular Protest and Political Reform in Africa," in *Comparative Politics,* Volume 24 (4), July 1992.

Bratton, Michael and Nicolas Van de Walle. "Patrimonial Regimes and Political Transitions in Africa" in *World Politics,* Volume 46, No. 4, July 1994. p. 453-489.

Bratton, Michael. *Democratic Experiments in Africa: Regime Transitions in Comparative Perspective.*(Cambridge: Cambridge University Press, 1997).

Brown and Schraub. *Resolving Third World Conflict: Challenges for a New Era.* (Berkley: U.S. Institute of Peace Press, 1991).

Cai-Anan, Samudavanik. "The Three Dimensional State," in James Manor, eds. *Rethinking Third World Politics.* (London: Longman, 1991).

Calhoun, C. "History and Sociology in Britain," *Comparative Studies in Society and History.* 1987.

Callaghy, Thomas. *The State-Society Struggle: Zaire in Comparative Perspective.* (New York: Columbia University Press, 1984).

Callaghy, Thomas. "The State and the Development of Capitalism in Africa," in Chazan and Rothchild eds. *The Precarious Balance.*(Boulder, Colorado: Lynne Reinner, 1989).

Carothers, Thomas. *In the Name of Democracy.* (Berkeley: University of California Press, 1991).

Cavarozzi, Marcelo, "Beyond Transition to Democracy in America," in *Journal of Latin American Studies,* Volume 23, Part 3, October 1992, pp.665-684.

Chabal, Patrick. *Politics of Power in Africa.* (London: Revolutionary Books, 1993).

Chazan, Naomi. *Civil Society and the State in Africa,* (Boulder Colorado: Lynne Reinner, 1994).

Chazan, Naomi and Donald Rothchild. *The Precarious Balance.*(Boulder Colorado: Lynne Reinner, 1989).

Cohen, Jean. *Civil Society and Political Theory.* (London: Verso, 1992).

Cliffe and Seddon. "Africa in a New World Order". *Review of African Political Economy.* Number 69, 1991.

Cohen, Robin. *Labor and Politics in Nigeria,* (London: Heinnemann Educational Books, 1974).

Coleman, James. *Nigeria, Background to Nationalism.* (Berkeley: University of California Press, 1965).

Collier, Ruth, and Collier, David. *Shaping the Political Arena.* (Princeton: Princeton University Press, 1992).

Dahl, Robert. *Polyarchy, Participation and Opposition* (New Haven: Yale University Press, 1971).

Decalo, Samuel. *Coups and Army Rule in Africa.* (New Haven: Yale University Press, 1990).

Diamond, Larry. "Democracy in Africa," in *Foreign Policy,* 85, 1991-92.

Diamond, Larry. Juan Linz and Seymour Lipset eds. *Democracy in Developing Countries,* Vol. 2. Africa. (Boulder: Lynne Reinner, 1988).

Diamond, Larry. "Nigeria's Search for a New Political Order," in *Journal of Democracy 2,* Spring 1991.

Diamond, Larry (ed.) *Political Culture and Democracy in Developing Countries,* (Boulder Colorado: Lynne Rienner Publishers, 1994).

Diamond, Larry and Marc Plattner, (eds) *The Global Resurgence of Democracy,* (Baltimore: John Hopkins University Press, 1993).

Diamond, Larry. Juan Linz and Seymour Martin Lipset. *Politics in Developing Countries,* 2nd edition. (Boulder: Lynne Rienner Publishers, 1995).

Diamond, Larry. Juan Linz and Seymour Martin Lipset. *Politics in Developing Countries* Vol.2 Africa; Vol. 3 Asia: Volume 4. Latin America (Boulder Colorado: Lynne Rienner Publishers, 1988 and. 1989).

Diamond, Larry. *The Democratic Revolution.* (New York: Freedom House, 1992).

Diamond, Larry and Gary Marks. (eds.), "Comparative Perspectives on

Democracy," in *American Behavioral Scientist,"* 35, 352-629.

Diamond, Larry. "Nigeria: The Uncivic Society and the Descent into Patriotism", in Linz, Martin, Lipset and Diamond eds. *Politics in Developing Countires: Comparing Experiences with Democracy,* (Boulder: Lynne Rienner Publishers, 1995).

Diani, M. "The Concept of Social Movement", *Sociological Review,* 40,1992, page1-5.

Di Palma, Guissepe. *To Craft Democracies* (Berkeley: University of California Press, 1990).

Doornbos, Martin. "The African State in Academic Debate: Retrospect & Prospect." *The Journal of Modern African Studies,* 28, 1990.

Dudley, Bill. *An Introduction to Nigerian Government and Politics.* (Bloomington: Indiana University Press, 1982).

Ekeh, Peter. "Colonialism and the Two Publics in Africa," in *Comparative Studies on Society and History*, 1975.

Enloe, Cynthia. *Ethnic Conflict and Political Development.* (London: Little Brown & Co., 1973).

Evans, Peter. "Predatory Development and Other Apparatuses: A Comparative Political Economy Perspective on the Third World State," in *Sociological Forum,* Vol. 4, 1989.

Evans, Peter and John Stephens. "Studying Development since the 1960s: the Emergence of a New Comparative Political Economy." *Theory and Society.* October 17, 1988, 713-735.

Fawehinmi, Gani. *June 12 Crisis: The Illegality of Shonekan's Government:* (Lagos: Nigerian Law Publications, 1993).

Forrest, Tom. "The Political Economy of Civil Rule in Nigeria 1979-84," *Review of African Political Economy,* 1986

Forrest, Tom. *Politics and Economic Development in Nigeria.* (London: Westview Press, 1993)

Gana, Aaron. *Old Breeds, New Breeds, and Moneybags: The Nigerian Political Class as an Obstacle to Democracy* (Lagos: AfriGov Monograph Series No.3, 1996).

Graf, William. *The Nigerian State.* (London: Heinemann Educational Books, 1988).

Gutto, Shadrack. "The Preconditions for Sustainable Development and People's Democracy," in *Africa Development,* 1988.

Gutkind, P.C.W. "From the Energy of Despair to the Anger of Despair: The Transition from Social Circulation to Political Consciousness among the Urban Poor in Africa," *Canadian Journal of African Studies*. Vol. 7. No. 2.

Gutkind, P.C.W. "View from Below: Political Consciousness from Below in Ibadan Poor," *Cahiers.* Volume 9. No. 5,1972.

Habermas, *The Structural Formation of the Public Sphere: an Inquiry.* (Cambridge: MIT Press, 1991).

Haberson, Rothchild and Chazan. Civil Society and the State in Africa. (Boulder: Lynne Rienner, 1994).

Haggard, Stephan and Robert Kaufman *The Political Economy of*

Democratic Transitions. (Princeton: Princeton University Press, 1995).

Hagopian, Frances, "After Regime Change," in *World Politics,* Volume 45, Number 3, April 1993, pp 464-500.

Hagopian, Frances, Mainwaring, Scott. "Democracy in Brazil: Perspectives and Problems," in *World Policy Journal,* 1987.

Hirsch, Ernest. "Structural Adjustment and Africa's Pro-democracy Movements." *Africa Today,* 1993.

Hodgkin, Thomas, *African Political Parties.* (Cambridge: Cambridge University Press, 1971).

Huntington, Samuel "Third Wave," in *Journal of Democracy,* Vol. 2, No. 2, 1984.

Huntington, Samuel *The Third Wave: Democratization in the Late Twentieth Century.* (University of Oklahoma Press, 1992).

Huntington, Samuel. *Political Order in Changing Societies.* (New Haven: Yale University Press, 1968).

Hyden, Goran. *No Shortcuts to Progress.* (Berkeley: University of California Press, 1983).

Ibrahim, Jibrin. "Obstacles to Democratization" in *Dilemmas of Democracy in Nigeria,* (Rochester: University of Rochester Press, 1997).

Ibrahim, Jibrin. "The Political Debate and the Struggle for Democracy in Nigeria," *Review of African Political Economy,* Volume 33, 1989.

Ihonvbere, Julius. "Where Is the Third Wave?" in *Africa Today,* Volume 43 (4), 1996.

Ihonvbere, Julius. "Are Things Falling Apart?" in *Journal of African Studies,* 34 (2) (Cambridge: Cambridge University Press,1996.)

Ihonvbere, Julius. "On the Threshold of Another False Start: a critical evaluation of pro-democracy movements in Africa" in Nyang'oro eds. *The State and Capitalist Development in Africa: Declining Political Economies,* 1989.

Ihonvbere, Julius. *Nigeria: the Politics of Adjustment and Democracy.* (New Brunswick: Transaction Books, 1994).

Ihonvbere, Julius. "The Military and the Derailment of the Transition to Democracy in Nigeria," in Eboe Hutchful, eds. *The Military and Society in Africa,* (Dakar: Codesria, 1997).

Ihonvbere, Julius. "Organized Labor and the Struggle for Democracy in Nigeria" in *African Studies Review* ,1996.

Iweriebor, Ehiedu. *Radical Politics in Nigeria: the Significance of the Zikist Movement:1945-1950,.* (Zaria: Ahmadu Bello University Press, 1996).

Jackson, Robert and Carl Roseberg. *Personal Rule in Black Africa.* (Berkeley: University of California Press, 1982).

Jackson, Robert. *Quasi-states: Sovereignty, International Relations and the Third World,* (Cambridge: Cambridge University Press, 1990).

Jega, Attahiru. "Professional Associations and Adjustment," in Olukoshi's *Politics of Structural Adjustment.*(Portsmouth: Heinneman, 1993).

Joseph, Richard. *Democracy and Prebendal Politics in Nigeria: the Rise and Fall of the Second Republic.* (Cambridge: Cambridge University Press, 1991).

Joseph, Richard. "Democratization under Military Rule and Repression in Nigeria," in Beckett and Young's *Dilemmas of Democracy.*(Rochester: University of Rochester Press, 1997).

Joseph, Richard. "Prebendalism and Military Dominance in Nigeria" manuscript for a conference on *Transition and Structural Adjustment in Nigeria* at the Hoover Institution (Tel Aviv: August, 1990).

Kaplan, Robert. "Was Democracy Just a Moment?" *The Atlantic Monthly,* December 1997.

Karl, Terry Lyn. "Dilemmas of Democratization in Latin America," in *Comparative Politics,* October 1990.

Kaufman, Robert. "Corporatism, Clientelism and Partisan Conflict," in Malloy's *Authoritarianism and Corporatism in Latin America.* (Pittsburgh: University of Pittsburgh Press, 1990).

Keene, John. *Civil Society and the State.* (London: Verso, 1988).

Kirke-Greene and Oyediran. *Transition Without End: Nigerian Politics and Civil Society Under Babangida* (Ibadan: Vantage Publishers, 1997).

Kitscheldt, Harry. "Political Opportunity Structures and Political Protest," in *British Journal of Political Science,* 1986.

Lancaster, Carol. "Democracy in Africa" *Foreign Policy,* No. 85. Winter '91,92

Lemarcharnd, Rene. "Uncivil States and Civil Societies: How Illusion Became Reality," in *The Journal of Modern African Studies,* 1992.

Lijphart, Arendt. *Democracy in Plural Societies.* (New Haven: Yale University Press, 1977).

Linz, Juan and Alfred Stepan. *The Breakdown of Democratic Regimes.* (Baltimore: John Hopkins University Press, 1978).

Linz, Juan. and Arturo Valenzuela (eds.) *The Failure of Presidential Democracy*, Volume I, *Comparative Perspectives and Volume II, The Case of Latin America.* (Baltimore: Johns Hopkins University Press, 1994).

Linz, Juan and Alfred Stepan, *The Breakdown of Democratic Regimes.* (Baltimore: John Hopkins University Press, 1994).

Linz, Juan. "Transitions to Democracy," in *The Washington Quarterly,* Washington, 1990.

Linz, Juan. "Change and Continuity in the Nature of Contemporary Democracies." in *Reexamining Democracy* (Newbury Park: Sage, 1992).

Lipset, Martin Seymour. *Political Man.* (New York: Anchor Books, 1960).

Lodge, Tom and Chris Rootes, *African Studies,* Volume 56 (1), 1997.

Lofchie, Mchael. "Representative Government, Bureaucracy and Political". In Doro and Schutz eds. *Governing in Black Africa.*(Englewood Cliffs: NJ, Prentice Hall, 1991).

Lucas, John. "The State, Civil Society and Regional Elites: A Study of

Three Association in Kano, Nigeria." *African Affairs,* 1994,93.

Luckham, Robert. *The Nigerian Military.* (Cambridge: Cambridge University Press, 1971).

MacEwan, Ian. "Transitions from Authoritarian Rule" in *Latin American Perspectives*: Issue 58, Volume 15, Number 3, Summer 1988, pp. 115-130.

Mafeje, Archie. "Ideology of Tribalism" *The Journal of Modern African Studies,* 1977.

Mamdani, Mahmood. "A Critique of the State and Civil Society Paradigm in African Studies" in *African Studies in Social Movements and Democracy,* (Dakar: Codeseria 1995).

Mahmud, Sakah. "The Failed Transition to Civilian Rule in Nigeria: its implications for democracy and human rights". *Africa Today,* 4th Quarter, 1993.

Mainwaring, Scott, "Democracy in Brazil and the Southern Cone: Achievements and Problems," in *Journal of International Studies and World Affairs,* Volume 37, Number 1, Spring 1995, pp. 113-179.

Mainwaring, Scott and Timothy Scully (eds.), *Authoritarians and Democrats: Regime Transition in Llatin America.* (Pittsburgh: University of Pittsburgh Press, 1987).

Malloy and Siegleson eds. *Authoritarians and Democrats: Regime Transition in Latin America.* (Pittsburgh: University of Pittsburgh, 1987).

Mamdani, Mahmood. "State Formation and Social Processes," *CODESRIA* working paper. (Dakar: Senegal, 1991).

Mamdani, Makadawire and Wamba Dia Wamba. "Social Movements, Social Transformation and the Struggle for Democracy in Africa". *CODESRIA,* (Dakar: Senegal, 1988).

Markovitz, Irving Leonard. "An Uncivil and Critical View of Civil Society in Africa", paper for a conference at the (Harry Truman Center for Hebrew University, Tel Aviv, 1990).

Melson and Wolpe. *Nigeria: Modernization and the Politics of Communalism.* (East Lansing: Michigan State University Press, 1971).

Migdal, Joel. *Strong Societies and Weak States,* (Princeton: Princeton University Press,1988).

Momoh, Abubakar .*The Rise of Civil Associations, Militarism and Popular Struggles in Nigeria.* (Dakar: Codersria, 1995).

Moore, Barrington. *Social Origins of Dictatorship and Democracy.* (Harmondsworth: Penguin, 1969).

Munck, Gerardo, "Democratic Transitions in Comparative Perspective," in *Comparative Politics,* Volume 26, Number 3, April 1994, pp.355-375.

Munck, Renaldo. *Latin America: The Transition to Democracy,* (London: Zed Press, 1989).

Ndegwa, Stephen. *The Two Faces of Civil Society: NGOs and Politics in*

Africa (West Hartford: Kumarian Press, 1996).
Nwabueze, Ben. *Nigeria '93: The Political Transition and the Future of Democracy.* (Enugu: Fourth Dimension Press, 1993).
Nwabueze, Ben. *Democratization.* (Owerri: Spectrum Books, 1993).
Nwankwo, Arthur. *Nigeria, the Political Transition and the Future of Democracy*. (Enugu: Fourth Dimension Books, 1993).
Nwabueze, Ben. *Military Rule and Social Justice in Nigeria.* (Owerri: Spectrum Books, 1993).
Nwankwo, Arthur. *Civilianized Soldiers: the Military Option to Democracy.* (Enugu: Fourth Dimension, 1994).
Nwankwo, Arthur. *Retreat from Power: the Military in Nigeria's Third Republic.*(Enugu: Fourth Dimension, 1995).
Nyang'oro, Julius and Timothy Shaw, eds. *Corporatism in Africa,* (Boulder: Westview Press, 1989).
Nyang'oro, Julius. *The State and Economic Development in Africa: Declining Political Economies.* (New York: Praeger. 1979).
Nzeribe, Chief Arthur. *Nigeria: Seven Years after Shehu Shagari,* (London: Kilamanjaro,1990).
Obasanjo, Olusegun and Akin Mabogunje. *Elements of Democracy.* (Lagos: ALF Publications, 1992).
O'Donnell, Guillermo. "Tensions in the BA State and the Question of Democracy." in Collier eds. *The New Authoritarianism in Latin America.* (Princeton: Princeton University Press, 1979).
O'Donnell, Guillermo and Phillipe Schmitter and Lawrence Whitehead (eds.) *Transitions from Authoritarian Rule.* Volume 5 (Baltimore: John Hopkins University Press, 1986).
O'Donnell, Guillermo. "Delegative Democracy," in *Journal of Democracy,* Volume 5, Number 1, January, 1994.
Offe, Clause. "Challenging the Boundaries of Institutional Politics: social movements since the 1960's" in Maier eds. *Changing Boundaries of the Political.* (Cambridge: Cambridge University Press, 1987).
Okwudiba, Nnoli. *Deadend to Nigerian Development: an analysis of the political economy of Nigeria, 1979-1989.* (Dakar: Codesria Book Series, 1993).
Okwudiba, Nnoli. "Ethnic Conflict in Africa." *CODESRIA* Dakar: Codesria, 1989).
Olagunju, Tunji, Adele Jinadu and Sam Oyovbaire. *Transition to Democracy in Nigeria, 1985 —1993.* (Lagos: Safari Books, 1993).
Olowu, Dele, Kayode Soremekun and Adebayo Williams. *Governance and Democratization in Nigeria.*(Ibadan: Spectrum Books Limited, 1995).
Olukoshi, Adebayo and Abdulrahmeen. "The Left in Nigerian Politics and the Struggle for Socialism." *Review of African Political Economy,* 1986.
Olukoshi, Abedayo. *The Politics of Structural Adjustment in Nigeria.* (London: Heinemann, 1993).
Olumhense, Sonala. "The Road to Democracy," in *Africa Report,* Volume

36, March/April 1991. pp. 51-53.

Olurode, Lai. *M.K.O. Abiola on June 12 Mandate,* (Lagos: FastData Nigeria Ltd.1993).

Osoba, Segun. "The Deepening Crisis of the Nigerian Bourgeoisie." *Review of African Political Economy,* 1979.

Otobo, Dafe. "The Nigeria General Strike of 1981". *Review of African Political Economy,* 1989.

Oyovbaire, Sam. "Political Developments in Nigeria" in Okon Edet Uya (eds.), *Contemporary Nigeria: Essays in Society, Politics and Economy.* (Buenos Aires: Artes Grafitias Eidtoriales Publiciterias EDIPUVLISA, 1992) pp.38-39.

Oyovbaire, Sam. *Democracy in Nigeria: Interpretative Essays.* (Benin City: Koda Publishers, 1990).

Oyovbaire, Sam. *The Democratic Experiment in Nigeria.* (Benin City: Omega Publishers, 1987).

Petras, James and Morris Morley, *Latin America in the Time of Cholera: Electoral Politics, Market Economics, and Permanent Crisis.* (New York: Routledge, 1992).

Post, Kenneth and Michael Vickers. *Structure and Conflict in Nigeria 1960-1966* (Madison: University of Wisconsin Press, 1973).

Przeworski Adam. *Democracy and the Market.* (Cambridge: Cambridge University Press, 1992.)

Przeworski, Adam. "Problems in the Study of Transitions to Democracy," in O'Donnell et al, *Transitions from Authoritarian Rule.* (Baltimore: John Hopkins, 1986).

Remmer, Karen. "New Theoretical Perspectives on Democratization," in *Comparative Politics,* Volume 28, Number 1, October, 1995.

Report of the Political Bureau, Lagos: Federal Government Printer, 1987, pp. 246-247.

Rootes, C. "Social Movements and Politics," in *African Studies,* 56.1.97.

Rotimi & Ihonvbere, in "Democratic Impasse: Remilitarization of Nigeria" pp 675 in *Third World Quarterly* 15, Number 4, 1994.

Rotimi and Ihonvbere, *Multiparty Democracy and Political Change.* (New York: Bookfield USA)

Rueschemeyer, Dietrich, Evelyn Huber Stephens and John D. Stephens. *Capitalist Development and Democracy:* (Chicago: University of Chicago Press, 1992).

Rustow, Dankwart. "Transitions to Democracy: toward a dynamic model". *Comparative Politics.* Page 337-363. 1970.

Sakah, Mahmud. "The Failed Transition to Civilian Rule in Nigeria," Africa Today, 1994, 4th Quarter.

Sandbrook and Cohen, eds. "The Lagos Proletariat", *The Development of the African Working Class: Studies in Class Formation and Action.* (Toronto: University of Toronto Press, 1975).

Sandbrook and Cohen eds. *The Development of the African Working Class, Studies in Class Formation and Action.* (Toronto: University of Toronto Press, 1975).

Sandbrook, Richard. "Liberal Democracy in Africa: a Socialist Revisionist Perspective" *Canadian Journal of African Studies,* Volume 22, Number 2, 1988.

Saro-Wiwa, Ken. *Journal of Democracy,* Volume 7, Issue 1, January 1996, pp.184-185.

Scott, James. "Patron-Client Politics and Political Change in Southeast Asia". *American Political Science Review.* 1972.

Schatz, Sayre. "The Inert Economy of Nigeria: from Nurture Capitalism to Pirate Capitalism," in *The Journal of Modern African Studies,* Volume 22, Number 1.

Schmitter, Phillipe and Gerard Lembruch, eds. *Trends Toward Corporatist Intermediation.* (London: Sage, 1979).

Schmitter, Phillipe. "The International Context of Contemporary Democratization", in *Stanford Journal of International Affairs,* Volume 2, Issue 1, Fall/Winter 1993, pp.1-34.

Schmitter, Phillipe and Terry Lyn Karl. "What Is and What Is Not Democracy," in *Journal of Democracy,* Volume 2, Number 3, 1991.

Schumpeter, Joseph. *Capitalism, Socialism and Democracy.* (New York: Harper and Brothers, 1942).

Skocpol, Theda, Dietrich Rueschemeyer and Peter Evans. *Bringing the State Back In,* (Cambridge: Cambridge University Press, 1985).

Segal, Aaron. "Can Democratic Transitions Tame Political Successions?" in *Africa Today,* 43(4)(1996).

Shafer, Michael. "Sectors, States, and Social Forces: Korea and Zambia Confront Restructuring" in *Comparative Politics,* Vol.22, No.2, 1990.

Sklar, Richard, "An Elusive Target: Nigeria Fends off Sanctions," in Polis, Volume 3, Number.1, 1997.

Sklar, Richard. *Nigerian Political Parties.* (Princeton: Princeton University Press, 1963).

Smith, Dennis. *The Rise of Historical Sociology.* (Philadelphia: Temple University Press, 1991).

Smith, William. Carlos Acuna, and Eduardo Gamarra (eds.) *Latin American Political Economy in the Age of Neoliberal Reform.* (New Brunswick: Transaction Publishers, 1994).

Stepan, Alfred and Juan Linz. "Political Crafting of Democratic Consolidation or Destruction: European and South American Comparisons" in Robert Pastor eds. *Democracy in the Americas: Stopping the Pendulum.* (NY: Holmes and Meter, 1989)

Stepan, Alfred. *Rethinking Military Politics.* (Princeton: Princeton University Press, 1979).

Stepan, Alfred. *Democratizing Brazil,* (Oxford: Oxford University Press, 1989).

Stepan, Alfred. "Paths Toward Re-democratization" in Schmitter et al eds. *Transitions from Authoritarian Rule.*

Stepan, Alfred. *The Breakdown of Democratic Regimes, Latin America.* (Baltimore:John Hopkins University, 1978).

Takaya, Bala and Sonni Tyoden. *The Kaduna Mafia: A Study of the Rise, Development and Consolidation of a Nigerian Power Elite.* (Jos: University of Jos Press, 1983).

Tarrow, Sydney. *Power in Movement,* (Cambridge: Cambridge University Press, 1995).

Tilly, Charles. "Social Movements as Historically Specific Clusters of Political Performances," in *Berkeley Journal of Sociology,* 38 (1993-4):1-30.

Tilly, Charles. "Contentious Politics and Social Change in Africa," in *African Studies,* 56.1.97.

Tilly, Charles. *As Sociology Meets History,* (New York: Academic Press, 1981).

Tilly, Charles. *From Mobilization to Revolution.* (Reading: Addison-Wessely, 1978).

Uwazurike, Chudi. "Politics and the Search for Accommodation in Nigeria: Will Rotational Consociationalism Suffice?" unpublished manuscript. (New York: CUNY, 1996).

Uwazurike, Chudi. "Ethnicity, Power, and Prebendalism: the Persistent Triad as the Unsolvable Crisis of Nigerian Politics," in *Dialectical Anthropology* 21: 1-20. 1996.

Van de Walle, Nicolas. "Political Liberalization and Economic Reform in Africa". *World Development.* 22 (4), 1994.

Waterman, Peter. "Consciousness, Organization and Action Among Lagos Port Workers," *Review of African Political Economy,*1979.

Whitaker, C.S. *The Politics of Tradition: Continuity and Change in Northern Nigeria, 1946-1966.* (Princeton: Princeton University Press, 1970).

Whitaker, Seymour. "The Unfinished State of the Nigerian State," *Worldview,* 1993.

Young, Crawford. "Patterns of Social Conflict: State, Class, and Ethnicity," *Deadalus* 3, Spring 1982.

Zakaria, Fareed. "The Rise of Illiberal Democracy," *Foreign Affairs,* November/December 1997 (Volume 76, Number 6).

Zolberg, Aristide, R. "The Military Decade in Africa," *World Politics* 25.2, January 1973.

Zolberg, Aristide, R. "Beyond the Nation State: Comparative Politics in Global Perspective", in *Beyond Progress and Development,* ed. Jan Bertiny, Will Blockmans and U. Rosenthal, 42-69. (Aldershot: Avebury/Gowen, 1987).

Zolberg, Aristide, R. *Creating Political Order.* (Chicago: University of Chicago Press, 1985).

Zolberg, Aristide, R. "The Structure of Political Conflicts in the New States of Tropical Africa," *American Political Science Review,* 1969.

News Magazines and International Publications

1998, June 1st, *Tell,* "Tension in the Military" see cover story page 16 "Rumbles in the Military".

1998, October 19th, *The News* "Race for Aso Rock" see page 12—"Salvos for the General" and page 18 "Abiola's Secret Letters to the Generals".

1996, December 23rd, *Newswatch,* "Government Versus NADECO" see page 14 "Eyeball to Eyeball with Ajasin".

1996, February 26th, Tell, "Abacha Desperate for Survival" see page 10 "Fit of Desperation."

1996, March 3rd, *TSM,* "Dark Secrets: Abiola Weeps in Jail" see cover story.

1996, March 4th, *Tell,* "Wanted Dead or Alive: the Junta Guns for Soyinka" see page 8 "Abacha's Most Wanted Man".

1997, March 17th, *Tell,* "MKO Writes Abacha: we must settle June 12 or else" see page 10 "The Right Way is June 12".

1996, December 2nd, *Tell,* "Gani: Freedom At Last" see page 16 "The Nation: Who is Next?"

1993, July 26th, *The Nigerian Economist,* "Will August 27 Be?" see cover story page 20.

1995, August 28th, *Newswatch,* "Debate on Draft: Abacha's Hidden Agenda" see cover page 10 "A Hidden Agenda?"

1994, April 11th, *Tell,* "How Abiola Was Double-Crossed" see cover "The Travails of Abiola" page 8.

1993, August 30th, *The Nigerian Economist* "What's IBB Up To?" see cover story page 22.

1993, August 2nd, *The Nigerian Economist* "Babangida: Crises Dog His Path" see page 18 and "A Disclaimer by Ambimbola Davis" page 11.

1993, October 4th , *The African Guardian,* "Soon, Mr. President?" see cover story page 12.

1993, July 12th, 1993 *Newswatch* "Why They Stopped Abiola: the Military Versus Nigeria" see page 9 "How the Military Flaunts its Might".

1994, December 5th, *Tell* "Why Abacha Won't Release Abiola" see page 8, "Playing Politics with Precious Life".

1996, April 29th, Tell , "I See a Revolution Coming: only the truth can save Abacha" see special interview with Archbishop of the Church of Nigeria, "I Pray for a Bloodless Revolution".

1995, August 6th, *TSM,* "Countdown: Yar'Adua's Life" see cover story page 12.

1995, November 20th, *Newswatch,* "Who Annulled June 12?" see cover "Who Killed June 12?" page 11.

1997, March 3rd, *Tell,* "Abiola: Dead or Alive?" see cover story page 10 "Abacha's Hostage".

1995, December 31st, *Democracy Echo,* "Pro-Democracy Groups Fight Back" page 1.
1998, March 17th, *Weekend Concord,* "Abacha Rally: a tale of two rallies in two cities" page 3.
1992, October 26th, 1992 *The African Guardian,* "When Will Babangida Go?" see "The Last Chance" page 20.
1997, July 14th, *Tell,* "I Foresee Armed Struggle-Wole Soyinka" see cover "Abacha Has Wasted My Generation" page 8.
1994, September 26th, *Tell* "Forces Against Me and June 12" see "Enemies of June 12" page 14.
1993, July 12th, *The African Guardian,* "Divided: Politicians Sell Out" see "Running Against the People" page 24.
1996, March 25th, *Newswatch*1996, March 25th, *Newswatch* "The Detainees" see cover story page 10.
1994, February 7th, *The News,* "Has Diya Lost Out: the power game in Aso Rock as Abacha consolidates" see cover story page 14.
1995, March 11th, *The Week,* "Abacha Frustrates NADECO" see "The Final Showdown: NADECO vs Abacha" page 8'.
1996, May 20th, *Newswatch,* "Abiola's Freedom" see Nigeria, "The Struggle Continues" page 16.
1993, March 1st, *The Nigerian Economist,* "Can They Win?" see cover story "What Chance?" page 26.
1994, August 15th, *Tell,* "Install Abiola Now: Col. Umar Warns Abacha" see cover "The North Is For June 12" page 12.
1998, June 22nd, *Tell,* "Death of a Tyrant" see special edition, "The Ultimate Coup: Against Abacha" page 8.
1998, August 17th, *Tell,* "The Plot to Kill Abubakar: How Diya Saved Him" see "How Diya Saved Abubakar" page 14.
1996, December 16th, *Tell,* "Killing Lagos: Abacha Punishes the West" see "The Plot Against Lagos" page 12.
1996, March 18th, *Tell,* "We Are Tired of Dictatorship: Catholic Bishops Tell Abacha", see "A Time to Go" page 10.
1997, July 14th, *Newswatch,* "We Must Resolve June 12 Now—Sunday Mbang" see cover story interview with prelate of Methodist Church of Nigeria page 8.
1998, May 25th, *Tell,* "There Will Be A Revolution: Bishop Gbonigi" see "Abacha is Thoroughly Wicked" page 12.
1997, May 19th, *Newswatch,* "1998 Presidency: Abacha's Men Divided" see "Babel of Voices" page 9.
1996, August 5th, *The News,* "North-South Divide Deepens" see "Yorubas Have A Hidden Agenda" page 10.
1996, August 5th, *Tell,* "NADECO Rocks the Military" see cover story page 9.
1997, November 24th, *Newswatch,* "Abacha: Four Year Verdict" see "Abacha's Maiden Speech: My Mission" page 8; "The Man Abacha: His Mystique, His Style" page 10.

1997, October 13th, *Tell,* "Fight to the Finish, Abacha Vows to Deal with the Opposition" see page 16, "Abacha Hangs Tough".
1997, November 10th, *Tell,* "How NADECO Floored the Junta" see "Victory for the Opposition" page 16.
1993, July 19th, *Tell,* "Nigeria Boils: the People Say No to Babangida" see "Dance on the Precipice" page 10.
1998, June 11th, *Tempo,* Volume 10, No. 23, "Why Abacha Will Go" see "The Forces at Work".
1998, September 24th, *Tempo,* Volume 11, No. 11, see "The Heart of the Matter—Power Shift: Ige vs Dikko" page 3.
1994, February 24th, *The News,* "Abacha Panics" see "On the War Path: the opposition is mounting" page 18. Also see "Yar' Adua's Arrest" "Why CD's Conference Was Stopped."
1995, August 14th, *Newswatch,* "War on Abacha: The American Connection" see "Campaign Against Abacha: Americans and some Nigerian residents.." page 10.
1995, July 10th, *Tell,* "No Handover Soon: Abacha Deceives the World" see Abacha's Days Are Numbered" and interview with Randall Robinson, page 12.
1996, April 29th, *Newswatch,* "Abacha's Wars: and the forces against him" see "War on All Fronts" page 8.
1997, January 13th, *Tell,* "The Junta's Hatchetmen: how Abacha uses them to destabilize the West" see cover story, page 10.
1997, January 13th, *The News,* "Southerners are Terrorists: responsible for bombings" see page 9.
1994, December 12th, *Tell,* "Abacha Must Go In 1995: Military Commanders" see "Trouble in the Rock" page 10.
1995, August 21st, *The Meridian,* "June 12 Divides Progressives" see cover story, page 10.
1995, August 14th, *Tell,* "Reign of Terror: Now Abacha Wages War Against Everybody" see, "Vengeance, Thy Name is Abacha!"
1994, April 11th, *The Nigerian Economist,* "The Way Forward: Nigerians Disagree" see cover story page 11. Also see "Eastern Political Elite Unite to Fight Marginalization" page 17.
1997, December 22nd, *Newswatch* "Death of Yar'Adua: More Trouble for Abacha" see "Death in Abacha's Gulag" page 12.
1998, July 20th, *The Post Express* in "Issues" page 26, "NADECO's Proposal on the State of the Nation."
1996, June 23rd, *The Guardian* in "Sunday Politics "NADECO's Fight Against Abacha" page A6.
1998, August 16, 1998, *The Post Express,* "Sunday Special", "Rumbles in Pro-Democracy" page 10.
1998, March 3rd, *National Concord,* "Abacha-must-go rally holds today—UAD" cover story.
1995, January 16, Tell "Why Abacha Met Enahoro" see page 8, "Aso Rock's Power Game."

1997, April 7, *Tell* "Abiola Must Be President" see cover story page 8, "A Boost for Abiola."

1998, October 26, *The News* "How I Escaped Abacha's Assassins—Wole Soyinka" see cover story page 5, "My Exile Story."

1994, May 30, Times Week 'Daring Abacha: Regional Groupings Hold Talks Despite the Federal Government', Page 10.

1994, June 27, *Tell,* "Abiola, Abacha Battle for Control" in "Politics Will Destroy the Military"—Akin Aduwo, page 14.

1995, July 31, *The Meridian,* "Abiola to Head National Government?" page 10 and "No Compromise on June 12: an interview with Balarabe Musa."

1994, July 4, *Newswatch* "Abiola's Arrest" in "The Longest Running Show" page 9

1994, June 6, *Newswatch* "Is Abiola Ready to Fight Abacha?" in "Abiola is Ready to Die" page 14.

1998, October 8, vol.11, no.13 *Tempo "Yar'Adua's Last Days."*

1997, July 7, no.27 *Tell,* "Northern Opposition to Abacha Thickens."

1992, June 25, *Africa Watch,* Volume 4, Issue 7—*"Nigeria: Silencing the Vocal Opposition."*

1997, October 4, *Amnesty International: Nigeria,* —"A Travesty of Justice: Secret Treason Trials and Other Concerns."

1994, October "Human Rights Watch: Africa" , Volume 6, No.8—Nigeria, *"The Dawn of a New Dark Age."*

1993, August 27, *Human Rights Watch/Africa,* —"Nigeria: Democracy Derailed."

1993, June *Human Rights Watch/Africa,* Volume 5, No.9—"Nigeria: Threats to a New Democracy."

1991, April 24, *Africa Watch,* Volume, No.3, Issue No.8—Nigeria: "Behind the Wall."

1991, October, *Africa Watch,* An Africa Watch Report—"Nigeria: On the Eve of Change: Transition to What?"

1995, *Human Rights Watch Africa,* "Nigeria: Contradicting Itself: an undemocratic transition seeks to bring democracy nearer."

1992, *Africa Watch,* Volume No. 4, Issue No. 10—"Nigeria, Crackdown on Human Rights and Pro-Democracy Groups as Transition Is Postponed Again."

1993, March 30, *Human Rights Watch/Africa,* Volume 5, No.4,—"Nigeria: Military Injustice."

1996, September, *Human Rights Watch/Africa,* Volume 8, No.3 (A) —"Nigeria, Permanent Transition."

1995, July , *Human Rights Watch/Africa Report,* Volume 7, No.5, —"Nigeria, The Ogoni Crisis."

1998, February-March, *Democracy Review* (CLO), Vol 1, Issue 3 —"The Face of Abacha's Transition Program."

1997, Oct-Dec, *Liberty* (a CLO publication), Volume 8, Number 4—"Killing Nigeria."

1997, September *Victims* (CDHR Newsletter), Volume 8, No.26, "Abacha Intensifies Rights Violation"

1996, September *Freedom Watch* (A CDHR Monthly) —"Weeping Soldiers: Crying for Power."

1997, October. *Human Rights Watch/ Africa* -, Vol 9, No. 6 (A) "Nigeria: Transition or Travesty?"

Endnotes

Preface

1 "A Dawn of a New Dark Age" NADECO press release, September 7, 1994.

Chapter 1

2 An acronym reflecting the opposition to the annulment of the presidential elections, claiming Chief Abiola as the winner.

3 NLC, ASUU, NUPENG and PENGASSAN are older professional organizations which before 1990 represented the vanguard for mobilizing democratic rights. They have experienced a tradition of mobilizing in support of democratic rights and interests among their professional constituencies.

4 "Oil and Democracy in Nigeria" *Review of African Political Economy.* volume 8. Page 25.1986.

5 I am referring to studies pioneered in the O'Donnell, Guillermo, and Schmitter volume: *Transitions from Authoritarian Rule: tentative conclusions about uncertain democracies.* (John Hopkins University Press, 1986). On the more narrow study of the civil society (associational) role, I specifically relate to Philip Schmitter's 1979 editorial "Still the Century of Corporatism" published in Lehmbruch and Gerhard eds. *Trends Toward Corporatist Intermediation,* London, 1979.

6 The Campaign for Democracy (CD); the National Democratic Coalition (NADECO); the United Democratic Front of Nigeria (UDFN).

7 The period is further sub-divided into: 1) 1986-1993 Representing the controversial Babangida transition-to-democracy project which spearheaded the crisis. This period identifies the social conditions—national governmental organization and economic re-structuring, which paved the way for the pro-democracy insurgency. 2) 1990 — 1993 representing period of climatic pro-democracy insurgency. 3) 1994-1997 represents the period of highly contested social movement activism against the General Abacha military regime, as well as the growth of international activism.

8 Nigeria, as a case study of political transitions, is more than often cited cross-regionally, being pulled out of the African context and compared to cases such as Algeria, Argentina, and Turkey, in an attempt to understand these countries' unique cyclical nature of democratic transitions, as well as their problems of military politicization and civil/military relations. (Huntington, 1990) Nevertheless, in support of the "uniqueness of the Nigerian case" theory, in the contemporary period, in comparison to the African countries already cited—countries with much smaller, lower income levels, and less political experience with democracy—Nigeria uniquely remains a non-democratic state. Since the

1960's Nigeria's political landscape has vacillated between intermittent periods of democratic regimes and longer periods of military government; and in the 1990's prospects for democracy remain bleak. Indeed, similar to Latin America in the 1960's, a study by O'Donnell 1976, Philip 1985, Nordlinger 1977 and Stepan 1971, distinguished between two patterns of relationships between civil society and the military in that region during the 40's to the 70's. One pattern, observed in Brazil and Peru, consisted of an initially weak civil society which underwent a process of rapid organization, with excluded groups pressuring for inclusion and in some cases trying to ally with sectors of the military, and established groups feeling threatened and appealing to the military to protect order and keep the excluded groups excluded.

9 *Human Rights Watch/Africa.* 1993.

10 Since 1960, the country has experienced two and a half democratic regimes, three major military coups overhauling democratic regimes, four dominant military regimes, and three elaborate democratic transition programs. Cited several times by Huntington's study on democratic waves, the author classifies Nigeria with Turkey, Argentina, Brazil, Peru, Bolivia, and Ecuador, as examples of countries with "wave democratization in cyclical patterns." In the cyclical pattern, countries alternated back and forth between democratic and more conservative military regimes.

11 In the 1970s, Nigeria's oil boom led the country in a 7% annual growth rate.

12 In the 1970s, Nigeria led Africa in the fight against apartheid in Rhodesia and South Africa. Nigeria continues to be the leadership force in West Africa through the Economic Community of West African States (ECOWAS).

13 Even though authoritarian governments in Zambia, Kenya, Benin, Tanzania, and somewhat in the Ivory Coast all clearly were swept under as a result of the wave of popular sentiment for political change; however, all these states existed under the African, "one-party rule" phenomenon. Nigeria, on the other hand, has always operated under somewhat different political regime circumstances. For example, the country's history documents a complex ethno-regionalism, which resulted in unique ethnic party and state structures in Nigeria , structures which facilitated against one-party rule, though producing its own brand of state authoritarianism—militarization.

14 Diamond, Kirk-Greene & Oyediran, 1997

15 Tunji Olagunu, Adele Jinadu, and Sam Oyovbaire. *Transition to Democracy in Nigerian (1985-1993).*(Lagos: Safari Books, 1993).

16 Major citation on this theory—the civil military paradox—is a study of the Babangida transition-to-democracy (Oyovbaire & Olagunju, 1993).

17 Data presented in the sections on alliances and the political opportunity of each agent pro-democracy movement organization offers some insight into the nature and extent to which the "climate of opinion" in favor of immediate democratization was raised as a result of effective

social mobilization during this period.

18 Olagunju et al's theory of 'anti-politics'.

19 In his book, *The Third Wave,* Samuel Huntington designates the period beginning in 1974 and enduring into the 1990s as the third wave of global democratization.

20 The 1970s scholarly reflections of democratic transitions in Spain and later Latin America, pioneered by Juan Rial, and later Whitehead, O'Donnell et al. 1979, 1986.

21 This body of work includes a wide body of seminal studies ranging from the works of Arato and Cohen on civil society in Eastern Europe to Chazan and Rothchild on civil society in Africa.

21 Doornbos, Martin, 'The African Sate in Academic Debate: Retrospect and Prospect' I *The Journal of Modern African Studies,* 1990

22 Larry Diamond, 1992

24 Patrick Chabal, *Politics of Power in Africa,* Revolutionary Books, 1993

25 Zambia, Tanzania, Uganda, Kenya, Benin, Ivory Coast, Ghana have all recently undergone some form of democratic transition.

26 Chazan and Rothchild, 1989

27 Most scholars who use the concept cite a number of early Western European classicist scholars —ranging from Hegel, Paine, De-Tocqueville, Marx to more recent scholars, Jurgen Habermas and Thomas Keene—as originators or "best users" of the term civil society. While even the early scholars each customized their application of the concept to Renaissance Europe, the term—usually deemed synonymous with democratization—generally applied to "the historically produced sphere of life in 16th century Western Europe, which arose as a result of the historical product of a multi-dimensional process precipitated by the spread of commodity relations and the emergence of the market." (Hegel). Jurgen Habermas accents this state of affairs as the "strategic initiatives of an embryonic bourgeois class who shaped an associational life along voluntary and democratic principles." (Habermas *The Structural Transformation of the Public Sphere: an inquiry,* Cambridge, Mass: MIT Press, 1991) Also, see John Keene's, 1988 study on "Civil Society and the State." Verso, London (Keene, 1998), where his main thesis lays out civil society as that "legitimate arena of defense against the state."

28 Defined as the civil society-political liberalization thesis.

29 Chazan & Rothchild, 1989

30 Chris Allen in "Who Needs Civil Society?" (Allen, 1997). John Haberson, "Is Civil Society Necessary?" (Haberson, Rothchild and Chazan,1994); Mahmoud Mamdani "A Critique of the State and Civil Society Paradigm in African Studies" in *African Studies in Social Movements and Democracy*. (Codeseria: Dakar.,1995).

31 Not all civil societal groups constrain state action. In fact, many collaborate with the state and facilitate its actions.

32 Mamdani, Mahmood , "A Critique of the Civil Society Variable" in *African Studies in Social Movements and Democracy.* (Codeseria:

Dakar,1995). Rita Abrahamsen in "Democratization: a Neo-Gramscian Perspective" *Journal of Modern African Studies,* volume 35. 1997, where the author argues that the "democracy project" is manifested by the common perception of a world-wide democracy movement where IFI's, western governments, and the developing world "poor" are seen to share the same goals and aspirations.

33 The author categorizes them as Non Government Organizations (NGO's), but emphasizes the organizational characteristics of these organizations as the distinguishing factor regarding their contribution to democratic struggles (Ndegwa, 1996).

34 Stephen Ndegwa.*The Two Faces of Civil Society: NGOs and Politics in Africa.* (West Hartford: Kumarian Press, 1996).

35 Stephen Ndegwa: *The Two Faces of Civil Society: NGOs and Politics in Africa.*(West Hartford: Nairobi. Kumarian Press, 1996).

36 As Arato and Cohen's 1993 study on the subject contends, "Is the driving force of democratization *everywhere* the contention between civil society and the state?"

37 Their alliances; their leadership structure; their ideology; their resources etc.

38 Sydney Tarrow (Tarrow, 1995) suggests that the expansion of "political opportunity" precedes a wave of mobilization in which organized publics challenge the status quo because the risks of such action are lower and the likelihood of success higher during such openings.

39 Tom Lodge, Chirs Rootes. *African Studies,* Volume 56 (1), 1997.

40 Charles Tilly, "Contentious Politics and Social Change in Africa" in *African Studies,* 56.1.97.

41 M.Diani, "The Concept of Social Movements" *Sociological Review,* 40,1992,1-5.

42 Michael Bratton. *Democratic Experiments in Africa: Regime Transitions in Comparative Perspective.* (Cambridge: Cambridge University Press. 1997)

43 According to Mamdani, the general application of civil society by many scholars of African democratic struggles has tended to avoid the question of agency, thereby side—stepping real African popular struggles.

44 C. Rootes, "Social Movements and Politics.'" C. Tilly in "Contentious Politics and Social Change in Africa" in *African Studies,* 56.1.97

45 As is the case with Bratton's definition of civil society in (Chazan, 1994 pg 169) ("civil society is an arena where manifold social movements ...attempt to constitute themselves.") most scholars seem to acknowledge no conflict in their usage of both concepts of civil society and social movements interchangeably. In fact, as Bratton's definition of civil society demonstrates, the concepts can enhance each other.

CHAPTER 2

46 Migdal, Joel. *Strong Societies and Weak States.* (Princeton: Princeton University Press,1988). Migdal's seminal study gauges state capacity

by the extent to which a state can guide its society by implementing the binding rules.

47 The soul of Northern hegemony was nurtured by the pre-colonial historical events, which led up to the successful fundamentalist uprising of Uthman Dan Fodio, a Fulani Muslim who lived among the Hausas at the turn of the century. This uprising broke-up Hausa self-rule into principalities and created a Fulani Caliphate with Sokoto at its center. The success of the Islamic Revolution of Dan Fodio spread beyond the northern Hausa states to several other kingdoms, reaching as far as Yoruba-land (Southwest). Kole Omojola. *At The Crossroads: challenges and options for Nigeria*. (Ibadan: Pulsemedia, 1992).

48 A system of colonial rule in which the colony was dependent on the native authority structure of each ethnic region/group.

49 As a result of British amalgamation of different peoples into the Northern Protectorate and the eventual metamorphosis of the protectorate into a single Northern Region, previously independent peoples and places were forcibly and unwillingly brought under the control of the Caliphate with consequent loss of identity.

50 "Nigeria: the uncivic society and the descent to praetorianism" by Larry Diamond (Diamond, Linz and Lipset, 1995).

51 Originally founded as a nationalist party by Lagosian Herbert Macaulay. However, with the death of Macaulay in 1947, Nnamdi Azikiwe took over the leadership of the party and formed the Ibo State Union (ISU), which was later to compromise the pan-Nigerian character of the NCNC.

52 Dickson Agedah. *The Military in Politics.* (Lagos: Perception Communications, 1993).

53 Beckett and Young argue that "permanent transition" turns on that paradoxical situation —visible over many years—in which Nigerian military rule is legitimated by a sense of progress toward creating its own alternative: civil democratic government (Beckett & Young, 1997); and Olukoshi's "The Left and the Struggle for Democracy" (Olukoshi, 1996).

54 The nine-year tenure of the Gowon regime sought to perpetuate its rule but the Murtala coup of July 1975 led to the acceptance of the agenda of civil society and eventually to the Second Republic. (Jibrin Ibrahim, 1997).

55 *Nigerian Tribune,* August 1st , 1975.

56 In fact, democratic transitions have become such an entrenched practice among the country's political democratic development that the Nigerian state is paradoxically referred to as a state in 'permanent transition'. (Beckett and Young, 1997).

57 In the words of the late Chief Abiola, "no amount of brute force will keep any unpopular government in power for any length of time...." (Agedah, 1995).

58 *West Africa*, January 13, 1986, pg.107.

59 The debate itself involved extensive consultation with Nigerians on

thirty aspects of governance including ideology, forms of representation, ethnicity, the military, women, labor, youth and students, traditional rulership, local government, corruption, and the mass media. A total of 27,324 contributions were made to the body. (*West Africa,* January 13, 1986 pg. 107). The seventeen member committee included of a diverse spectrum of representatives from civil associations and constituencies, labor, women, the media, intellectuals, and ethnic groups.

60 The Babangida administration, through its "White Paper Report on the Political Bureau," adopted 90% of the bureau's recommendations in its political transition program (PTP).Sam E. Oyovbaire, "Political Developments in Nigeria" in Okon Edet Uya (eds.) *Contemporary Nigeria: Essays in Society, Politics and Economy,* Buenos Aires: Artes Grafitias Eidtoriales Publiciterias EDIPUVLISA, 1992, pp. 38-39).

61 A tendency toward a "state class" (Hartmut Elsenhans,1986) was reflected in the evolution of a brand of state capitalism in Nigeria, the increase of federal powers, and the influx of oil revenue particularly during the 70s and the early 80s. Sometimes described as the neo-colonial elite, separated into sub-categories of politicians, civil servants and administrators, soldiers, and a commercial-national bourgeoisie of traders, contractors, independent professionals,. Solidarity among these groups developed from their utility to each other, and from a common awareness that their self-enriching activities must be carried on through the political machinery.

62 A strain of Nigerian political thought born out of a fear of the growing military advocacy among the military and sectors of civil society alike, and of the degeneration of Nigerian political thought to more narrowly defined democratic models, such as the civil-diarchy and military-proscribed, limited democratic structures for Nigeria. Jibrin Ibrahim describes this advocacy as a looming ideology of institutionalizing autocracy, whereby debate on political models for the country during the 1989 -1992 transition to the Third Republic era centered around choosing among autocratic political forms such as diarchy, triarchy, one or two party systems. (Beckett and Young, 1997).

CHAPTER 3

63 Tarrow, Sydney. *Power in Movements.* (Cambridge: Cambridge University Press.1995).

64 As a state, which has traditionally exhibited characteristics of cyclical and episodic political alternation between militarism and democracy, state-building and social engineering has become an embedded feature of Nigeria's political history (Diamond, Kirke-Greene, Oyediran,1995).

65 Sydney Tarrow (Tarrow, 1995) suggests that the expansion of "political opportunity" precedes a wave of mobilization in which organized publics challenge the status quo because the risks of such action are lower and the likelihood of success higher during such openings.

66 Political opportunity structures may be distinguished among a) the formal institutional structure of the state: b)the informal procedures and prevailing strategies used to deal with challengers, and c)the configuration of power in the party system—civil society (italics my emphasis).

67 The dominant model is: Strong states plus weak civil societies lead to constrained participation, punctuated by violent outbursts of movements, while weak states in strong civil societies lead to open participation and conventional collective action. But underneath these differences, are complex dynamics of state structures. Whereas a military state may appear to be characterized as a strong authoritarian "closed" state, Nigerian militarism—by comparison—has been relatively "open" in the past. Prior to 1986, the Nigerian military state's "corporate" structure has exercised "inclusive" rather than exclusionary strategies to deal with its challengers in civil society (Chapter 2).

68 State-building creates an opportunity structure for collective action of which movements take advantage. (Sydney Tarrow, 1995).

69 The 1986 state-building project (transition-to-democracy program), titled Political Transition Program (PTP); the economic restructuring program, titled Structural Adjustment Program (SAP); and the Post Cold War era of the diffusion of democracy movements, especially in Africa (The Second Wave of African Renaissance).

70 As Tarrow insists, movements not only seize opportunities they often create them. The CLO, CDHR & Campaign for Democracy (CD) acted as diffusion and repertoire effects for the proliferation of pro-democracy insurgency in Nigeria. In turn, the efforts of these SMOs were facilitated by international NGO's and governments in support for democracy.

71 Defined as the changing aspect of the structural elements of the state and civil society, which act as the instigator of social change.

72 In 1983, after the general public had revealed a profound exhaustion and disgust with the greed, corruption, and opportunism of the 2nd Republic, the Nigerian military under the Buhari/Idiagbon regime sought to restore accountability to public life by imposing on civil society several draconian decrees subverting democratic rights. These acts by the once-popular military regime lead to its de-legitimization. (Aaron Gana, 1998).

74 Larry Diamond "Nigeria: the Uncivic Society and the Descent into Praetorianism" in Linz, Martin Lipset & Diamond. *Politics in Developing Countries: comparing experiences with democracy.* (Princeton: Lynne Rienner Publishers, 1995).

75 Decree 4 prohibited journalists from criticizing the government.

76 All who had previously been banned as a result of their collective action against the prior military regime for its subversion of rights.

77 In order to explore the agenda of this political and economic restructuring, as well as to gain support and legitimacy for his transition program, a mark of the Babangida military regime, tried to forge links with

individuals and professional groups within the civil population. By way of the National Agenda Committee on the IMF Loan and the Political Bureau, two military created advisory committees made up of an expansive spectrum of civil societal groups and civilian individuals, the Babangida regime captivated the minds and imaginations of millions of Nigerians by the candor with which it announced its transition time-table, and its manner of dramatizing political debates and participatory political involvement in a military setting. (Nwankwo, pg 19, 1993).

78 Babangida, *Portrait of A New Nigeria.* (Lagos: Precision Press, 1989).

79 General Babangida's political transition program provided a political opportunity for civil societal activists expressed the traditional openness of Nigerian military rule as well as the Nigerian military's historical propensity to observe the politics of inclusion by soliciting active participation of civil society sectors in its authoritarian politics. The Babangida administration conducted a second elaborate transition to democracy program demonstrating the relatively openness of Nigerian military regimes. However, where social movement contention had occurred—labor groups, professional groups—the traditional response by the military was an attempt to co-opt and ban collective action. Detention, incarceration, and para-military murders of civil society activists represented an impending 'closure' of the Nigerian military in its repression-facilitation strategies.

80 Nigeria's 1970s oil boom had transformed into an oil glut where net earnings from oil revenues had declined so much that the nation's economy had been pushed into recession.

81 When a dramatic drop occurred in the international price of oil in the early 1980's as a result of the glut in the world market; the corresponding fall in Nigeria's oil revenues triggered an unprecedented crisis of immense dimensions in the economy. From a peak of $22.4 billion in 1980, Nigeria's oil earnings fell to $16.7 billion in 1982 and $10 billion in 1983 (National Economic Council Expert Committee, 1983). Subsequently, Nigeria's balance of payments account went into the red, public finances were thrown into disarray, the country's GDP rapidly dropped by 4.4% in 1983, and the budget deficit stood at a staggering 6.231 billion naira. Social consequences of the declining economy immediately followed in later years as between 1983—1985, about 50% of the factories operating in the country collapsed outright, while the remainder dropped to about 40% capacity utilization. As a result of this, tens of thousands of industrial workers and public service workers were laid-off. In addition to all this, the economy was further saddled with a heavy debt burden. Internal public debts rose from 4.6 billion naira in 1979 to 22.2 billion naira in 1983. At the external level, repayment of principal and interest on the country's foreign debt rose to 1.3 billion naira. (Olukoshi, 1993.)

82 The effect of structural adjustment would be to change the structure of the economy in terms of the labor employed and output in favor of

the modernizing sectors of the economy. However, the IMF/World Bank application of the notion of SAP policies has been to encourage the economies in question in the attainment of equilibrium in international transactions, thus restructuring the Nigerian domestic economy, thereby producing a liberalized national market more in synchronicity with the global market.

83 *Monthly Business and Economic Digest,* July 1987.

84 World Bank publication, 1989. Also, Robert Bates in "Socio-economic Bases of Democratization" in *Africa in African Governance in the 1990's* (Atlanta: Emory University, 1990), where he argues within the public choice framework applied to Africa. Bates advocates the elimination of state controlled market boards so that agrarian interests can be liberalized. This theory is prevalent among social scientist and best epitomized by Larry Diamond in "Roots of Failure, Seeds of Hope" in *Politics in Developing Countries,* (Princeton: Lynne Reinner, 1995) where the author argues that economic liberalization will expand entrepreneurship, create a resurgence of the profit motive and foster individual initiatives toward the evolution of a meaningful democracy.

85 On September 15, 1989, Gani Fahwehinimi, prominent pro-democracy crusader, was arraigned before the Transition to Civil Rule Tribunal with the main charge against him being his opposition to SAP.

86 *West Africa.* June 12, 1989, page 94.

87 *West Africa,* January 13, 1986, page 106. See Diagram I for schedule.

88 Federal Government of Nigeria. *Report of the Political Bureau.* (Federal Government Printer. Lagos, 1987).

89 Government document: *Decree 19 of 1987:* a decree which empowered the Federal Military Government to take measures to ensure the implementation of the political program set out in schedules 1 to 6 of the decree.

90 Sam E. Oyovbaire, "Political Developments in Nigeria". Okon Edet Uya. *Contemporary Nigeria: Essays in Society, Politics and Economy.* (Buenos Aires: Artes Grafitias Eidtoriales Publiciterias EDIPUVLISA, 1992) pp. 38-39.

91 *Tell Magazine.* "I See Bloodbath Ahead". No. 45 November 9, 1992, p.11.

92 Many felt that the minority decision by two bureau members had been induced by the military leader as a means for prolonging military rule.

93 "A little to the right," the Social Democratic Party (SDP) and the other "a little to the left", the National Republican Convention (NRC) — General I.B Babangida "The Dawn of a New Socio-Political Order", address to the Nation on Saturday, October 7, 1989; and *Newswatch,* October 23, 1989, pp. 13-26

94 In a 55-page report issued in October 1991, "On the Eve of Change: A Transition to What?", *Africa Watch* detailed the concerns of the transition as the government's tight control of the transition program, its abandonment of the rule of law and the level of government inter-

ference with civilian institutions during the transition program, greatly weakening their effectiveness as alternative voices in the transition. *Africa Watch,* 1991.

95 A *Financial Times* article presented data to show that Nigeria had become one of Sub-Saharan Africa's poorest countries with an unemployment rate of 40 percent. Despite the stringent and unpopular structural adjustment program that had all but eliminated Nigeria's middle class, the budget deficit and foreign debt remained high.

96 Turning the democratization program into a weapon of oppression, General Babangida used the Decree from time to time to silence government critics. In 1989 it was used to convict and imprison Gani Fawehinmi, a human rights lawyer, who had been seeking to prosecute two top officers of the security forces for the murder of Dele Giwa, the outspoken editor-in-chief of *Newswatch* magazine who was killed by a parcel bomb in 1986. The decree was threatened to be used again in 1990 against the leaders of a group known as the National Consultative Forum who were planning a national conference on the political future of the country. Police canceled the conference amidst charges that the conference threatened to interrupt the transition program.(Section 8 of Decree 19: "Any person who organizes, plans, encourages, aids, cooperates, or conspires with any other person to undermine, prevent, or in any way, do anything to forestall or prejudice the realization of the political program as set out in the Schedules to this decree shall be guilty of an offense." Subsection 3 cautioned against organizing any resistance to the program.) *1992 Annual Reports on Human Rights in Nigeria.* (Lagos: Civil Liberties Publication, December, 1993) and *Human Rights in Retreat: A Report on the Violations of the Military Regime of General Ibrahim Babangida.*(Lagos: Human Rights Watch, 1993).

97 An interesting mix of old cleavages and coalitions and some new breeds emerged, the two parties reproducing to some extent the emergent cleavage between southern-led progressives and northern-led conservatives. (Diamond, Larry,1994) The pattern of electoral outcomes demonstrated by the elections scheduled in Schedule Three and Four (local council elections, state gubernatorial elections, and national assembly elections), showed some promise of generating the more national, cross-cutting alignments that seemed to have been the objective of two-partyism, and which had also seemed to be the trend taking shape in the first two republics.

98 Rotimi & Ihonvbere. "Democratic Impasse: Remilitarization in Nigeria" pg 675 in *Third World Quarterly* 15, no.4 .1994.

99 See 1993 Annulled Presidential Election Results in Appendix.

100 **Diagram II** maps out the developmental stages of organization among civil society. The chart depicts the nation's forty year history demonstrating the manner in which social movement organizations have reconstituted into diverse group formations, ranging from the foundational ethnic union civil associations to the nationalist movements

that developed in the sixties to form the cornerstone political parties that were to continue their ideological strains into the contemporary era. **Diagram II** also demonstrates the manner in which professional associations and early political organizations continued their activism into the post-colonial regimes, but especially how new organizational formats—NGOs and political reform movements—were developed in the mid-eighties and nineties, all organizations which have spearheaded the contemporary pro-democracy movement.

CHAPTER 4

101 Values and claims, leadership, actions and events; and resources.

102 Differentiation among group type within civil society.

103 Bjorn Beckman, "Expanding Democratic Space" in *Dilemmas of Democracy.* (Rochester: University of Rochester Press, 1997.) pg 25.

104 C.W Whitaker *The Politics of Tradition.* (Princeton. Princeton University Press. 1970).

105 Previous sections have already discussed the development of ethnic politics in early Nigeria. It is significant however, to mention that 'tri-polar' politics (the tendency of Nigerian politics to be based on three regional ethnic parties) has also made way for bi-polar politics. Since 1964 with the NPC/NNDP alliance in the form of the NNA, and the NCNC/AG/NEPU alliance in the form of the UPGA, shifting bipolar alliances, particularly formalized by Babangida's 'two party' mandate, is a common tendency among Nigerian politics. Of particular note is the 1999 bipolar tendency with the alliance of the AD/APP versus the PDP.

106 The first trade union in Nigeria, the Southern Nigeria Civil Service Union was formed as early as 1912. Subsequently, the inauguration of the Railway Workers Union marked the beginning of militant unionism in Nigeria. In 1921, the artisans employed on the government railroad, who had joined with other technical workers, struck against a threatened reduction in wages. Moreover, radical social movements could be identified under the colonial regime as early as 1946 when the Zikist movement, an independent organization of the National Council of Nigeria and the Camerouns (NCNC), initiated the mobilization for radical nationalist politics for the entire nation (Ehiedu Iweriebor, 1996). Also, during the same period, NEPU, a movement of petty traders, peasants, and artisans led by a populist intelligentsia that appealed to the masses to effect political change, reflected the concerns of a poor, middle-belt agrarian society dominated and exploited by the Anglo-Fulani Native Authorities.

107 John Lucas' research on civil society in Kano demonstrated that despite the commanding presence of the state, elite in Kano used associations—the Kano State Foundation and the Kano Traders Multi-purpose Cooperative Society—to pursue their development of a class.

108 Attahiru Jega in "Professional Associations and Structural Adjustment"

in Olukoshi eds. *The Politics of Structural Adjustment in Nigeria.* (Portsmouth. Heinemann, 1993).

109 A group that counterbalanced the more conservative National Council for Nigerian Women.

110 Yusuf Bangura and Bjorn Beckman, the "Politics of Structural Adjustment in Nigeria" in *Authoritarianism, Democracy and Adjustment.* (Upsala: Nordsika Africanistitutet, 1992).

111 Documents drafted by the labor and students' unions that outline a list of prescriptions to improve the economic and political development of the country.

112 By 1985, Nigeria was undergoing a recession caused by a global oil glut with a drop by half in the country's oil revenue earnings.

113 Established in 1990 to promote respect for human rights and the rule of law in Nigeria.

114 Momoh, Abubakar. *The Rise of Civil Associations, Militarism and Popular Struggles in Nigeria* (Dakar: Codersria,1995).

115 The tradition of social movement activism among Nigerian civil society has implications for the contemporary Nigerian democratic movement. Throughout critical stages of Nigerian history, organizations among civil society have re-constituted in leadership and in ideology in defense of their interests. In the contemporary period, these organizations have proliferated and developed new organizational techniques for the purpose of re-democratizing the Nigerian state.

116 On June 12, 1993, the annulment of the Third Republic presidential elections result, declaring Chief M.K.O Abiola the winner, established a watershed in Nigerian political history. The annulled election results led to a wide-spread reaction among Nigerian civil society, which condemned the shocking blatancy of arbitrary military rule. It propelled forward social movements with a significantly enhanced ideology defining Nigeria's political future.

117 "June 12" symbolized the illegal annulment of what was considered Nigeria's freest, fairest, and most progressive presidential election. Chief Abiola was acclaimed the winner by undercover press publications of the results and by the NEC. The June 12 Movement calls for the reinstatement of those results and the swearing-in of the winner, Chief Abiola as Nigeria's duly elected President of the Third Republic.

118 See Diagram III for complete listing and categorization of Nigerian pro-democracy organizations, 1990-1998.

119 All entail vast public involvement and support for the democracy claim.

120 Refer to Diagram IV.

121 CLO Human Rights Report.1990.

122 Ken Saro-Wiwa's Movement for the Survival of the Ogoni People.

123 Also, significantly representative of Group A is the Gani Fahwehinmi Solidarity Association—though a member of the CD collective in its initial foundation. Probably Nigeria's leading social critic, activist, and crusader for justice and true democracy, lawyer Gani Fawhinmi, gained momentum during this phase of Nigerian pro-democracy struggles.

No single activist has initiated law suits against the military government, all class-action suits on behalf of the Nigerian populace's democratic and civil rights, as many times as Fawehinmi. Fawehinmi's law suits against the military government range from suing the government for the postponement of the Third Republic elections, suing Babangida for annulling the elections, suing General Abacha for the murder of the Ogoni Five—Ken Saro-Wiwa et al—and especially a suit against General Abacha for the illegal detention of Chief Abiola and all other political prisoners. Gani Fawehinmi, incorporated his social leadership zeal into the National Conscience Party, a movement organization advocating a combination of human rights, civil rights, and democratic rights for the Nigerian masses.

124 Socio-economic factors crystallized between 1986-1990, giving rise to a counter-hegemonic bloc of lower middle class of middle-level civil servants and independent professionals, displaced political elite, and a disenfranchised "popular" class, all became increasingly antagonistic toward militarization as the limits of its capacities in government became clearer. For the former political elite, the implementation of liberal-democratic governing and administering institutions offered a rational parity, a means of being heard, and a more rational system of government.

125 Julius Ihonvbere. "Are Things Falling Apart?". *Journal of African Studies* .1996.

126 Later the group was to modify its position and focus on the organizational form for a future Nigerian democracy, advocating alternative political systems of federalism and con-federalism.

127 Significantly, the MUP leader, Balarabe Musa, had declared that MUP's aim was to convince Nigerians that the traditionally conservative north was not against democracy, and that the victory of the winner of the Presidential elections, Chief Abiola, should be realized.

128 Ihonvbere, Julius. 'Where is the Third Wave?'. *Africa Today.* Volume 43.1996.

129 The working-class movement has unavoidably been drawn into the dynamics of alliance politics. Workers provide leadership for a broad range of social groups. The struggles of academics and students for a just and democratic educational system (ASUU, NANS), those of doctors for an improved health care system (NMA) and of journalists (NUJ) and lawyers (NBA) for a free press and civil liberties have all resulted in the formation informal networks with the NLC since 1978. Bangura & Beckman "African Workers & Structural Adjustment" in Olukoshi. *The Politics of Structural Adjustment in Nigeria* (Portsmouth: Heinemann,1993).

130 The growing relevance of the ASUU in the 1980s is explained by the rapid expansion of the Nigerian educational sector and the crises that began to engulf the Nigerian economy in the 1980s. Under the leadership of Dr. Festus Iyayi, ASUU's activism was a thorn in the Nigerian government's flesh. The association remained a significant and effec-

tive force in broad-based national struggles, consistently calling out its members on general strikes, each time, halting work in Nigeria's thirty-odd universities. An exceptional alliance between the ASUU and the NLC took place in 1984 when ASUU became a formal affiliate of the NLC. In 1986, a very strong alliance among the NLC, the ASUU and NANS (the student body) was established, with the NLC planning nation-wide demonstrations to underline its concern for civil liberties and democratic rights. In 1986 the anti-government demonstrations had reached such level proportions that a government tribunal had been set-up to investigate the crisis. At that tribunal, state security agents testified that the NLC as the political party, NANS, the youth wing, and ASUU, the intellectual vanguard wanted to overthrow the government.(The Akanbi Tribunal which dismissed agents' accusations —Allahiru Jega. "Professional Associations and Structural Adjustment" in Olukoshi 1993).

131 In membership, mobilization reach, effectiveness of events, and sustainability and consistency of action.

132 Nwankwo, Arthur, *Retreat from Power, the Military in Nigeria's Third Republic*. (Enugu: Fourth Dimension,1995).

Chapter 5

133 *Newswatch*. September 25. 1989.

134 *Human Rights Watch,* April 21, 1992, "Nigeria: Contradicting Itself: an undemocratic transition seeks to bring democracy nearer".

135 Text of press conference held on Monday, November, 11, 1991 at the NUJ Press Center, Lagos, announcing the inauguration of the Campaign for Democracy movement in Nigeria.

136 CD Constitution—Appendix.

137 The Nigerian left consists of radical intellectuals represented through ASUU, Nigerian students NANS, and Nigerian professional and labor groups, NLC, NMA.

138 See the Kano-based "Unity Forum for Peace and Democracy," and the Jos-based "Democratic Forum," and the Kaduna-based "Kaduna Alliance for Democracy," and all regional affiliate groups who organized during its apex rallies.

139 Establishing a sovereign national conference was to become the cornerstone of the objectives and the demands by the Campaign for Democracy and later by the pro-democracy movement.

140 CD communique's preamble -Appendix.

141 CD primary document—Appendix.

142 CD primary document—Appendix.

143 CD primary document—Appendix.

144 CD text of October 28, 1992—Appendix.

145 CD document —Human Rights Watch, 1994.

146 Tunji Olagunju and Sam Oyovbaire. *For Their Tomorrow, We Gave Our Today: Selected Speeches of IBB.* (Lagos: Safari Books, 1991).

147 See Chapter 3 which concludes that the setting of the stage for the pro-democracy movement network, was initiated by the agency of older social movement organizations, like the Nigerian Labor Congress (NLC), Academic Staff Union for Universities (ASUU) and the Nigerian Medical Association (NMA), which mobilized and organized nationwide strikes and demonstrations against the debilitating economy and the introduction of an economic, structural adjustment program (SAP).
148 All three organizations were at separately proscribed, co-opted, and persecuted by the Babangida military government for their agitation activities.
149 Popular forces began to make an organic link between economic structural adjustment and the transition-to-democracy process, between the worsening social conditions and the continued stay of the military. The slogan became, "Down with military rule." (Momoh,1998).
150 In August, 1993, General Babangida announced that he had, "Offered as his personal sacrifice to voluntarily step aside as president and commander-in-chief of the Armed Forces of the Federal Republic of Nigeria." (CD Press Release).
151 The United Action for Democracy —founded in 1996 —see foundation declaration in Appendix.
152 "Opening and Access" refer to factors, which contribute to access by pro-democracy agents and organizations to force concessions from the military regime.
153 BBC Summary of World Broadcasts, June 18, 1993.
154 The Association for Better Nigeria (ABN) was a pro-military organization advocating a longer, more enduring military-guided transition to democracy.
155 "The Chicken Has Come Home to Roost", CD publication, June 17—Appendix.
156 CD publication —Appendix.
157 *West Africa,* June 28, 1993.
158 "Over a hundred persons had been killed, from Lagos to Kwara and Delta States. In Lagos, alone, about 75 persons were reported killed. Over 200 persons were wounded and undergoing treatment." (CLO Report, 1994: 178).
159 *West Africa,* June 28, 1993.
160 *Human Rights Watch: Africa,* August 27, 1993 "Nigeria: Democracy Derailed."
161 "A Call to Activism" CD press release—Appendix .
162 "The Resistance Must Be Intensified", June 30, 1993 —Appendix.
163 "June 12 is Non-Negotiable"—CD Bulletin —Appendix.
164 Several reports correlate the popular resistance organized by the CD with the military's decision to quit. (Ihonvbere, 1996 Momoh, 1997).
165 CD Press Release n.d. (Abubakar Momoh, 1997).
166 *Human Rights Watch,* 1993 (op.cited).
167 In Kano the Unity Forum for Peace and Democracy organized a pro-

cession on August 12. In Jos, the "Democratic Forum" organized to begin mass protest. In Kaduna, the "Kaduna Alliance for Democracy," an umbrella organization for eleven mass democratic organizations, engaged in protest.

168 "Three Days of National Protest"—CD communique—August 22, 1993—Appendix.

169 Including the arrests of CLO members—Wale Shittu, Femi Adeluga and Emma Nweke for being in possession of CD leaflets, as well as the raiding of CD headquarters by security agents (by August 12, over 200 CD activists were arrested all over the country—*Africa Watch,* August 1997).

170 The Nigerian democracy movement became synonymous with the June 12 mandate.

171 *Newswatch,* July 12, 1993; *The African Guardian,* July 12 "Running Against the People".

172 *The Nigerian Economist.* "Babangida: Crises Dog His Path", August 30, 1993.

173 Babatope, Ebenezer—*The Abacha Regime and the June 12 Crisis.* (Lagos: Ebino Topsy, 1995).

174 General Abacha and Oladipo Diya.

175 Chima Ubani, 1994 (Abubakar Momoh, 1997; Ebenezer Babatope, 1995; Aaron Gana, 1996.).

176 *CD Democratico.* Vol.1 No.1.

177 "A Call to Action—D-Day", Monday May 9, 1994.

178 The New York-based Campaign for Peace and Democracy was one of the first to establish demands of the Nigerian government as a result of the exposure from the CD rallies.

179 CD Newsletters —Appendix.

180 Ihonvbere, Julius. "Are Things Falling Apart ?". *Journal of African Studies,* 1996.

181 Disseminating controversial political literature. Used widely by the Nigerian media—especially in local regions.

Chapter 6

182 "The Lagos Declaration". NADECO, 1994 —Appendix.

183 "Abiola is Ready to Die". *Newswatch.* June 6, 1994 in an interview with Bola Tinubu—NADECO member.

184 *Newswatch,* July 4, 1994

185 Human Rights Watch, *Permanent Transition.* 1996.

186 The Nigerian governmental Presidential villa located in Abuja, Nigeria's capital city.

187 Tell no.3, January 20, 1997. NADECO's pro-democracy activity had penetrated the Abacha regime to such a consequential extent, that key ministers with the military regime were beginning to advise the junta to negotiate with NADECO as the representatives of the pro-democracy opposition. Alex Akinyele, chairman of the Abacha regime's

National Reconciliation Committee, NARECOM, advised the regime to resist the temptation of demonizing NADECO as the source of all its woes. (Tell no.3, January 20, 1997).

188 When General Babangida stepped aside from power on August 27, 1993 after a massive popular campaign by the CD to force the military out of power, he installed in power an Interim national Government headed by a civilian, Ernest Shonekan,. He also left General Sani Abacha, at the time his Chief of Defense, as the sole military administrator in the ING. On November 17, 1993, Abacha used the continued popular pro-democracy resistance against the ING as a symptom of the declining chaotic status of the Nigerian nation as a rationale for a bloodless coup d'etat against the ING under the leadership of General Sani Abacha. Soon after General Abacha declared himself head of state and chief of staff of Nigerian armed forces, the general abolished all remaining political structures of the defunct Third Republic. He significantly included members of defunct national assembly and the newly elected civilian governors.

189 "NADECO-The Way Forward"—declaration statement —Appendix.

190 "NADECO-The Way Forward"—declaration statement —Appendix.

191 The Middle Belt Forum, the South-South Forum, the Northern Leaders Forum, and the MNR are just some of the progressive organizations that have pledged support for NADECO. Individual members such as Enahoro, Lawal Dambazzau, David Ejoor and Mohammed Arzika were included as signatories in the NADECO foundation statement.

192 A long-standing tradition for the Owo Meeting group—and other civilian clubs—was to recommend civilian ministerial appointments to military regimes. The Owo group held significant influence with most military regimes, which usually appointed the group's civilian referrals. Structures like the Owo Meeting represent the social force behind the mutually reinforcing civil-military alliance—a landmark of Nigerian politics.

193 "NADECO—The Way Forward" 1994.

194 Abubakar Momoh. *The Rise of Civil Associations, Militarism and Popular Struggles in Nigeria:1986-1994.* (Dakar. Codesria. 1995).

195 It is worth mentioning in detail some of the more prominent members of NADECO. More importantly, the membership base of this group distinctly represents the Nigerian civilian elite/political class, a social group that has traditionally allied with successive military regimes. NADECO is lead by octogenarian, veteran nationalist and former state governor, Chief Pa Ajasin. A leading chieftan of NADECO includes veteran nationalist activist and politician Chief Anthony Enahoro, former Chief of Defense Staff in the Second Republic retire General Alani Akinrinade, former Foreign Minister in Babangida regime, Professor Bolaji Akinyemi. NADECO Chairman for its overseas wing is a former governor and health minister Dan Suleiman.;former minister of works and housing, Wahab Dosumu; former Sokoto state governor, Yahaya Abdulkadir'; former Third Republic Senate President, Ameh Ebute;

former presidential aspirant for Social Democratic Party (SDP), Ralph Obioha, former Second Republic Senator, Abraham Adesanya; NADECO General Secretary Ayo Opadokum; former health minister, Chief Ralph Uwechie; former Chief of Army Staff, Commodore Ebitu Ukiwe; former Presidential aspirant, SDP, Olabiyi Durojaiye; former governor of Lagos state, Admiral Kanu; former governor of Anambra state, Chukwuemeka Ezeife and president of the Eastern Mandate Union, EMU; a catholic priest and former Governor of Benue State, former naval officer, Vice-Admiral, Akin Aduwo; Reverend Moses Adasus, former governor of Benue State. Retired Major-General Adeyinka Adebayo; Chief Bola Ige, former state governor; former senator, Bola Tinubu; Alhaji Mohammed Hamza; Mohammed Arzika, former leader of the defunct Social Democratic Party. Also included as the foundation signatories are Malam Lawal Dambuzzau, a prominent ally of the late Malam Aminu Kano of the NEPU fame; Colonel Yohanna Madaki, a former governor of Gongola State. Some prominent affiliate members of NADECO include: Dr. Beko Ransome-Kuti, Chairman of CD; former governor of Kaduna State and President of Movement for National Unity and Democracy, Balarabe Musa; elected governor of Edo State, Chief John Oyegun; and Spokesperson for NALICON, Professor Wole Soyinka.

196 The National Party of Nigeria model represented the ideal party structure that approximated true federal character for Nigeria's multi-ethnic population.

197 The socio-political coalitions formed through the Owo Meetings—including the Chief Olu Falae presidential campaign and the MKO Abiola organization leading the SDP progressive coalition and victory in 1993.

198 Some "June 12" advocates and members of the progressive coalition joined the Abacha regime, but remained in advocacy of June 12—former Lagos State governor Lateef Jakande, prolific writer, Ebenezer Babatope, and Walter Onogoruwa—were all described by the NADECO opposition as "turncoats." Moreover, some military politicians such as, chief of general staff Oladip Diya, remained in subversive alliance with the opposition.

199 A sovereign national conference was a cornerstone objective initiated by the Campaign for Democracy and adopted by most pro-democracy organizations. By the time NADECO addressed the issue, it had become a primary objective of the pro-democracy movement.

200 In its charter, NADECO resolves "Whereas, the Nigerian people have been demanding for a long time a sovereign national conference as a mechanism for discussing and resolving the fundamental questions confronting the nation".

201 *The Week*, "Abacha Frustrates NADECO" February 7,1994.

202 However, some traditional rulers of the West, including ten activists signed a statement on May 22 1994 on behalf of the group, Afenifere, urging the people of Nigeria not to boycott the elections into the con-

stitutional conference. Excerpts of the statement read, " We the undersigned committed and loyal members of the Afenifere would want to appeal to our highly respected and admired father and leader, Papa Michael Ajasin, to call off the order that has been imposed on our people for a boycott of the Monday, May 23 1994 delegates election to the proposed National Constitutional Conference through a decision taken by NADECO.......We are guided in our stand (and on this appeal) by a very strong conviction that any boycott of the proposed National Constitutional Conference will be inimical to the long-term political interest of our people, aside from being a disservice to the June 12 struggle to which we are irrevocably committed. " (*This Week.* May 30, 1994).

203 " Voter turnout for the ward election was abysmally low with less that 17 percent of eligible voters responding to the NCC election." *Newswatch,* June 6, 1998.

204 *Newswatch,* June 6, 1994.

205 *Tell Magazine* "Walking a Tight Rope", June 27, 1994, no.26.

206 *Tell,* June 27, No.26.

207 In 1993, immediately after the annulment, Chief Abiola categorically declared that he was not prepared to be a dead hero over June 12. "Why should I be ready to die? Was that part of the qualifications? Was it a clause in the electoral register? The only loser of any war is the man who will not live to tell the story of what happened." *Newswatch.* June 4, 1994.

208 *Tell Magazine.* June 27, 1996.

209 *Tell Magazine.* June 27, 1996.

210 *Newswatch.* "The Longest Running Show". July 4, 1994.

211 *Constitutional Rights News* ."Nigerians Agitating for Democracy Get Repression"...August 5, 1994.

212 Excerpts from the proclamation speech by M.K.O Abiola on Saturday, June 11, 1994. Tell June 27, 1994, no.27 —Appendix.

213 *Tell Magazine,* June 27,1994.

214 The National Union of Banking and Financial Institutions, the National Union of Air Transport Services Employment, and the National Union of Local Government Employees. The Lagos state branch of the Nigerian Bar Association joined briefly on July 12. The National Union of Teachers also joined the strike in early July. The Academic Staff Union of Universities (ASUU) embarked on a strike in August 22, and the national labor leadership, the NLC, finally joined the strike from August 3-5.

215 "Oil and Gas Workers Union Threatens Strike Action in Support of Abiola from 4th July" *AFP in English,* June 27, 1994, BBC Summary of World Broadcasts, June 29, 1994.

216 By August, the strike had eroded oil export earnings—'Oil and Gas Worker's Union Threatens Strike Action in Support of Abiola from Huly 4' in AFP in English, June 27, 1994, BBC Summary of World Broadcasts (SWB).

217 General Abacha's chief of general staff, Lieutenant General Oladipo Diya, had often been used by the general to reach out to leading figures of the NADECO and Afenifere to create a base for General Abacha at the grassroots. Such forays in the early days of the Abacha government had yielded positive results in the recruitment of pro-democracy and progressive civilian activists into the Abacha regime. Referred to as the progressive ministers, some of these prominent politicians included Ebenezer Babatope, Lateef Jakande, Olu Onagoruwa, and Alex Ibru. These ministers became very active in bridging the access between NADECO and General Abacha. For example, the 'Progressive Ministers' urged the military leader to invite NADECO leaders for a meeting with view to resolving the June 12 crisis. On July 24, 1994, such a meeting was held to negotiate Chief Abiola's release, and was coordinated by Mr. Alex Ibru, the then Minister for Internal Affairs and a member of the Provisional Ruling Council.

218 Chief of Staff Diya also maneuvered support at the grassroots level for the regime's constitutional conference. On May 21, after a meeting with Yoruba traditional leaders, the Yoruba Oba's Council endorsed the proposed constitutional conference elections despite the objection of NADECO. (Tell. no.26, June 27, 1994).

219 *The Meridian,* No.8, July 31, 1995.

220 NADECO members continued to use their former leverage with military administrations to maintain dialogue in the resolution of the Nigerian crisis.

221 *The Meridian.* "Abiola Heads National Government". No. 8, July 31, 1995.

222 The Government of National Unity was presented to the 1998 Abubakar regime as one of the most fully supported alternatives to another transition—to—democracy program by the military.

223 At the grassroots level, NADECO and Afenifere began to reassess their political alliances with some Northern progressives and conservatives, including coalition outreach to Malam Ciroma and Alhaji Umaru Shinkafi. A West-North rapprochement was to effect Chief Abiola's release and enter into a workable compromise to pave the way for a revised model for the actualization of June 12.

224 The Abacha regime acknowledged that NADECO was right on the issue of the government not coming out with an enabling decree on the NCC. (Babatope, 1995. pg.163).

225 Prominent politicians and pro-democracy activists who joined the Abacha administration. (Babatope, 1995).

226 An active role was also played by NLC leader, Pascal Bafyau, whose organization also actively consulted with Chief Abiola in setting conditions for his release (Babatope, 1995. page 166).

227 G.K.O Ajayi, Chief Abiola's lawyer.

228 *The Meridian,* July 31, 1995, no.8.

229 *The Meridian,* 1995, no.8.

230 Bolaji Akinyemi, Wole Soyinka, and other exiled members—Anthony Enahoro and Ralph Obioha.
231 Radio Nadeco address: NEWS FROM CUMBRE—www.cumbre.
232 *Tempo Magazine,* February 20, 1997: 'Interview with Alani Akiniriade" NADECO activisit.

CHAPTER 7

233 Chapter Six, "Democracy Now" on the initiation of NADECO's exiled movement in Great Britain and the United States.
234 *Newswatch.* "NDAC Letter to President Clinton". August, 1995.
235 Other groups include the "failed" World Congress of Nigerians, the Nigerian Pro-Democracy Network (only ten groups with a more specific mandate—organized against African American pro-Abacha lobbyists) The UDFN, however, formed the largest and most sustained group, bringing together as many as 100 pro-democracy organizations throughout the U.S., Canada, Great Britain, and other Western European cities.
236 A survey conducted at the September 20-21, 1997 world conference of Nigerian pro-democracy organizations, hosted by the UDFN, revealed structural attributes of UDFN affiliates. The survey sampled twenty Nigerian pro-democracy organizations abroad, asking organization representatives to comment on a range of issues, including each organization's objectives, ideological persuasions, accomplishments, and events carried out. (Survey entitled "Democracy Now" — Appenidix). Survey participants included: the African Democratic League, National Conscience Party, Nigerian Democratic Alliance, Canadian African Democratic Movement for Nigeria, CODHN, Canadian/African Democratic Movement for Nigeria, Organization of Nigerians in the Americas, Nigerian Freedom Foundation, Yoruba Development Cultural Organization, the Voice Forum, the Nigerian Community in Greater Pittsburgh, NALICON, Nigerian Forum for Democracy, Democratic Alliance for Nigeria.
237 The sheer volume of pro-democracy organizations abroad created some obstacles for pro-democracy activism in the international arena. Due to the vast size of the movement, non-Nigerian, pro-democracy human rights organizations looked upon it as a lack of clear unity among Nigerian civil society abroad, claiming that the splintering effect demonstrated a distraction from the main agenda. As a result, the UDFN aggressively and consistently sought to dissolve all affiliate pro-democracy organization membership and consolidate the body into a single individual membership, transforming the UDFN into the sole and forefront pro-democracy organization abroad. Advocates of this measure cited confusion among international allies as to who to deal with and fund regarding pro-democracy advocacy in Nigeria. However, this measure was voted down. Most organization members cited advantages to the "group membership" structure in mobilizing a mass

movement beginning at their local constituency levels. The extensive pluralism of the Nigerian pro-democracy movement abroad has been cited by advocates of the consolidation move as a cause for the limited impact that the international community has had on influencing change in Nigeria under the Abacha regime.

238 UDFN "Restarting the Nation Clock: Communique of the First Nigerian Pro-Democracy Summit", March 29, 1996.Affiliate organizations claimed as their main objective the "restoration of democratic/accountable government re-establishment for Nigeria." Many also cite the advancement of Nigerian democracy in some way, while others listed broader human rights objectives for oppressed Nigerians. All organizations defined as pro-democracy organizations express a firm commitment to the resolution of the principle of 'June 12' being the single means for restoring democratic governance in Nigeria, similarly showing the same commitment to the rejection of the Abacha military regime's transition to democracy program.

239 "Restarting the National Clock" —UDFN communique —Appendix.

240 "WCFN Washington Declaration," September 29, 1996.

241 "Justice" was agreed upon to be established as the basis for the movement, something which incorporated democratic struggle, "June 12," and human rights advocacy in Nigeria. —September 1997 Pittsburgh Conference.

242 The NDAC, which has affiliated bodies throughout the US holds a "war room" session in the dead of the night once a week to link all its affiliates together by way of a tele-conference on the week's developments in Nigeria.

243 Newswatch, August 14, 1995.

244 Nigerian Pro-Democracy Group Research Survey: "Democracy Now" —Appendix.

245 The November 10, 1995 executions of Ken Saro-Wiwa and eight other Ogoni activists from MOSOP caused a huge outcry from the international community, thereby setting off the unprecedented degree of isolation of Nigeria. The Nigerian international-based pro-democracy groups took advantage of the international campaign against Nigeria to sustain international attention and exert pressure on the Abacha military administration.

246 Although, after the June 12, 1993, annulment of the Nigerian elections, the international community, lead by Canada and the United States, made a limited effort to put in place punitive steps against the Nigerian military regime. This effort included the cancellation of all but humanitarian aid. Military relations between the two countries were reduced. Also, American visas were denied to " immigrants and non-immigrants who formulate or implement policies impeding a transition to democracy in Nigeria or who benefit from such policies and the immediate families of such persons." On July 27, Jesse Jackson arrived in Nigeria as President Clinton's special envoy and met with General Abacha, Chief Abiola, and members of the human rights community. He failed

to make any progress in easing the deadlock and stated upon his return home that the U.S. and other countries should begin "assertive, aggressive diplomacy" to prevent civil war. Less active than the U.S. in promoting human rights in Nigeria, the European Union has made statements condemning human rights abuses. For example, on August 26, 1994, the EU urged the Nigerian government to halt a campaign against its political opponents. The EU also implemented visa restrictions to Nigerian governmental personnel.(HRW-Africa, September, 1996). In concert with the Commonwealth Heads of Government's (CHOGM) punitive steps against Nigeria, Canada has implemented and enforcing punitive measures, in many cases taking unilateral action similar to that of the United States and the EU.

247 The October 20, 1991 Harare Declaration commits members to certain fundamental principles, including liberty of the individual, equal rights for all citizens, and the "individual's right to participate by means of free and democratic political processes in framing the society in which he or she lives."

248 "United Democratic Front of Nigeria Memorandum to Commonwealth Heads of Government (CHOIGM)," October 1997—Appendix.

249 UN document *A/RES/50/199,* March 11, 1996, reporting General Assembly resolution 50/199 on the Situation of Human Rights in Nigeria, of December 22, 1995.

250 UN document 51st session General Assembly Agenda item *110 A/51/538* October 22, 1996.

251 UDFN's London affiliate member —Kayode Fayemi has consistently addressed British governmental bodies on the pro-democracy crisis in Nigeria; and a UDFN Canadian affiliate, CODHN, has been very active working with Canadian Parliament —Appendix.

252 Letter by Congressman Donald Payne to Warren Christopher and a letter to Chief Abiola by Congressman Bill Jefferson—Appendix.

253 HR 1786 http://www.nagdhr.com/hr.html.

254 Other radio broadcasts include NADECO—abroad's Radio NADECO; the Indiana-based Free Nigeria Movement's Voice of Free Nigeria, which broadcasts from Algeria; and Radio Free Nigeria broadcast from Germany.

255 Both launchers of the station.

256 UDFN newsletter, September 1997.

257 Document on Oakland Sanctions, sourced from http://www.nagdher.com/oak.html —Appendix.

258 New York City Council Resolution http://www.nagdhr.com/nyres.html —Appendix.

259 World Cup Soccer organizers based in France.

260 *Tempo,* February,1997. Interview—NADECO-abroad member, General Akinriade.

261 Fund raising was a controversial item discussed at the 1997 UDFN Pittsburgh Conference. UDFN III Conference minutes—Appendix.

CHAPTER 8

262 The five-year repressive regime of General Abacha came to an end in June 1998 with the death of General Abacha. The initiation of the military's successor regime headed by General Abubakar marked a total reversal of the excessive dictatorial characteristics of the Abacha regime. General Abubakar declared the official end of military vanguardism, announcing the intention of the military's quick exit from Nigerian politics once and for all. Representing liberal forces of the military, Abubakar immediately released most pro-democracy political prisoners and disbanded the unpopular military transition-to-democracy program initiated by General Abacha. Though falling short of releasing the winner of the June 12 1993 presidential elections and reinstalling him as president of a Government of National Unity in May 1999, General Abubakar put forward an independent transition-to-democracy program with full participation by pro-democracy activists. However, despite General Abubakar's liberalization policies, in June 1998, marking the fifth anniversary of the June 12 movement, the pro-democracy movement was still battling against the Nigerian military and its state apparatus. The Nigerian pro-democracy movement organized under a new umbrella—the Joint Action Committee on Nigeria (JACON), the CD, NADECO, and the UDFN-abroad, continued to present civil society as a threat perception to the military regime, compelling the Abubakar regime and any successive military regimes to fully democratize the Nigerian state.

263 *Tempo.* June 11, 1998—"Abacha at the Crossroads".

264 *Tempo.* June 11, 1998—"Abacha at the Crossroads".

265 The CDHR, CRP and the CLO were the first human rights organizations in Nigeria's history to expose prison conditions, unjust trials, illegal decrees, and other human rights abuses imposed upon Nigerian citizens. See the CLO report.

266 The justification for military intervention in politics—to guard against corruption, to redirect the economy, to unify ethnic divisions and to provide for stability—Beckman (ROAPE).

267 Increasing state repression and the absence of real commitment in elite political circles to resist authoritarianism precipitated the proliferation of various civil rights groups, among them the NADL, the CDHR, the CRP, the CLO, and the crowning Campaign for Democracy, CD.—Chapter Five, "Democracy Now".

268 Between 1990 —1993, with politicians repeatedly humiliated by the military but still prepared to go along with them despite their unhappiness with the transition program, organizations and coalitions of the Nigerian left became the main visible source of opposition to the ruling military oligarchy. The Campaign for Democracy thereby became the vanguard of national sentiment against continued military rule and for democracy (Jibrin Ibrahim, 1997).

269 For its advocates, the "June 12 movement" symbolized the re-estab-

lishment of the aborted Third Republic transition-to-democracy process, thereby reflecting the principle for the future of democracy in Nigeria.

270 In the following year, 1994 and later in 1995, NADECO and the UDFN-abroad succeeded in establishing the reversal of the "June 12" annulment essential for any future democratic government in Nigeria.

271 *The Guardian*. November 12, 1993.

272 *Tell Magazine.* "Abacha Vs Abacha". 1994; and *Human Rights Watch.* 1994.

273 *Tell Magzine.* May 18, 1998 "Abacha, Diya and the Coup."

274 *Tell Magazine.* No.27, July 7, 1997 ."Northern Opposition to Abacha Thickens."

275 *Human Rights Watch/Africa Report* .Vol.9 No.6(A), October 1997.

276 Some of these pro-military movements include: the Association for a Better Nigeria led by Arthur Nzeribe: the National Movement for Vision 2010, led by Oladosu Oladipo. Youths Earnestly Ask for Abacha, led by Kanu. The Movement for Abacha for President, launched by Chief Orji Kalu, the National Mobilization and Persuasion Campaign (NMPC) headed by Godwin Daboh—cited in Movements Launched to Persuade Abacha to Run for President, text of report by Agence France Presse (AFP).

277 *Tell Magazine.* December 22, 1997.

278 *Tell Magazine.* August 14, 1995.

279 CLO special report on list of 105 detainees. List of all detainees—Appendix.

280 *Tell Magazine.* December 22,1997.

281 *Human Rights Watch Africa*. June, 1993.

282 HRW/Africa documented at least five firebomb attacks on members of the opposition including the homes of Gani Fawehinmi, leader of the Solidarity Movement, and the CD, and at the headquarters shared by the CD/CDHR.

283 *Tell Magazine*. August 14, 1995.

284 In 1994, NADECO established the reversal of the June 12 annulment as the mobilizing principle of any future democratic government in Nigeria.

285 The Abacha regime detained Chief Anthony Enahoro, a Nigerian nationalist, the late Chief Adekunle Ajasin octogenarian and Nigerian politician, and Olu Falae, former finance minister. Similarly, Abacha has hounded into exile Nobel Prize Winner Wole Soyinka, General Akinrinade, the former Chief of Army Staff, Professor Bolaji Akinyemi, former Minister of External Affairs. Also, the Abacha regime has been linked to the inexplicable assassination of Chief Abiola's pro-democracy activist wife, Kudirat Abiola, and Alfred Rewane, head of NADECO, the attempted assassination of Abraham Adesanya, a deputy leader of NADECO, and Alex Ibru, publisher of the Guardian newspapers.

286 Other exiled members included Cornelius Adebayo, former governor

of Kwara State, John Odigie-Oyegun, former governor of Edo State, Professor Bolaji Akinyemi, former minister of external affairs, Wahab Dosumu, former minister of works and housing, Commodore Dan Suleiman, former governor of Benue State, and Ralph Obiora, a former presidential aspirant of the outlawed Social Democratic Party (SDP).

287 Traditionally Yoruba speaking regions—NADECO's foundation base.

288 *Tell Magazine.* January 20, 1997.

289 *The Week*,.September 16, 1996.

290 Trumped-up coup attempt charges, which resulted in the sentencing of Obasanjo, Yar 'Adua, Beko and others.

291 *Tempo,* June 11, 1998, Vol.10 "Abacha at the Crossroads" by Esosa Igele. The article asserts that Generl Abacha had lost the resolve to pursue his self-succession bid and before his death was preparing to announce the abandonment of this plan. The article also asserts that the credit for the change of heart must go the democratic opposition.

292 Through active social mobilization by pro-democracy organizations, the movement identified allies for other military/state challengers, such as the mass media, the clergy, and guerilla movements.

293 *National Concord.* February 21, 1994 ."The Campaign for Democracy Split".

294 In fact, when General Babangida canceled the results of the party primaries in late 1992, a number of political leaders accepted his actions and strove to meet his new demands and regulations. The CD, which acted as an umbrella of support for about 35 popular organizations, was prepare to chase out Babangida in January 1993. However, CD member Femi Falana explains, 'our dilemma was that the politicians that were disqualified were not prepared to champion any cause', Tell, 13 September 1993, "The Struggle Has Just Started" Femi Falana.

295 Julius Ihonvbere —"Are Things Falling Apart? The Military and the Crisis of Democratization in Nigeria". *Journal of Modern African Studies.* 34,2 (1996) pp. 193-225.

296 *CLO Report.* 1994.

297 Campaign for Democracy Bulletin, "Be Ready for More Action on Monday July 5, 1993", Lagos, CD Secretariat, July 1993.

298 Referring to the Northern (Muslim) and Southerner (Christian) power dichotomy in Nigerian politics, usually referred to as the problem of northern Hegemony.

299 Ibid.

300 The number of pro-democracy organizations increased from a handful of human rights organizations in the 1990's to a proliferation of groups by 1994, including many who advocated the use of arms and violence to attain their goals.

301 The other group was thought to be NADECO. Although consistently refuted by NADECO leaders, violent resistance has been persistently associated by the military regime with NADECO. Following a May 31, 1995 bomb explosion during the launching of the family support pro-

gram of the wife of General Abacha, the state police arrested and interrogated Chief Cornelius Adebayo and at least two other members of NADECO. Prominent NADECO leaders such as General Akinrinade, Wole Soyinka, and Abraham Adesanya have been publicly accused by the military of being terrorists. Bomb blasts have allegedly been tied to NADECO by the military with police officers claiming that Wole Soyinka's NALICON is the military wing of NADECO (*The News.* January 13, 1997).

302 *Tell.* January 20, 1994.

303 *The News.* January 13, 1997.

304 *Tell Magazine.* January 20, 1997.

305 *Tell,* January 20, 1997.

306 Julius Ihonvbere "The Military and the Derailment of the Transition to Democracy in Nigeria" in Eboe Hutchful eds. *The Military and Society in Africa.* (Dakar: Codesria, 1997).

307 This process of the expansion of progressive forces among elite during this period of democratization in Nigeria is evidenced by a dialecticism of sorts, resulting from a growing dissatisfaction among civilian elite for continued military dominance. This observation is a reflection of the civil-military paradox, the contradiction embedded in the long-standing existence of an interlocking relationship between Nigerian's vibrant civil society and a politicized military state.

308 Well-known civilian and military politicians and members of the elite civil society sector.

309 The membership of Nigerian nationalists Anthony Enahoro, veteran politician Bola Ige, former military politicians, such as General Alani Akinrinade and Colonel Gwadabe, Nobel Prize winner, Wole Soyinka and a host of others.

310 NADECO membership list —Appendix.

311 A sovereign national conference would bring together all elements of Nigerian civil society in a dialogue and debate on the desired political structure of Nigeria. The SNC, as it was often referred to, also had the objective of social reconciliation and Nigerian national unity. Again, initiated by the CD, adopted by NADECO and other pro-democracy organizations, advocacy for a sovereign national congress took its cue from democratic upsurges by civil society in neighboring African countries, such as Benin and Zambia, where authoritarian governments were overthrown by the convening of sovereign national conferences. By 1998 in a post-Abacha regime, the SNC became synonymous with a Government of National Unity (GNU) as a government based on the "June 12" mandate.

312 The Nigerian media's bold and consistent critique of the regime throughout the period has also afforded this civil society sector a significant role in the pro-democracy movement. Sympathetic press coverage of pro-democracy activities also afforded the press a liaison role between the pro-democracy forces and the mass public—including elite, popular and international and has promoted democratic aware-

ness among the populace.

313 Ignoring the demand by the pro-democracy movement for the convening of a sovereign national conference, the Abacha regime launched a state-guided, National Constitutional Conference, whose objective was to deliberate a future democratic government for the country. By manipulating the agenda to its own ends, the military's conference once again exemplified the Nigerian military's inclination to continue its fostering of civil-military alliances by attempting to co-opt elite sectors within civil society.

314 The NADECO boycott strategy sought to discourage voting by the populace, as well as participation by civilian politicians in the Constitutional Conference.

315 NADECO derives its membership from the People's Consultative Forum.

316 These groups' membership traditionally was made up of the civilian elite class, especially civilian politicians; they have always existed as civil societal associations formed for the basis of political and social networking and dialogue among civilians during Nigerian military regimes.

317 By 1995, commitment to June 12 as a coalition platform became a basis for the ideological division of the movement into those groups who became June 12 stalwarts, and opponents who necessarily espoused a democratic vision for Nigeria beyond June 12.

318 By 1995, a leading Nigerian political pundit and leader of the pro-democracy group the Movement for Unity and Progress (MUP), Alhaji Balarabe Musa, described the progressive ideological landscape among the progressive civilian elite sector this way, "We should use commitment to the June 12 mandate as a standard for measuring the progressiveness of individuals or groups." (*The Meridian,* August 21, 1995).

319 The Progressive Coalition is a social club force originating from the social democratic foundations of the Owo Meeting and the Action Group. NADECO was founded and made-up of a web of organizations among Nigerian civil society and individuals reflecting a complex network of progressive discourse groups, ethno-regional groups, and political associations rooted in the prior democratic regimes in Nigeria.

320 NADECO has been able to draw its urban popular support from alignments with the Campaign for Democracy and its affiliate human rights organs. With the CD severely weakened by the time NADECO was just coming to prominence, and since they had the same fundamental goals, the CD was happy to organize with NADECO for the 1994 rallies on behalf of Chief Abiola and NADECO's subsequent campaign to boycott the National Conference.

321 NADECO had national character due to the presence of members from the Middle-belt, Northern, Eastern, Western and Southern parts of Nigeira.("NADECO's Fight Against Abacha"—*The Guardian.* Sunday, June 23, 1998).

322 In 1990, the Babangida regime's mandatory two-party system of the famed theme "a little to the left and a little to the right" grouped political associations among civil society into the progressive-based Social Democratic Party (SDP) and the conservative National Republican Party (NRC).

323 The All Nigeria Congress, ANC, pulling the biggest weight within the conservative phalanx.

324 General Obasanjo also funded and chaired the Association for Democratic and Good Governance in Nigeria (ADGGN).

325 Political prisoner died in jail.

326 *Newswatch.* April 29, 1996.

327 For example, MOSOP, the Movement of the Survival of Ogoni People lead by the world-famed author, late Ken Saro-Wiwa, while primarily interested in the issues related to the minority ethnic group in Ogoni Land, also allied with the Campaign for Democracy and pro-democracy advocacy. Moreover, groups like Mkpoko Igbo and the Eastern Mandate Union (EMU) contain both progressive and moderate forces, united by their commitment to Igbo power, but disunited on their stance on "June 12". Northern elements among the pro-democracy network such as the Turaki Committee and the Northern Elders Forum, are committed to the need for a broad dialogue to move the nation forward, but encourage moving beyond discussions on "June 12" and Chief Abiola to achieve democracy in the country. (Umaru Dikko, Pg 12, *The News,* 25 December, 1995).

328 *The Meridian,* August 21, 1995.

329 Organized professionally by the Nigerian Union of Journalists (NUJ), which acted in support of the pro-democracy movement. In 1995, the private press organized its own pro-democracy movement, Journalists for Democratic Rights (JODER).

330 Y.Z. Ya'u, "The Mass Media in the Struggle for Democracy in Expanding Democratic Space" in Beckett and Young. *Dilemmas of Democracy.* (Rochester. University of Rochester Press.1997).

331 Owned by Chief Abiola.

332 Tradition of distributing thousands of political pamphlets documenting political concerns.

333 For three years of the pro-democracy struggle, *TEMPO's* editors published the radically pro-democracy magazine on a weekly basis from the underground. During this time, the magazine educated the Nigerian populace on controversial but accurate activities of the Nigerian military and the Nigerian pro-democracy movement.

334 Y'au "Expanding Democratic Space". In Beckett and Young. *Dilemmas of Democracy.* (Rochester. University of Rochester Press,1997).

335 1. Mrs Chris Anyanwu, publisher, the Sunday Magazine (TSM) 2. Kunle Ajibade, editor, the News magazine 3. Ben Charles Obi, editor, Classique 4. Alumona Jenkins, editor, the News magazine 5. Onome Osifo-Whiskey, editor, Tell magazine 6. Hamid Danlami, publisher of

Al-Mazan. 7. Femi Ojudu, editor, the News Magazine 8. Akin Adesokan, snr writer, the Post Express 9. Tokunbo Fakeye, defense correspondent of the News:10. Salawu Rafiu, admin manager, the News.11. Bagauda Kaltho, Kaduna correspondent, the News magazine. 12. Mohammed Adamu, Abuja correspondent, African Concord magazine:13. Moshood Fayemiwo, editor, Razor Weekly. 14. Soji Omotunde, editor,, African concord.

336 Additional allies identified during the pro-democracy period for alternative and future challengers include minority rights claims, which since the international visibility attained by Movement of the Survival of Ogoni People (MOSOP), and this organization's participation in the pro-democracy struggle have generated the creation of many more minority rights organizations who have adopted the model of political contention and collective action to realize their objectives of 'power shift' and equitable allocation of Nigeria's oil resources in the country. Also, Nigeria's religious leaders began to join the pro-democracy movement in condemning the country's declining political state. Nigeria's Catholic bishops, organized under the bishops of the Association of Episcopal Conference, called on the Abacha regime to hand over power to democratic rule earlier scheduled to avoid continued deteriorating conditions in Nigeria. The Christian Association of Nigeria (CAN), represented by Sunday Mbang, a prelate of the Methodist Church was even more critical of the Abacha Regime and the general's self-succession bid, pronouncing its support for June 12 and genuine democracy. Another religious critic of the Nigerian junta was the Anglican Church, represented by Emmanuel Gbonigi, the church's lord bishop at Akure, who was often mistaken to be a NADECO member due to his wide support of the pro-democracy movement.
In a sweeping victory for the clergy, in March 1998, the Pope visited Nigeria. Addressing millions of Nigerian Christians, the Pope called for an end to military rule in Nigeria and demanded the release of all political detainees.

337 Oyelele Oyediran, "Transition Without End: from Hope to Despair:reflections of a participant-observer". in Beckett & Young's *Dilemmas of Democracy.* (Rochester: University of Rochester Press, 1997).

338 Due to the exile of some NADECO stalwarts, including Wole Soyinka, Anthony Enahoro, Alani Akinrinade, Bola Tinubu, Ralph Obioha, Dan Suleiman, Tokunbo Afikuyomi, and Bolaji Akinyemi, NADECO-abroad was able to cultivate foreign resources and organize profound satellite offices in the U.S. and the U.K. NADECO-abroad forged alliances with scores of Nigerian-based pro-democracy organizations and international-based human rights organizations in the U.S., Canada, and Western Europe.

339 NADECO-abroad is an affiliate member of the United Democratic Front for Nigeria (UDFN).

340 Executive committee.

CHAPTER 9

341 General Abacha's declaration of a transition to democratic plan culminating in national elections in October 1998, threatened to characterize a significantly different transition from previous military transition programs. An unprecedented move to succeed himself as a civilian President of a Fourth Republic, General Abacha imitated his colleagues in West Africa, Jerry Rawlings of Ghana, and Jameh of Gambia. Not ruling out the possibility, the general is quoted to having said,

"The decision is my own constituencies. It is not new in Africa, neither is it new in the sub-region, where military people have stepped into politics."(*Tell,* Feb, 1997) What made this unprecedented (for Nigeria) notion of General Abacha's self-succession plan fulsome was the Abacha-for-President campaign, with political society (the political parties organized for Abacha's transition) competing to recruit the military leader as their political party's Presidential candidate.(*Tell,* 1997 Feb.)

Disqualified from contesting in General Abacha's interminable transition-to-democracy because they were perceived as anti-Abacha forces (Jibrin Ibrahim, 1997), the opposition (in the form of the National Democratic Coalition (NADECO), the broad union of political associations, human rights groups, nationalists, ethnic groups, complemented by the activities of the Campaign for democracy—the coalition of human rights groups, student organizations and labor unions) has resorted to legal actions, strikes, demonstrations, and in some cases counter-violence in an effort to block
General Abacha's new transition program, and forcing the acceptance of the June 12 election results. This course by the opposition has been perceived by the military regime as a frontal attack on the General's refusal to discuss the resolution of the June 12 question outside the parameters of his own transition program, and therefore led to the attempted subversion of the opposition by the Abacha regime.

342 Jibrin Ibrahim "Obstacles to Democratization". Beckett and Young. *Dilemmas of Democracy.* (Rochester: University of Rochester, 1997).

343 In March 1999, former General Olusegun Obasanjo won the presidential elections organized under Abubakar regime's transition-to-democracy program. Upon announcement of the results, violent demonstrations erupted in the South-West, Obasanjo's native region. Supporting the protests, Chief Olu Falae, the Presidential aspirant representing the competing party, the AD (re-constituted from the NADECO opposition) claimed that the former general's "rigged victory" represented another military maneuver to perpetuate the military in power. (WBAI Report, March 4, 1999).

344 The first time was the 1960 colonial led, transition The second time was the 1979 Obasanjo-led transition.

345 In earlier sections of this study, it was suggested that the uniqueness

of the Nigerian case as a case of a democratic transition in Africa is attributable to the civil-military paradox, a concept which attempted to explain a process whereby very close and sometimes non-distinguishable alliances and coalitions forged between civil society and the military have fostered the professionalization and expanded politicization of the Nigerian military, thereby undercutting stable democratic government and democratic consolidation in the country. However, at the same time the civil-military alliance and rich associational activity among civil society has kept tyrannical authoritarian rule at bay in Nigeria.

346 Long-standing and mutually interactive relationship between civil society and military, a relationship which also mutually limits the extremist tendencies of both sectors.

347 The Nigerian pro-democracy movement suffered from the tendency of being threatened by a lack of clear dominant leadership and by a tendency toward an anarchy, which was exploited by a resistive ruling elite.

348 Aaron Gana. *Old Breeds, New Breeds.* (Lagos. AfriGov Monograph Series.1996).

349 Pita Agbese "Nigeria: how to derail a transition program." *Multi-party Democracy and Political Change in Africa.* (Houston. Bookfield Press.USA.1998).

350 Sklar, Richard. "An Elusive Target: Nigeria Fends off Sanctions" in *Polis,* Volume 3, no 1. 1997.

351 Organizations have emerged around the charismatic personality that leaders—Chief Abiola, Beko Ransome-Kuti, Wole Soyinka, Gani Fahwehinimi—and yet these organizations have failed to root themselves in grassroots social empowerment for the purpose of effecting democratic change.

352 Ebenezer Babatope. *The Abacha Regime and the June 12 Crisis.* (Lagos: Ebino Topsy, 1996). page 53.

353 *Newswatch.* vol 18, no.24, December 14,1993.

354 Abubakar Momoh. *The Rise of Civil Associations, Militarism and Popular Struggles in Nigeria:1986-1994* (Dakar: Codesria, 1995).

355 Disagreements among the top leadership—Wole Soyinka and Anthony Enahoro—over the financial management of the movement abroad caused the breakup of the original movement abroad, the World Congress of Nigerian Democracy.

356 *The Guardian* "Sunday Politics". June 23,1996.

357 Stephen Ndegwa. *The Two Faces of Civil Society: NGO's and Politics in Africa.* (West Hartford: Kumarian Press. 1997).

358 Stephen Ndegwa. *The Two Faces of Civil Society: NGO's and Politics in Africa.* (West Hartford: Kumarian Press. 1997).

359 Although the pro-democracy movement is very much alive, the greatest challenge, however, remains its inability to forge and solidify a coalition of the voluminous pro-democracy organizations and other progressive forces under a unified platform in opposition to the

Nigerian military regime.

360 General Obasanjo was a victim of General Abacha's repression of pro-democracy activists. Alongside Dr.Beko Ransome-Kuti, CD chair, the general was sentenced to 15 years imprisonment on trumped—p charges of an alleged coup-attempt.

361 *Post Express.* November 30, 1998. Mma Agbagha "Buying Up the Transition."

362 In their founding meeting, the Conference of Fused Associations, an expansive coalition to found the APP, including Umaru Shikafi's ANC (an offshoot of the late Yar 'Adua's Peoples Democratic Movement (PDM), Dr.Olusola Saraki's National Unity Forum, Chief Emmanuel Iwuanyanwu's United Nigeria People's Party, Afenifere, the People's Consultative Forum (PCF) and its allies in the Eastern Mandate Union (EMU) and the Solidarity People's Party (SPP).

363 *Nigerian Vanguard.* "Politics This Week" "AD Can Produce Next President—Tinubu" by Tunji Olawuni. November 26, 1998.

364 The NADECO (AD)-APP coalition broke down when pro-military elements, such as Arthur Nzeribe and Chief Lamidi Adedibu were given front-line status within the party. Propelling the issue of leadership character to the political debate, the AD ran on credible and honest leadership who will serve the interests of the masses. (*Vanguard,* "Politics This Week". Tunji Olawuni-11/26/98). The AD is also in the forefront of raising the question of Northern hegemony—framed as "power shift" —in the 1999 political discourse. Also avoiding an alliance with the PDP because that party was ambivalent about the question of ensuring a southern presidential leader, the AD is at the forefront in advocating the "rotational presidency" model for the next Nigerian constitution. Such a model attempts to allocate national executive political power—in the form of the presidency—equally among ethnic regions by period.

365 JACON Blueprint on *The Way Forward for a Democratic Nigeria,* Thursday, July 6,1998.

366 The United Action for Democracy (UAD), of which the Civil Liberties Organization (CLO) is a member, is not a member of the JACON. The UAD views itself as a forum for radical pro-democracy and human rights organizations, and has chosen to stay outside of the organized political platform. Instead, the UAD has created a democracy monitoring group, which will monitor the fairness of the transition program.

367 Gani Fahwehinmi was highly critical of General Obasanjo's donation to the PDP of N130,000,000 naira. In his usual activist style, Fahwehinmi requested an investigation into the source of the general's donation.

368 Abubakar address to the nation—launching his transition program.

369 General Babangida approved a constitutional bill forbidding military takeover of civilian governments. Before the general annulled the 1993 elections, he pledged that his regime would be the last military regime in Nigerian history.

370 A term defined by Robert Kaplan as a middle version of politics between liberal and neo-conservative moralists concerned with human rights and tragic realists concerned with security and economy.("Was Democracy Just a Moment?", Robert Kaplan in the *Atlantic Monthly*).

LIST OF CITED INTERVIEWS WITH PRO-DEMOCRACY ACTIVISTS

1. "Coup Against the Civilians: My Role, My Regrets" (unedited press statement delivered by Mr. Abimbola Davis, National Director of Organization of the ABN at Allen Avenue, Ikeja to the world press on July 16th, 1994 (*The African Guardian:* "Conspiracies; New Plans to Abort August 27—ABN Unmasked", July 26, 1993).
2. New Year Message broadcast on Radio Kudirat, Nigeria (RKN) by Professor Wole Soyinka, UDFN Activist/NADECO exile.
3. "We Are Near Disaster" Interview with Bashorun MKO Abiola, detained symbol of pro-democracy movement, in *The News* "Man of the Year". June 12, January 10, 1994.
4. "Abiola Speaks—from the archives that is" Interview of Chief Abiola, detained symbol of pro-democracy movement "Nobody Can Stop Me" by *African Concord,* June 6, 1994.
5. "My Date with Destiny" interview with Bashorun Abiola, detained symbol of pro-democracy movement, in the African Guardian in August 27 "I Will Be Sworn in As President-MKO" August 16, 1993.
6. "Why I Wrote Abacha" Interview with Bolaji Akninyemi, NADECO-abroad Activist/Exile by Osa Director, *Tell Magazine,* August 4, 1997.
7. "The North is for June 12" Interview with Abubakar Umar, NADECO Activist, *in Tell Magazine,* August 15, 1994.
8. "The Secret Pact" Interview with Omo Omoruyi in *Tell Magazine,* September 29, 1997.
9. "Interview of General Alani Aknrinade" Interview with Alani Akinrinade, NADECO Activist, in *Tempo Mazazine,* February 20, 1997.
10. "Hope Betrayed" Interview with Brigadier-General David Mark, NADECO Activist by *Newswatch,* "The Abacha Coup: Our Original Plan by David Mark", April 11, 1994.
11. "Abacha Voted for Abiola" Interview with Bola Tinubu, NADECO Activist, by Osa Director in *Tell,* September 8, 1997.
12. "My Political Agenda Continues" Interview with Gani Fawehinmi, radical pro-democracy/human rights activist, in *Tell,* November 7, 1994 by George Mbah and Dayo Ajigbotosho.
13. "No Case for Fresh Elections" Interview with Anthony Enahoro, NADECO-abroad activist/exile in "Nigeria Boils: the people say no to Babangida" *Tell,* July 19, 1993.
14. "No Surrender" Interview with Balarabe Musa, pro-democracy activist in Newswatch, April 8, 1996.

15. "We Must Get Rid of the Military" Interview with John Odigie-Oyegun, NADECO Activist in *Tell,* July, 1996.
16. "1998 is Irrelevant" Interview with Femi Falana, CD/UAD Activist in *Tell,* December 9, 1996.
17. "The Military Can Be Defeated" Interview with Hafsat Abiola, daughter of slain NADECO Activist, Kudirat Abiola (also Director of KIND) in *The News,* August 4, 1997
18. "Nigerians Must Fight for Their Freedom" Interview with Bola Ige, NADECO Activist, in *Tell* November 11, 1996.
19. "I Will Fight On" Interview with Ken Saro-Wiwa, international human rights activist (MOSOP leader) in *Tell,* June 5, 1995.
20. "Enough of Military Rule" Interview with Olisa Agbakoba, CLO/UAD Activist in *TheWeek,* July 28,1997.
21. "Salute to the Nigerian Press" Excerpts from Chris Anyanwu's (publisher TSM and pro-democracy activist) address read in Paris on the occasion of UNESCO's award to her of the second Guillermo Cano World Press Freedom prize.
22. "Talk Now or Fight Later" Interview with Wole Soyinka, UDFN/NALICON Activist, with Dare Babarinsa in "We May Go To War"—*Tell Magazine*, November 2nd, 1998.

DIAGRAM II

CONTEMPORARY - PAST LINKAGES: NIGERIAN CIVIL SOCIETY, 1914 – 1998

	1914 - 1966 GUIDED DECOLONIZATION	1967 - 1983 POST-COLONIAL AUTHORITARIANISM	1984- 1998 CONTEMPORARY DEMOCRATIC STRUGGLES
CIVIC ASSOCIATIONS	The Igbo Union (Nnamdi Azikiwe) Egbe Omo Oduduwa (Obafemi Awolowo) Jamiyyar Mutanen Arewa (Tafewa Balewa) The Northern Elements Progressive Association (NEPA)	the Movement for Progressive Nigerians the Nigerian Democratic Movement Women in Nigeria	the Northern Elders Union the Igbo Elders Union the Yoruba Elders Union Afenifere, Ohanze, MOSOP, Turaki..
POLITICAL PARTY	NPC (Balewa) (Northern Autonomy) AG (Awolowo)(Liberal Socialist Agenda) NCNC (Azikiwe, Enahoro (Nationalist Party) NEPU (Aminu Kano) (Radical Socialist)	NPN (Nationalist/Republicanism/Northern) UPN (Liberal Socialist Agenda/Ethnic) NPP (Ethnic sectional party/Igbo) GNPP, PRP (ideological/non-trad North)	SDP (a little to the left) NRC(a little to the right) UNCP, CNC, GDM, DPN (ABACHA PARTIES) PDP, APP, AD (ABUBAKAR TRANSITION 1998)
PROFESSIONAL ASSOCIATION	Nigerian Medical Association (Beko Ransome-Kuti) Trade Unions Congress (TUC) Nigerian Associations of University Teachers National Union of Nigerian Students (NUNS)	Nigerian Medical Association (NMA) Nigerian Labor Congress (NLC) Academic Staff Union of Universities(ASUU) National Association of Nigerian Students	ASUU NLC NUPENG PENGASSAN
NON-GOVERNMENTAL ORGANIZATION (international connections)			Constitutional Rights Project Civil Liberties Organization Committee for the Defense of Human Rights Gani Fahewihinmi Solidarity/NCP
POLITICAL REFORM MOVEMENT	National Council for Nigeria's and Cameroons (NCNC) The National Youth Movement (NYM) The Zikist Movement		Movement for the Survival of Ogoni People Campaign for Democracy (CD); UAD National Democratic Coalition (NADECO) United Democratic Front of Nigeria ,UDFN ADGGN, MUP, NALICON

DIAGRAM III

THE NIGERIAN PRO-DEMOCRACY MOVEMENT 1990 -1998

GROUP CATEGORY	GROUP NAME	PROMINENT LEADERS	DEMOCRATIC IDEOLOGY	ORGANIZATIONAL TYPE	MEMBERSHIP TYPE
GROUP A: POPULAR CIVIL LIBERTIES	CLO	Olisa Agbakoba	human rights, democracy	NGO, 1986	radical professionals
	CDHR	Clement Nwankwo	human rights	NGO, 1986	radical professionals
	CRP	Clement Nwankwo	constitutionalism, human rights	NGO, 1988	radical professionals
	NADL	Femi Falana	constitutionalism, democracy	Political Association/Professional , 1988?	radical lawyers
	Human Rights Africa (HRA)	Tunji Abayomi	human rights -	NGO- Internationalist	middle class professional/ foreigners
	Campaign for Demo.(CD)	Dr. Beko Ransome-Kuti	democracy, anti-militarism	Political Association-Umbrella Org, 1990	radical professionals
GROUP B: POLITICO-ETHNIC	Egbe Afenifere (PCF)	Bola Ige, Adesanya, Ajasin	democracy- June 12, Awoist, ethnic	Cultural/Political Association	former Action Group, ethnic
	Mbpoko Igbo	Chuba Okadigbo	democracy- moderate, ethnic	Cultural/Political Association	Igbo elite
	the Northern Elders Council	Sultan Dasuki	stability, democracy, ethnic-conservative	Cultural /Political Association	Northern elite
	the Middle Belt Forum	Bala Usman, Balarabe Musa	economic justice, democracy, ethnic	Cultural/Political Association	radical ethnicists
	National Unity Club (NUC)	Mbakwe, Rimi, Jakande, Gana	nationalism, democracy- progressive	Political Association	former politicians
	MOSOP	Ken Saro-Wiwa	economic/social justice, democracy-ethni	Political Association	grassroots ethnic

DIAGRAM III CONTINUED

GROUP C: POLITICAL REFORM MOVEMENTS	NADECO	Ajasin, Ige, Tinubu, Ezeife, Akinyemi, Akinriade	democracy- June 12 - progressive	Political Association-Umbrella Org., 1994	former politicians, military off., middle class professionals
	MNR	Anthony Enahoro	democracy-political structure/federalism	Political Association- 1991?	former nationalists
	ADGGN	General Olusegun Obasanjo	democracy- moderate	Political Association- 1992?	former military officer
	PDM Movement/New DM	Shehu Yar'Adua, Sarunmi	democracy-moderate	Political Association- 1994?	former military officer
	Peoples Comm. for Liberty	Ebenezer Babatope	democracy-moderate	Political Association-1994/5?	former politicians
	Solidarity Association/NCP	Gani Fahwehimi	social justice, human rights, democracy	Political Association- 1990 - 1994?	radical socialist professionals
	United Action Demo (UAD)	Olisa Agbakoba	democracy-June 12- human rights	Political forum/Umbrella group	human rights, democrats
	Move .Nat. Unity (MNR)	Balarabe Musa	democracy, social justice - progressive	Political Association- 1994?	radical intellectuals, nationalists
	Democratic Alternative	Chima Ubani	democracy-	Political Association- ?	middle class professionals
GROUP D: OLD LABOR AND PROFESSIONALS	NLC	Hasan Ciroma, Pascal Bafyau	economic justice, democracy	Professional, Umbrella Org.-42 affiliations, 1947	working class-national
	ASUU	Atthiru Jega	economic/social justice, democracy	Professional, National, 1950	elite intellectuals
	NUPENG	Frank Kokori	economic justice, democracy	Professional, Sectoral, 1975?	oil workers
	PENGASSAN	Chief Milton Dabibi	economic justice, democracy	Professional, Sectoral, 1975?	oil workers
GROUP E: INTERNATIONAL NGO	NDAC	Professor Oparaoji	democracy - internationalist	Political Association	Nigerian diaspora - USA
	NDM	Mobolaji Aluko	democracy-June 12, internationalist	Political Association	Nigerian diaspora- USA

DIAGRAM IV

A PROFILE OF THE NIGERIAN PRO-DEMOCRACY MOVEMENT ABROAD

GROUP NAME	HEAD LOCATION	AFFILIATED GROUPS	REGIONAL OFFICES
ACTION GROUP FOR DEMOCRACY, AGD		UDFN	
AFRICAN DEMOCRATIC LEAGUE, ADL	HOUSTON, TEXAS	UDFN	
CAMPAIGN FOR DEMOCRACY, CD	LAGOS, NIGERIA	UDFN	PARIS, FRANCE
COALITION FOR DEMOCRATIC AWARENESS		UDFN	
DEMOCRATIC ALTERNATIVE		UDFN	
NATIONAL DEMOCRATIC AWARENESS COMMITTEE	BOSTON, MASS	WCFN, UDFN	
NATIONAL DEMOCRATIC COALITION, NADECO	LAGOS, NIGERIA	CD, UDFN, WCFN	WASHINGTON DC- USA, LONDON-UK
NIGERIAN DEMOCRATIC MOVEMENT	WASHINGTON DC- USA	UDFN, WCFN	LONDON- UK
NATIONAL FREEDOM FOUNDATION	PITTSBURGH- USA	UDFN	
NATIONAL LIBERATION COUNCIL, NALICON	LONDON-UK	UDFN	OSLO, NORWAY
NIGERIAN LIBERATION GROUP			
NEW NIGERIA FORUM, NNF	LONDON- UK	UDFN	
ODUDUWA MOVEMENT	LONDON- UK	UDFN	
ACTION GROUP FOR DEMOCRACY	USA	UDFN	
EGBE ISOKAN YORUBA	USA	UDFN	
CANADIAN ORGANIZATION FOR HUMAN RIGHTS AND DEMOCRACY IN NIGERIA, COHDN	MONTREAL- CANADA	UDFN, WCFN	LONDON, TORONTO, MONTREAL, VANCOUVER
CANDADIAN ASSOCIATION FOR DEMOCRATIC MOVEMENT IN NIGERIA	ONTARIO- CANADA	UDFN	
ORGANIZATION OF NIGERIANS IN AMERICAS, ONA	HOUSTON, TEXAS	CD, UDFN	
NIGERIAN PEOPLE'S FORUM	BROOKLYN- USA	NADECO, UDFN	
CALL-2-ACTION	USA		
EGBE OMO YORUBA	USA	UDFN	
MOVEMENT FOR THE REFORMATION OF NIGERIA, MNR	LONDON- UK	NADECO, UDFN	

DIAGRAM IV CONTINUED

NIGERIAN DEMOCRATIC TASK FORCE	USA	UDFN	
THE COCOONS	USA	UDFN	
SOLIDARITY MOVEMENT FOR SOUTHERN MINORITIES	LONDON- UK	MOSOP, UDFN	
ODUDUWA YOUTH MOVEMENT	USA	UDFN	
DEMOCRATIC ALLIANCE OF NIGERIANS IN CANDADA	CANADA	UDFN, CODHN	
COALITION OF NIGERIAN DEMOCRATS IN GERMANY, CONDIG	GERMANY	UDFN	
NIGERIA FORUM	SCOTLAND- UK	UDFN, WCFN	
THE NIGERIAN CAUCUS, GERMANY	GERMANY	UDFN	
COALITION AGAINST DICTATORSHIP IN NIGERIA		UDFN	
NATIONAL CONSCIENCE PARTY	LAGOS-NIGERIA	NADECO, UDFN	CALIFORNIA-USA, WASHINGTON DC, CANADA
ORGANIZATION OF NATIONAL UNITY		UDFN	
LEAGUE OF PATRIOTIC NIGERIANS		UDFN	
ACTION GROUP FOR DEMOCRACY	OSLO- NORWAY	UDFN, NALICON	
NIGERIAN FORUM FOR DEMOCRACY	MICHIGAN- USA	UDFN	
KUDIRAT INSTITUTE FOR NIGERIAN DEMOCRACY, KIND	BOSTON- USA	UDFN	
CANADIAN/AFRICAN DEMOCRATIC MOVEMENT FOR NIGERIA	TORONTO- CANADA	UDFN, NALICON	
NIGERIAN DEMOCRATIC ALLIANCE, NDA	BOSTON- MASS	UDFN	OSLO, DC, DETROIT, ATLANTA, BALTIMORE, CHICAGO, LONDON, NIGERIA
THE VOICE FORUM	GERMANY	NALICON, UDFN	NIGERIA, LONDON
ASSOCIATION OF NIGERIANS ABROAD, ANA	LONDON- UK	UDFN, NDM	
Nigerian Advocacy Group for Democracy and Human Rights (NAGDHR)	Boston, Massachusetts	Sierra Club	
Free Nigeria Movement, FNM	Indianapolis, Indiana		

DIAGRAM V
PRO-DEMOCRACY NETWORK ORGANIZATIONAL ALLIANCE FLOW

IDEOLOGICAL PERSUASION / *ORGANIZATION CATEGORIES*	*PROGRESSIVE*	*MODERATE*	*CONSERVATIVE*
JUNE 12 POLITICAL PARTY COALITIONS – 1993	SOCIAL DEMOCRATIC PARTY (SDP)		NATIONAL REPUBLICAN CONVENTION (NRC)
IDEOLOGICAL ORGANIZATIONS (FREINDSHIP CLUBS)	PEOPLE'S CONSULTATIVE FORUM (PCF)	NATIONAL UNITY CLUB (NUC)	ALL NIGERIA CONGRESS (ANC)
PRO-DEMOCRACY ORGANIZATIONS	CD-NCP-MNR-NADECO-UDFN	MOVEMENT OF UNITY AND PROGRESS (MUP) PEOPLES DEMOCRATIC MOVEMENT (PDM) ASSOCIATION OF GOOD GOVERNANCE AND DEMOCRACY (ADDGN)	NDP-NCN-NPM (all Igbo-based) NATIONAL CONGRESS OF NIGERIA NIGERIAN DEMOCRATIC PARTY NIGERIAN PROGRESSIVE MOVEMENT
ETHNIC POLITICAL ORGANIZATION	AFENIFERE-MOSOP-ETP/INC IGBO UNIONS- EMU	THE MIDDLE BELT FORUM-MKPOKO IGBO	NORTHERN CONSULTATIVE FORUM TURAKI COMMITTEE NORTHERN ELDERS FORUM
POSITION ON JUNE 12	*DEMOCRACY CANNOT PROCEED WITHOUT THE REALIZATION OF THE JUNE 12 ELECTIONS*	*JUNE 12 IS DEAD; DEMOCRACY IS ACHIEVABLE BEYOND JUNE 12*	*JUNE 12 IS DEAD; DEMOCRACY IS ACHIEVABLE BEYOND JUNE 12*

Index

NLC, 2, 16, 34, 43, 49, 54, 60, 78, 84-85

NUPENG, 2, 16, 49, 54, 73, 78, 84-85

PENGASSAN, 2, 16, 49, 54, 73, 78, 84

Political opportunity, 12, 16-17, 19, 29-30, 40-41, 45, 47-49, 51, 53, 56, 64, 78, 96, 137